Killing God's Enemies

The Secret History of the Crazy War Against Jews, African-Americans and the U.S. Government

By John Lee Brook

Published by:
Trine Day LLC
PO Box 577
Walterville, OR 97489
1-800-556-2012
www.TrineDay.com
publisher@TrineDay.net

Library of Congress Control Number:

Brook, John Lee
 – 1st ed.
p. cm.
Includes references
Epub (ISBN-13) 978-1-63424-072-7
Mobi (ISBN-13) 978-1-63424-073-4
Print (ISBN-13) 978-1-63424-071-0
1. 2. . 3. . I. Brook, John Lee. II. Title

First Edition
10 9 8 7 6 5 4 3 2 1

Printed in the USA
Distribution to the Trade by:
Independent Publishers Group (IPG)
814 North Franklin Street
Chicago, Illinois 60610
312.337.0747
www.ipgbook.com

Contents

Chapter 1

Land of the Free

According to the Southern Poverty Law Center, fifty new right-wing militia groups have been formed in the U.S. in the last two years. More than a few of them are located in Alaskan cities. For example, the Second Amendment Task Force in Fairbanks boasts 7,000 members. All of who carry guns and rifles on Saturdays and Sundays, when they're not at work. These groups post speeches and combat exercise videos on YouTube. The speeches promote fear and spread extremist propaganda, while the combat exercise videos advance violence as an alternative. Most of these groups claim to be Christians. And many of them subscribe to the beliefs of Christian Identity.

The April 2009 murder of three police officers in Pittsburgh was perpetrated by a white supremacist, whose personal belief system was based on the doctrinal tenets of Christian Identity. The cop-killer was afraid he was going to lose his right to "keep and bear arms." And Political Research Associates – a Massachusetts think tank – states that right-wing extremists are responsible for nine murders since the election of President Obama.

The Department of Homeland Security has identified these right-wing militia groups as "the most dangerous domestic terrorist threat."

Why? Because they are defiant, dangerous and well-armed. Since most of them subscribe to the teachings of Christian Identity, they have identified the government as their enemy. For they believe the government is the pawn of Jewish bankers, who desire to rule the world. The only thing standing between the Jewish bankers and their goal is a small cadre of white Aryan warriors, who are ready, willing and able to lay down their lives for the white way of life. Killing the enemies of God is merely doing God's Will.

* * * * *

The lunch hour was almost over. It was hot and humid. People walked back to their places of work, eager to get out of the heat and into air-conditioned buildings. Eighty-eight year old James Wenneker von Brunn steered his car into a parking place near the 14ᵗʰ Street entrance of the United States Holocaust Memorial Museum in Washington D.C. It was June 10, 2009.

Von Brunn double-parked his car. It didn't matter, because he knew he wouldn't be coming back. The car would be towed. Then it would sit in some impound yard, waiting to be claimed. It would never be claimed.

The old man got out of the car and walked toward the building. He carried something long and slender in his right hand.

Seeing the elderly gentleman approaching the entrance, Stephen Tyron Johns politely opened the door and held it. Johns was a museum security guard. His job was to protect the premises and all those in it. Johns liked his job and he liked people, so he instinctively held the door open.

Von Brunn raised a .22 caliber rifle and shot Johns at point blank range. Mortally wounded, Johns sank to the floor like a wet sock.

Two nearby security guards heard the gunshot and saw Johns fall. Pulling their pistols, the two guards fired at the man with the rifle. Bullets hit him. Von Brunn dropped his rifle and clasped his wound. Blood bubbled over his hands.

Within minutes, the D.C. police, the U.S. Park Police and the FBI Terrorism Task Force had surrounded the building. Dressed in black and wearing body armor, they bristled with weapons. The building was evacuated, including large numbers of visiting schoolchildren, who had arrived in yellow buses.

Von Brunn was placed under arrest. A search of his person turned up a notebook. The notebook had the names and locations of other buildings written in it. One of the buildings listed was the National Cathedral. Bomb squads were sent to ten of the buildings in von Brunn's notebook.

Von Brunn had written a message in the notebook. At the end of the message von Brunn had scrawled his signature. The message read: "You want my weapons – this is how you'll get them. The Holocaust is a lie. [Barack] Obama was created by Jews. Obama does what his Jew owners tell him to do. Jews captured America's money. Jews control the mass media. The First Amendment is abrogated henceforth."

The FBI searched von Brunn's apartment, where they discovered another rifle, ammunition, computers, a hand-written last will and testament, along with a painting of Jesus Christ standing next to Adolf Hitler. One of the computers contained child pornography.

Who was James von Brunn and how did he come to this?

Born in St. Louis, Missouri, von Brunn was a good student, who was artistically inclined. As a child, his dream was to become a famous painter. Later, he attended the University of Washington, where he played varsity football and joined a fraternity. Most of his friends thought of him as handsome and athletic. His dream of being a painter had fallen by the wayside. He majored in journalism.

During World War II, he served in the Navy, commanding a PT boat. His crew respected him, for he was handsome and fearless and brave, caring for others more than himself. He received three battle stars. After the war, von Brunn got a job in advertising in New York City. Because he was smart and talented, he was soon a successful executive. In the 1960s, he moved to Maryland, where he became involved in Christian Identity, because he didn't like the way the country was going. No one knew their place anymore. Everyone claimed they had "rights." It became a movement. Civil rights! Something had to be done. White people needed to stand up and say something or else the whole country would go right down the toilet. Christian Identity was the only hope.

Much later, after he retired, he lived in Hayden Lake, Idaho, in 2004 and 2005. Until 2001, Hayden Lake had been the headquarters of the Aryan Nations, which was a neo-Nazi, white supremacist group.

At the time of the museum shooting, von Brunn lived in Annapolis, Maryland. He had moved back to what he knew. He was more comfortable in the East.

Von Brunn had an extensive criminal record. In 1966, after a fight in a restaurant, he was pulled over by police. The police determined that he was drunk and arrested him for driving under the influence. He got off with a fine. Two years later, he spent six-months in jail for resisting arrest.

James von Brunn decided that something needed to be done. No more talk. It was time to put up or shut up. The U.S. government was nothing more than the puppet of Jewish puppet masters. White Americans had lost all their God-given rights. So von Brunn determined he would take up the hood of Phineas, becoming a lone warrior. The honor of God had to be protected.

In 1981, von Brunn walked into the Federal Reserve's Eccles Building armed with a loaded revolver, a knife and a sawed-off shotgun. He was there to make a citizen's arrest of the Federal Reserve's Board of Governors for treason. They were responsible for "high interest rates."

Threatening a security guard with the revolver, von Brunn was jumped from behind by other security guards and restrained. Von Brunn told the guards he had a bomb. He did not. What he did have, though, was a device that looked like a bomb.

Federal authorities arrested him for attempted kidnapping and hostage-taking. Tried and convicted, von Brunn served six-and-a-half years in prison.

According to von Brunn, he was convicted by "a Negro jury, Jew/Negro attorneys and sentenced to prison for eleven years by a Jew judge. A Jew/Negro/White Court of Appeals" denied his subsequent appeal.

Nineteen years later, in 2009, once again James von Brunn decided it was time to do something. No more talk. Put up or shut up time. He was 88-years old, miserable, alone and lonely, and had nothing to live for anymore. The very least he could do before he died was protect the Honor of God. So he bought a rifle and some ammunition. Then he drove to Washington, D.C. It was a sunny day. He'd never seen the sky so blue. He felt good, almost young again.

God was watching.

After he murdered Stephen Johns, von Brunn was tried and sentenced to life in prison. They shipped him off to the Federal Correctional Complex in Butner, North Carolina. Von Brunn died in a Butner Hospital on January 6, 2010.

Big Boy and Little Feather

It was a crappy house on a crappy street in the crappiest part of the city. The city was Houston, Texas. A vast metropolis full of big oil money and lots of humidity. It had some other things too. Things like drugs, violence, and poverty. East Houston was the worst part of the city. The lowlifes congregated there because the rents were cheap.

The house sat on Cypress Street. A low chain link fence surrounded the front yard, which had a grass lawn in desperate need of water and weed killer. The inside of the house wasn't in much better shape. Old furniture with frayed upholstery, empty beer bottles and a Persian cat named Cindy, which was short for Cinderella. There were also five or six assorted handguns, ammunition and, over in the corner near the dining room table, an AK-47 assault rifle.

AK-47: a rather simple name, where AK is short for the Russian *avtomat Kalashnikova*, "Kalashnikov's automatic," and 47 refers to the year in which it was selected as the official weapon of the Soviet Union.

"It can turn even a monkey into a combatant," said Laurent Kabila, the fearsome Congolese political leader, referring to the AK-47.

The rifle belonged to Dennis "Big Boy" Clem, who lived in the house with his girlfriend. Her name was Tanya Smith, but most of her friends knew her as Little Feather, because – supposedly – she had some Indian blood in her. Anyway, so she said. Tanya claimed she had shamanistic powers, that she was an obeah doctor. Nobody knew what the hell she was talking about. According to her, this meant she was clairvoyant. She said she had extrasensory powers. According to her, that's why she dressed the way she did. Most of the time she was all Gothed-out. Every once in a while, she traded the Goth look for an American Indian look. Which consisted of a leather dress with lots of fringe hanging all over it and a feathered headdress.

Whenever Tanya started talking about her powers and shit, Big Boy just shook his head and rolled his eyeballs. But he was smart enough not to say anything. Tanya had a real bad temper. It didn't pay to piss her off.

Besides being lovers, Big Boy and Tanya were members of the Aryan Circle, which was a white supremacist gang. The Aryan Circle was into violence, drugs, guns, money, and a virulent brand of racist ideology. They hated anyone whose skin wasn't white.

Which was why, when a pick-up truck parked in front of the house, things went from bad to worse. Seated in the cab of the truck were two African-Americans. One was 15-years old. He was in the passenger's seat. The other, the driver, was 19-years old. Both were local gangbangers – members of the notorious Bloods – who hustled drugs for walking around money. They were looking for Big Boy, because he owed them some money for some crystal meth. Only they chose the wrong day to come collecting.

For a bunch of Big Boy's friends were standing around the front yard drinking beer. All were white. All were heavily tattooed with swastikas and lightning bolts. Most were drunk. And none of them liked African-American gangbangers.

One of the beer drinkers, who went by the name of "Tricycle," took note of the truck as it came to a stop in front of the house. When he saw who was in the truck, he pointed at the truck with his beer bottle, shouting, "Get the fuck outta' here!"

Everyone in the front yard turned to look in the direction Tricycle's beer bottle was pointing. A few seconds later, someone shouted, "Goddamn niggers. What the hell ya' think you're doing?" Pretty soon, all the whites were screaming racial slurs at the two gangbangers.

Inside the house, Tanya heard the noise. She walked outside to see what was going on. She was dressed all in black, with heavy black eyeliner.

When she saw the gangbangers in the truck, she went ballistic. "Hey, you in the truck. Ya'll niggers need to leave. And I mean right now!"

The gangbangers just sat there. The passenger said something to the driver, causing him to flash a big smile.

Tricycle saw the smile and took it as disrespect. He began walking toward the truck. As Tricycle got closer, the passenger turned a little, raising his hand. In his hand was a 9mm Glock. The gangbanger extended his arm out the side window of the truck and fired. The bullet hit Tricycle in the thigh, spinning him around and down.

Big Boy was in the house, making a sandwich when he heard a gunshot. Pausing, he cocked his head, listening. He held a jar of mayonnaise in one hand and a spoon in his other hand. Then he heard a shrill scream, which he recognized. Sounded like Tanya was all worked up about something.

Putting the jar down on the counter, he dropped the spoon in it. Licking mayo from his thumb, he walked over to the AK-47. It was loaded and ready to rock n' roll – always. When growing up, Big Boy had been a Boy Scout. He believed in being prepared. He picked up the lethal looking weapon and jacked the bolt back.

Walking to the front window of the house, he took a quick look-see. Tricycle was on the lawn, holding his leg, which was bleeding. Tanya, middle finger raised, was screaming something at a pickup truck. Big Boy recognized the truck. He knew who was in it. Adrenaline surged through him.

Two seconds later, Big Boy burst out of the house. Raising the AK-47, he sprayed the cab of the pickup with bullets. Rifle ready, Big Boy advanced on the truck. Peering through the truck's open window, he saw two dead gangbangers and a lot of blood.

Lowering the rifle, Big Boy walked back toward the house. As he passed Tricycle, he said, "Somebody get 'im outta here. Cops'll be here soon." Big Boy knew his neighbors. By now, most of them had already dialed 911.

"You got about ten minutes," he told everyone in the front yard. "You best be gone in five." Everybody began scrambling around.

He walked over to Tanya, who stood there glaring at the truck. "We gotta' go. An' I mean right now. Get your shit together."

Five minutes later, the house was empty. Even the cat was gone. Except for the pick up truck with two dead gangbangers in it, no one could have guessed anything had happened.

The cops arrived. They took one look at the truck and called for a forensics team. Then they called the morgue. Then they knocked on the front door of the house. Nobody home. So they went to the house across the street, where two widowed sisters lived. The sisters invited the officers in, sat them down, poured coffee, and told them what they had seen and heard.

Meanwhile, Big Boy and Tanya were hiding out at a friend's house. The friend was a member of the Aryan Circle. After they told him what had gone down, he said they could stay as long as they needed. Two days later, Big Boy decided they should move, because news of the two dead gangbangers was all over the television. And the newscasters were happily providing names and descriptions of the suspects: Dennis Clem and Tanya Smith.

So Big Boy and Tanya changed locations. They moved in with another friend, who was also part of the Aryan Circle. As payment, Big Boy gave the friend an elaborate tattoo. Tattooing was Big Boy's thing. He was a true artiste when it came to body art.

The heat was on, though. The Houston police were questioning everybody, especially known members of the Aryan Circle, following up on every lead. Tanya and Big Boy had to stay inside the house. If they didn't, someone would spot them, put two and two together, and call the cops. Even so, Big Boy knew that – sooner or later – somebody would let something slip, and then they'd be in deep shit.

Three weeks after the shooting, Big Boy decided it was time to get out of Dodge. If they didn't, they'd be caught. He made arrangements to stay with Aryan Circle members in Louisiana. On August 5, he and Tanya drove across the state line into Bastrop, Louisiana. In the back of their borrowed SUV, they had handguns, a sawed-off shotgun, and an SKS assault rifle. And thousands of rounds of ammunition. Big Boy wanted to be prepared, just in case.

They spent their first night in Bastrop at the home of Donald Brendle. Brendle, a righteous member of the Aryan Circle, lived in the house with his girlfriend. Her name was Chrystal Harrell. Because of his reputation, the local police kept a close eye on Brendle. In fact, Brendle was suspected of a recent theft, involving drugs and money. For this reason, Brendle advised Big Boy and Tanya that it would be safer if they moved to a downtown motel. Big Boy agreed. So Brendle drove downtown and registered for a room at the motel. Only he made a mistake, which would soon discombobulate the whole thing. He registered under his own name. Big Boy and Tanya moved into the motel.

Meanwhile, the Bastrop police decided to bring Brendle in for questioning. But they couldn't find him. So they started contacting Brendle's family members, trying to find out where he was. One of Brendle's relatives told the police that Brendle might be staying at the motel downtown. The relative had heard Brendle mention something about a motel downtown.

At two o'clock in the afternoon, Bastrop Police Detectives Chuck Wilson and John Smith arrived at the motel. They were there to question Brendle. Checking with the desk clerk, they asked if Donald Brendle was registered. The clerk said yes and gave them the room number.

Detective Wilson knocked on the door of the room. He and his partner expected Brendle to answer the door. They had no idea what they were walking into. Brendle was not in the room. Instead, two heavily armed, extremely volatile fugitives were in the room.

A young woman answered the door. Dressed in black, she wore heavy black make-up. "Yeah?" she asked, standing in the open doorway.

The two detectives looked at each other. Wilson shrugged. "I'm Detective Wilson," he said. "This is Detective Smith. We're looking for Donald Brendle. Is this his room?"

"Yeah," said Tanya. "Only he ain't here."

Inside the room, Big Boy was listening. And he didn't like what he was hearing. Cops. Picking up two handguns, he moved to the bed, where he slid the guns under the bedspread. Then he positioned himself on the bed between the two guns, his back against wall, as if he had been watching television.

"Well, would you mind if we came in and had a look around? It'll only take a minute and we'll be out of your hair," said Detective Wilson, smiling.

Tanya hesitated. Turning her head, she glanced over at Big Boy. She could see him seated on the bed. The cops couldn't because of the door's angle. Big Boy gave his head a slow, definite nod – let 'em come in.

Tanya looked at Detective Wilson. She smiled. "Sure. Why not?" she said. "I got nothing to hide." She stepped back so the two detectives could enter.

Once inside, the detectives automatically scanned the room. The big guy with a shaved head and Nazi tattoos was hard to miss. He was not Brendle. That was for sure. Whoever he was, he looked like bad news. The kind of guy you did not want to meet in a dark alley.

"Hey," said Big Boy.

Detective Wilson nodded. Detective Smith just stared. He had a bad feeling about this. "We're trying to locate Donald Brendle," said Wilson.

"Hmmm," grunted Big Boy. Tanya stood near the still open door. Her arms were crossed over her chest. The look on her face was that of a snake watching a mouse.

"You wouldn't happen to know where we might find him, would you?" asked Wilson.

Big Boy shook his head. "No."

"Are you a friend of his?" asked Detective Smith.

"No."

Detective Wilson stopped being polite. "You got any ID?" he asked, looking at Big Boy, then at Tanya.

"Yeah," said Big Boy. He slid his hands under the bedspread. When he pulled them back out, there was a 9mm pistol in each hand.

Both detectives held their hands out in front of their chests, making the universal gesture of 'take it easy.' "Whoa now," said Wilson. "You don't wanna' do anything crazy."

Big Boy fired both guns. One of the bullets hit Wilson in his shoulder, spinning him around. The other bullet hit Smith in his elbow, knocking him back. Smith made a grasping motion toward Wilson. "Go! Go!" he shouted. Both detectives ran out the open door into the hallway.

As the two detectives moved down the hallway toward the exit, Big Boy emerged from his room. Still holding a gun in each hand, he fired repeatedly at Wilson and Smith. He kept firing until both men fell to the floor. Wilson and Smith were dead.

Big Boy stood looking at his handiwork. He smiled. Then, hearing something behind him, he turned. Tanya walked past him without a word. When she got to the exit, she opened the door and walked across the parking lot to the motel office. She walked up to the desk, where the motel manager stood staring at her. He had heard the rolling thunder of gunfire. It sounded as if a war was being fought across the way.

"You need to call 911," announced Tanya. "Two cops are wounded. I think they're dead."

As the manager reached for the telephone, Tanya walked back out the office door. Once outside, she trotted over to the borrowed SUV, got in, started the engine and drove off with squealing tires.

Both the Bastrop Police Department and the local Sheriff's Department responded to the 911 call. The motel manager told the emergency dispatcher that two detectives had gone to the room registered to Donald Brendle. There was a lot of gunfire. The detectives had not come out.

Police officers and deputies showed up ready for the worst. All wore body armor and carried shotguns and pistols. As they fanned out and moved toward the building, an ambulance arrived. The med-techs grabbed their kits and ran toward the building.

Big Boy emerged from the building, surprising everyone. With a gun in each hand, he started firing at the med-techs. Police officers and deputies immediately returned fire. Ducking behind a nearby parked car, Big Boy shot back at the cops.

Wounded, the med-techs dropped their kits and scurried out of the field of fire.

Slapping new clips into both his handguns, Big Boy jumped out from behind the car and blazed away at the cops. Half-a-dozen shotguns boomed. Big Boy staggered as sledge hammer-like blows pounded him. Gathering his strength, Big Boy leaped forward once again, blasting away with both guns. The shotguns boomed again and again. Patches of red bloomed on Big Boy's shirt. Falling to his knees, he kept firing until his guns were empty. Another booming volley followed. Big Boy crashed forward, dead.

Meanwhile, Tanya Smith drove down the freeway back toward Houston. She had no idea Big Boy was dead.

Once the police identified Big Boy as Dennis Clem, it wasn't hard to figure out who his female companion had been. Or that she was probably going back to Houston, where she had friends. The Houston Police were alerted and began working all their sources and informants. Two days later, Houston police officers surrounded a double-wide mobile home in a trailer park. The trailer park accommodated a number of Aryan Circle members, who, because of their socio-economic status, gravitated to trailer parks. And like most people, members of the Aryan Circle were attracted by the luxury of emotional and psychological commitments. They wanted to associate with likeminded people, people who thought and acted like they did. Thus, when one member moved to a trailer park, others tended to follow.

Tanya Smith aka Little Feather was hiding out in the double-wide trailer, owned by a member of the Aryan Circle. The cops knew she was there because someone had tipped them off. Tricked out in her usual Gothic Queen costume, Tanya elected not to do a 'Big Boy' – shoot it out with the cops. Instead, she strolled out of the double-wide nonchalantly, as if on her way to the store to buy a quart of milk. The cops arrested her and transported her to jail.

News of Big Boy's final vicious gunfight with the cops circulated rapidly through the Aryan Circle's membership. Prayers offered up for Big Boy referred to him as "a soldier for our cause and a good man." The Aryan Circle newsletter announced that "Dennis Clem is home in the Heavens."

Summer Heinz proudly displayed the tattoo Big Boy had given her, telling everyone, "My best friend did it. Seven days before he was in a shootout with two cops and killed them but died too. It means a lot to me."

A few months later, Summer was arrested for her involvement in another murder.

Five months later, in January 2009, Tanya Smith was convicted on federal weapons charges. The judge sentenced her to 27 years in prison. Before she could begin serving her sentence, she was transported to Louisiana, where she stood trial for second degree murder and drug charges. The jury found Tanya Smith guilty on all counts. She received two consecutive life sentences, along with concurrent sentences for the less significant charges.

James von Brunn, Dennis 'Big Boy' Clem, and Tanya Smith aka Little Feather were connected by more than the ideology of white supremacy. All three subscribed to the doctrinal teachings of the Church of Christian Identity. More importantly, all three were members of the ultra-elite holy order called the Phineas Priesthood.

Chapter 2

A Lust For Vengeance

To fully understand the Phineas Priesthood, it is necessary to go back to the year 1300 B.C., because that's where the whole thing began. At about that time, Moses was leading the Hebrews through the wilderness toward the Promised Land. Moving from bivouac to bivouac, the Hebrews came to a place called Shittim, on the plains of Moab. It was from Shittim that the Hebrews would cross the Jordan River.

The nation of Moab boasted a centralized form of government, at the top of which sat a king. Most of the inhabitants of Moab were farmers. There were, however, several large cities with splendid buildings. To protect its citizens and its cities, Moab had constructed fortifications, primarily small fortresses, which were placed at strategic points along Moab's borders. Many Midianite tribes had migrated to Moab from Arabia. Just prior to the Exodus of the Hebrews from Egypt, the Amorites, who were ruled by King Sihon, had invaded and occupied Moab. The religion of the Moabites was paganism. Specifically, they worshipped Baal Faur, also known as Baal Peor.

The cult of Baal Peor was a phallic cult, which meant they worshipped sex. According to St. Jerome, the idol of Baal Peor had a priapus (an erect penis) sticking out of its mouth. Baal Peor was a Syrian god on whose phallus every female worshipper was obliged to sacrifice her virginity.

While camped at Shittim, the Hebrews began socializing with the local Midianites, whose females were as promiscuous as they were beautiful. And they were very beautiful. Due to a shortage of young Hebrew women, the Hebrew men began sleeping with the Midianite women. Which, of course, went against the Law of the Hebrew God – Jehovah Elohim – and the explicit orders of Moses, who had warned the Hebrew men against sexual intercourse with "strange women." Moses' warning fell on deaf ears.

Zimri ben-Salu, who was the leader of the Hebrew tribe of Simeon, and who was expected to set an example, was one of the first and possibly the worst offender. For Zimri took as his mistress none other than Cozbi bath-Zur, who was the daughter of a Midianite prince. Zimri's act opened the floodgates. Patterning themselves after him, thousands followed his example, sinning before Jehovah Elohim by fornicating with "strange women."

When Moses confronted Zimri with his sin, Zimri replied hotly to the self-righteous Prophet, "Yes indeed, Moses, you're free to make use of such laws as you like. But you won't have me as one of your followers in your tyrannical commands. All you've ever done, under a pretense of laws and of Jehovah, is wickedly impose slavery on us and gain power for yourself, while depriving us of the sweetness of life, which consists in acting according to our own wills – the right of free men."[1]

After this rebellious outburst, later, in the Tent of Meeting (the Tabernacle), which was a gathering of the tribal elders and, in cases like this, served as a formal legal hearing, Zimri told the elders, "Indeed, this man (Moses) is harder on the Hebrews than were the Egyptians themselves! I think it right to come at truth by inquiring of many people, and not like one who lives under tyranny – to suffer the whole hope of my life to depend upon one man."[2]

That being said, Zimri stalked out of the meeting and went back to his own tent, where his mistress awaited him. Thunderstruck by the man's vehemence, Moses and the other elders sat stone-still. They didn't know what to do.

Talmudic tradition, which was an ongoing commentary on the Law and its interpretation, and which was accepted by some as authoritative and rejected by others as flight of fancy, discussed in great detail the enormity of Zimri's sin. To the point of counting the number of times Zimri and his lover successively copulated. The Talmud referred to Zimri as "that wicked man."

* * * * *

There was a man who did know what to do. His name was Phineas ben-Eleazar, a young Levitical priest. As he sat in the Tent of Meeting, Phineas had heard the words of the defiant Zimri. He had witnessed the trespasser's blasphemous insolence. Filled with righteous indignation, the priest reached for a spear and marched out of the Tabernacle to discharge his priestly function, which was to defend the honor of God. Philo Judaeus described what was about to happen as "a deed at once memorable for youthful daring, and worthy of a hero."[3]

---

1   Flavius Josephus, *Jewish Antiquities.*
2   Ibid.
3   Philo Judaeus, *Life of Moses.*

Going directly to Zimri's tent, he walked in and discovered Zimri and Cozbi naked, in the very act of breaking God's Law. Without hesitation, he thrust his spear into the embracing couple. Its point pierced Zimri's anus and sliced into and through Cozbi's womb. "He pierced them through," wrote Philo Judaeus, "and also cut off the genitals with which they were satisfying their sinful passion."

Phineas castrated the dead body of Zimri. Fixing the man's genitals to his spear, Phineas carried the spear with its blood trophies to the Tabernacle. There he drove the butt of the spear into the ground, where it stood day after day, thus displaying what happened to those who disobeyed Jehovah.

Electrified by Phineas' feat, Moses resumed command. He ordered the Levitical police to kill every Hebrew who had broken Jehovah's Law and had sex with a Midianite woman. The sands of Shittim ran red with Hebrew blood, as the Levitical police hunted down and slaughtered 24,000 Hebrews.

Inspired by so much death and blood, Moses decided that the Justice of God required more blood. So he had the Levitical police butcher every Midianite adult male, including Prince Zur, who was Cozbi's father. Moses also gave instructions that all the Midianites' wealth should be confiscated. And the Midianites were extremely rich.

Initially, Moses had meant to spare the Midianite women and children. But on second thought, he decided that they were too evil to live. The women were nothing more than sirens, who lured men to sin. And the male children would grow up to be pederasts and homosexuals, which was an abomination. So he ordered them put to the sword too. The only Midianites he spared were 32,000 virgin girls, who were later meted out, along with the monetary spoils.

After the carnage was over, Jehovah Elohim spoke to Moses, approving of Phineas' zeal. In this instance, 'zeal' may be defined as 'jealous.' Phineas was jealous for the honor of God, doing whatever was necessary to protect it. As a reward, Jehovah gave Phineas a "covenant of peace" and granted Phineas and "his seed" a priesthood that would have no end.

* * * * *

Within the context of the Bible, the story of Phineas is minor and unremarkable. Yet this relatively obscure event would later be shanghaied, distorted, and adopted by members of the church of Christian Identity to promote their own supremacist agenda, which revolved around race religion. The church of Christian Identity put forth Phineas as the template for their concept of "solitary warriors," thus fomenting violence and terrorism. Thus, the next step in understanding the Phineas Priesthood involves an examination of Christian Identity.

The term 'Christian Identity' comes from the following doctrinal statement: "We believe the Bible identifies the Anglo-Saxon people with the Old Testament nation of Israel." The statement, of course, is wrong. It reflects a misinterpretation of what happened to the Lost Tribes of Israel after their dispersion.

The Bible records – and historical evidence corroborates – that around 721 B.C. the Northern Tribes of Israel also known collectively as Samaria, were conquered by Assyria and carried away into captivity. This was Assyria's way of punishing Samaria for failing to pay tribute (taxes).

What happened to these 'lost tribes' has always been a controversial topic among Biblical scholars, amateur theologians and Christians.

According to some, the Ten Lost Tribes of Israel migrated to Great Britain, where they gave origin to the Anglo-Saxon or Caucasian race, which is also referred to as Aryan. The term given to this erroneous interpretation is British-Israelism.

The first person to really buy into the idea was John Sadler, who was a member of the British Parliament. He published a book called *Rights of the Kingdom* in 1649. In his book, Sadler put forth his belief that Europeans, Anglo-Saxons, Germans and Slavs were the descendants of the Lost Tribes of Israel. Since this was the period of British Imperialism, when the British Empire had hegemony over much of the world, Sadler's claim wasn't astounding. Most of England held the position they were not only racially superior to the rest of the world, but they were also "God's chose people." Indeed, circumstances served to prove the point.

Then in 1723, a Protestant apologist from Amsterdam, whose name was Dr. Abadie, observed, "Unless the ten tribes have flown into the air or have been plunged into the center of the earth, they must be sought for in the north and west, and in the British Isles." His remarks were reported widely in the British newspapers.

The idea of British Israelism really gathered momentum when, in 1792, Richard Brothers delivered letters to the King of England, the ministers of state, and the Speaker of the House of Commons. In his letters, Brothers advised the readers that in five days the fulfillment of the prophecy made by the Prophet Daniel in the Old Testament would occur. The prophecy Brothers referred to was in the seventh chapter of the Book of Daniel, which predicted the coming of four world powers – called "beasts" – the rise of the Anti-Christ, the Tribulation, and the Second Coming of Jesus.

According to Richard Brothers, God had called him two years before, in 1790. Prior to his call, Brothers had been a lieutenant in the British Navy. He abruptly resigned his commission in 1789 and, because of religious scruples, refused to accept his retirement money from the navy. Soon after hearing the voice of God calling to him, Brothers had begun having visions.

None of the letters' recipients took the matter seriously, writing the author off as another religious nutcase. Eight months later, in 1793, Brothers was back and again making fantastic predictions. He proclaimed the imminent death of King George III. And that after the King's death, the crown would be given to him, "the Nephew of the Almighty, and prince of the Hebrews, appointed to lead them to the land of Canaan." In other words, Brothers believed he was a direct descendant of King David. Which meant that only he could lay claim to the title of King of England. Subsequent to these crazy statements, Brothers published his book *A Revealed Knowledge of the Prophecies and the Times*, 1794.

The English government could no longer turn the other cheek. Forecasting the death of the King was serious stuff. So they tossed him into Newgate Prison. After he got out, he wrote more books. Most of his books trumpeted the validity of British Israelism, i.e., that the Anglo-Saxon people were the true Israel, descended from the Lost Tribes. Brothers also spoke at public gatherings, where he made wild political prophecies. Some of them actually came true, which increased his notoriety and attracted disciples to his religion. Most of his disciples were uneducated, poor and easily manipulated, the kind of people looking to get something for nothing. Apparently, Brothers was an accomplished rabble-rouser, because he was able to persuade many of his disciples to sell their meager earthly possessions so they could come with him to the New Jerusalem, which he was going to build on the River Jordan.

In 1795, the English government decided Richard Brothers was a lunatic. They ordered him committed to the Bedlam Asylum, where Brothers remained for eleven years. Released in 1806, Brothers discovered his religion was flourishing. British Israelism had caught on.

The next person to ride the British-Israelite wave was John Wilson. In 1840, Wilson published his book *Lectures on Our Israelitish Origin*, which was well-received and went through four subsequent printings.

John Taylor caught the wave in 1859, when he published *The Great Pyramid, Why Was It Built and Who Built It?* Taylor maintained that the

Israelites had built the Pyramid of Cheops. His argument rested upon the fact that British feet and inches formed the basis of the pyramid's construction.

By 1871, the waves of British-Israelism were getting larger and coming more frequently. For that was the year Edward Hine, who was a banker made a big splash with the publication of his book *The Ten Lost Tribes of Israel*, which became a bestseller, selling 250,000 copies. Later, in 1884, Hine boarded a ship bound for America, where he intended to spread the gospel of British-Israelism. And he did. While traveling around, Hine advanced the notion of Americans being the lost tribe of Manasseh. A few years later, a man named Howard Rand, who hailed from Massachusetts, borrowed Hines' gospel as his own. Only Rand made one significant change. He supplemented Hines' gospel with the centuries-old disease called anti-semitism. For Rand believed the Jews were responsible for the ills of the world. Rand called his gospel "Christian Identity."

The wave of British-Israelism crested in 1946. That was the year that Wesley Swift started his own church in Lancaster, California. Baptizing his church with the peculiar name of the Church of Jesus Christ-Christian, he rapidly established sister-churches in San Francisco, Oakland, Riverside, Hollywood and San Diego.

Swift, the only child of a prominent Methodist preacher, was born in New Jersey in 1913. God called him to preach while he was a teenager. By the time he was 18 years old, Wesley was a licensed preacher in the Methodist Church.

Not long after his ordination, Wesley attended an inspiring lecture by a Kingdom Indentity preacher. It was there that Wesley Swift discovered his "true heritage and the covenants that God had made with the White Race."[4] Galvanized into action by his new understanding, Wesley Swift moved to Los Angeles to attend Bible College, where he was further indoctrinated with the idea of true Israel, who were Aryan, and the concept of the "warrior priest." This indoctrination resulted in Swift joining the Ku Klux Klan. He began preaching in the Foursquare Church in Los Angeles, which was the headquarters of Amy Semple McPherson's holy-rolling denomination. Only the people weren't responding the way he wanted. So he decided to go it on his own.

It was then that he started his church – Church of Jesus Christ-Christian.

---

4   This quote about Wesley Swift was taken directly from the literature published by Kingdom Indentity Ministries, Harrison, Arkansas.

The Church of Jesus Christ-Christian was a racist sect, which mutated into Christian Identity. The core doctrine of Christian Identity revolved around the idea of only two races living on the face of the earth. A priestly white race, which was descended from the first man Adam, and the 'mud races' – anyone who was not white – which were the spawn of Satan. This latter idea came from the perverse idea that Eve had been impregnated by Satan. According to this theory, the white races were the descendants of Adam and Eve. Whereas the 'mud races' were the offspring of Cain, whose real father was Satan, who, disguised as a serpent, had mated with Eve.

Jews were the descendants of Cain. Aryans were the descendants of Adam and Eve through Abel. Aryans were God's chosen people. And any mixing of the races was nothing more than a Satanic plot, designed to destroy God's people – the white race.

Some Christian Identity ministries did not accept the two-race theory, because they did not hold that Eve was impregnated by the Devil. Rather they embraced the notion that the Jews were descended from Esau, who rejected God. Thus, Esau's offspring – the Jews – were those whom God had not elected. Which meant that as a race the Jews were evil. At a minimum, this theory demanded racial separation.[5]

By the 1950s, Swift was delivering his ideology by means of daily radio broadcasts. A dynamic and charismatic speaker, Swift's message appealed to more and more people, slowly spreading across the country, appealing primarily to malcontents, those disaffected by their lot in the social and financial pecking-order of life. These converts felt success and happiness were being taken from them by a vast conspiracy, which was composed of the government and its life-sucking taxes; the Jews, who were perceived as controlling the government; and the "mud people," who stole the jobs rightfully belonging to white people. Righteous anger at what was happening was the common denominator among Swift's adherents.

Somewhere in there, Swift hooked up with Colonel William Potter Gale, who organized anti-tax and paramilitary groups in the United States, including the California Rangers and the Posse Comitatus. Colonel Gale introduced Swift to Richard Girnt Butler, who later founded the Aryan Nations. Butler was an ardent white supremacist, who had never really considered the advantages of combining his racist philosophy with religion. But he was willing to listen. Once he heard the verbal pyrotech-

---

5   The best explanation of the two different theories is provided by Leonard Zeskind in his monumental *Blood and Politics*.

nics of Swift's message, Butler saw the light. Race and religion were the way to go. For religion added a spiritual urgency to the hate of racism. The result was an unprompted and spontaneous fanaticism – the army of God's chosen people.

With Swift at the helm, aided by Butler and Colonel Gale, Christian Identity continued to grow, slowly but surely. Then things started to fall apart for two reasons. First, Wesley Swift died in 1970. It quickly became apparent that Christian Identity was a much a cult of personality as it was a religion. The movement was only as strong as its honcho. Butler assumed control, but didn't have the force of personality or flair of Swift. Membership began to sag as members looked for someone to prop them up.

In the end, all that remained were the most rabid dupes – hardcore white supremacists energized by fear and hatred. Butler changed the name of the group, calling it The Church of Jesus Christ-Christian/Aryan Nations. The new name reflected the changing emphasis of the church. Butler wanted the group to take a more proactive stance. A separate national entity – populated by whites only – was the order of the day.

As a first step toward that ultimate, Utopian goal, Butler purchased a piece of property in Hayden Lake, Idaho. He and his remnant moved there, establishing an "armed white compound," where they separated themselves from the "mud people."

With Wesley Swift's death and Butler's inability to fill the dead man's big shoes, the second reason things fell apart lurched into the open. A green-eyed monster called jealousy. Christian Identity was made up of small groups scattered across the U.S. Each group or "church" had a local leader or "pastor." These leaders were ambitious and held themselves in high esteem. Every leader felt he should be in charge. So when Swift died and Butler failed to consolidate his eminence, the local leaders began jockeying for position. In other words, there was a power struggle, with each local leader trying to win as much support as possible. Which resulted in antagonism and division within the ranks of God's army.

Eventually, the local leaders decided it was better to be a big fish in a little pond rather than take orders from someone else, which would make them a little fish in a big pond. So a multitude of parochial groups sprang up. With minor variations, all were Christian Identity in their beliefs, but each had its own name, its own organization, its own recruiting program and its own power structure. And they all had their own agendas.

Chapter 3

Race and Racism

It was Solomon, the favorite son of King David and heir to the throne of Israel, who wrote, "There's nothing new under the sun." And the idea that the white race is superior to the so-called colored races is no exception. It's been around a long, long time. To demonstrate this fact, it is necessary to take a quick look at the idea of "race" and the general history of "racism."

Race, which is defined as "any of the major biological divisions of mankind, distinguished by color and texture of hair, color of skin and eyes, stature, bodily proportions, etc.: many ethnologists now consider that there are only three primary divisions, the Caucasian (loosely, *white race*), Negroid (loosely, *black race*), and Mongoloid (loosely, *yellow race*), each with various subdivisions: the term has acquired so many unscientific connotations that in this sense it is often replaced in scientific usage by *ethnic stock* or *group*."

White was first used in the racial sense, as an adjective, in the year 1604. Whoever it was that used it, did it like this: "of those races (chiefly European or of European Extraction) characterized by light complexion." Certainly it was used prior to that, but this is the first recorded usage. And it is assumed that this usage was quite common at that time, which shows how long 'racism' has been around.

William Perry, in 1676, distinguished between blacks and whites, calling blacks a totally different and separate species. Blacks differed from Europeans not only in skin color "but also in natural manners and in the internal qualities of their minds." No one challenged Perry's conclusions. In fact, Europeans agreed. There was nothing startling about these remarks. It was common knowledge.

Then in 1708, William Tyson, who was a physical anatomist, discovered the evolutionary missing link. He determined, scientifically of course, that it was the African Pygmy. Whom Tyson called "wholly a brute," halfway between an ape and a man.

Ninety-one years later, in the year 1799, a medical doctor from Great Britain validated the superiority of whites. His name was Charles White.

Dr. White published a profusely illustrated book in which he certified, without qualm and with meticulous decisiveness, that the white race is exalted over those of color. Mostly, his proof consisted of pointing out the cosmetic refinement of white faces – their "rosy cheeks and coral lips." Again, no one argued with the incredible virtuosity of the doctor's genius. But it *was* nice to know that an expert confirmed what everyone already knew.

Following in Charles White's "scientific" footsteps was Robert Knox. Knox, in his book *The Races of Man* declared it perfectly acceptable for whites to wipe out whole populations of blacks. Because "the texture" of the black "brain is, I think, generally darker." And because there is "a physical and consequently, a psychological inferiority in the dark races generally."

Essentially, by dint of abstract reasoning, Knox arrived at these exaggerated, quaint and absurd conclusions. Conclusions which Knox believed supported genocide.

Knox's conclusions were supported by A.R. Wallace, the codiscoverer of the theory of evolution. Put simply, Wallace explained that extermination of the colored races was nothing more than natural selection at work. In other words, racial eradication was a self-acting, scientific law, nothing to be concerned about. This was how the world worked.

Frederick Farrar took the idea of extermination even further, if possible. Farrar divided the races of mankind into three distinct groups: "savage, semi-civilized and civilized." And of all the races on the face of the earth, the Aryan and the Semitic were the only examples of civilized races. There was only one semi-civilized race: the Chinese, who, admittedly, were sliding down the slippery slope toward savage. All other races were savage, and "irreclaimable," because despite the whites' superhuman efforts, the savage races were beyond hope. They were "doomed."

Paul Rohrbach summed up the white man's attitude toward the "rising tide of color" in his 1912 best-selling book *German Thought in the World*. "Not until the native learns to produce anything of value in the service of the higher race, i.e., in the service of its and his own progress, does he gain any moral right to exist." Translation: it is morally proper to wipe out the colored races.

What none of these esteemed white men bothered to mention, as they set forth their logical and scientific excuses for genocide, was the real reason for such European posturing: real estate. They wanted what the blacks had, land and natural resources. In the end, then, the racism of some boiled down to money. Others truly believed the colored races were of lesser value than whites.

To me, it is fascinating that there is no universal definition of what is meant by whiteness, being white, white man, white race, or whites. Which only serves to emphasize just how parochial men are after all. In fact, about the only thing the experts agree upon with regard to whiteness is that it designates people with pale skin. After that, though, it all falls apart, because they can't agree on what "pale skin" means. This is because everyone, for some reason, wants to be whiter than they are. Especially rich people. Rich people with darker skin tend to consider themselves "whiter" than they really are. And poor people tend to agree with them. It's almost as if the poor people believe the reason the rich people are rich is because they're white, which means they're somehow better. Therefore they deserve to be rich.

One extreme example of this whiter way of thinking, I discovered, took place in Haiti, during the late 1700's. At that time, Haiti was known as Santo Domingo. One half of the island was governed by the French, the other half was governed by the Spanish. And England was looking for a way to gain part of the island, because there was so much money to be made from the sugar and coffee plantations. Anyway, the blacks on the island, most of who were slaves, came up with a skin-color classification system with 136 different names for each of 136 different shades of black. The lighter you were the higher your status.

In 1923, some guy named Bhagat Singh Thind so desperately wanted to be whiter than he was that he sued the United States government over it. In the end, the case came before the U.S. Supreme Court. The court decided that the people of India could not claim the title of "free white men" and all the perks that went with it. With little concern for Mr. Thind's wanna' be vanity, the court stated: "swarthy brunette[s] ... are darker than some of the lighter hued persons of the brown or yellow races."

Under this ruling, which I call the Snow White Clause, white women are the freest of all, generally speaking, because women have lighter skin than men in all races. But even in the fairest races, the women come in second, since Albinos produce almost no melanin and have the palest of all skins. They are the fairest of the fair.

As I previously observed, no one, especially the experts can agree upon what defines being white. But boy, do they try. Most countries of the world have, at one time or another, instituted programs to keep the riff-raff, that is, people of color, out.

In the late 1800's, Australia decided to restrict all permanent immigration by non-Europeans. It became knows as the White Australia Policy. They called their program the Immigration Restriction Act, which was a fancy way of saying, keep out. That means they were getting sick and tired of all the Chinese people coming into the outback. The way it worked was this: the immigration officials gave everyone trying to enter the country a language test. Applicants had to prove they could read, speak and write a European language. And the immigration guys got to specify the language. So one day it could be French, the next day it could be Italian. It wasn't until 1973 that the White Australian Policy was cancelled, because that's when it became politically advantageous to be non-racist.

Canada has a unique and somewhat confusing way of classifying whites and non-whites. In one census, the government wants to know about each person's "cultural or ethnic origin." Supposedly, this question does not refer to skin color. On the second census, people are either designated as white or non-white in color. And note that it is never whites and people of color. Rather, the people of color are called 'members of visible minority groups.' All three terms are demeaning. 'Non-white' implies immediate inferiority because you're not white – you're deficient already. People of color implies the same lack, but from the opposite direction: since you are a person of color, that means you're not white, and that means you're second-class. And the phrase 'visible minority' might be the worst of all, because it screams freakishness: you stand out because you're not the same as most everybody else, and since you're not a member of any majority, you must be genetically deviant. Each of the terms excludes, isolates, separates, and humiliates.

As far as I can tell, Canada has never had an official or active "whites-preferred" immigration program. However, it's my understanding that many whites in Canada despise the influx of Chinese immigrants. And it's no secret that the French-speaking whites of Quebec believe themselves vastly superior to all other Canadians, regardless of skin tone. If you're not white, don't speak French and don't live in Quebec, you're trash.

Brazil, though, is a whole different kettle of fish. Since most Brazilians are mixed racially, Brazil's definition of whiteness is more "broadly applied," which means it's vague, and if you want to be white, you just check the appropriate box. Really, that's how they do it. The census in Brazil operates on self-identification. In the year 2006 census, 53%, or 100 million Brazilians were white. However, as it becomes more and more acceptable to be of African descent (black), fewer people are identifying themselves as white. This pleasing trend indicates either a sense of healthy imminence, or signifies truculence and bellicosity. I suspect it represents a growing spiritual and racial serenity. Brazilians are becoming more at ease with who they are.

The definition of white in the United States is "people having origins in any of the original peoples of Europe, the Middle East or North Africa. For all practical purposes, though, it refers to people of European origin with pale complexions. In other words, if you look white (have a pale complexion), then you are white. But wait a moment, there is also the 'one drop' rule. This rule declares any person with any trace of non-white ancestry is not white. Which means that even if you look white, you may not *be* white. You might be tainted.

I suspect the "one drop" rule was to discourage what is called miscegenation, which is a fancy term for interbreeding, in the U.S. anyway, between whites and blacks.

"White race" or "white people" did not enter European dictionaries until around 1600, the result of widespread colonialism by the major nations. The use of the term "white people" was to assuage the guilt complexes of the whites as they proceeded to methodically and deliberately rape the earth of its wealth, and, simultaneously, wipe out whole races who happened to get in their way.

Put simply, whites were superior to people of color. They were superior intellectually, spiritually, physically and morally. This meant that lying to colored people was okay. Cheating colored people was okay. Stealing from colored people was okay. Enslaving colored people was okay. Murdering them was not only okay, it was encouraged because it improved the whole of mankind by reducing the unsound, who tended to drag everyone else down. The only thing discouraged was interbreeding with coloreds.

For example, some guy named Carl Peters founded the German East Africa colony. In carrying out his duties as commissioner, Peters did whatever was necessary to make money for the fatherland. He had the son of the Sultan flogged; murdered countless others, burned their villages and destroyed everything that wouldn't burn. Years later, in 1897, Peters was indicted and found guilty of the murder of his black mistress. Obviously, no one cared about the thousands of blacks he had murdered or the death of one lone black woman. What they did care about was Peters' unseemliness in his choice of female companions.

In April 1897, the same year as Carl Peters' trial, an English newspaper called the *Social-Democrat* published a remarkable piece entitled "Bloody

Niggers." And since the adjective 'bloody' in England is equivalent to our 'fucking' in America, the real title of the article was "Fucking Niggers."

Chapter 4

Biblical Origin of Race and Racism – Supposedly

W hich brings up the question: why on earth did God create mankind in different colors? Was it a bad joke or is God trying to make some kind of point? And if so, what's the joke? What's the point?

Where did all this racism begin? According to one interpretation of the Holy Scriptures, it happened like this:

The Bible relates the historical event called the Flood, a global cataclysm which wiped out all human life on the planet earth. Except for eight people: Noah, his wife, their three sons, and the sons' wives.

Noah's three sons, then, will re-populate the earth. Their names were Ham, Shem and Japheth.

According to the story, immediately after the Flood, after all the waters had receded, Noah became a farmer, "planting a vineyard." The historical reality is that Noah was a vintner. After the grapes were ripe and had attained the proper sugar content, he harvested them, pressed them and produced wine. After the wine had aged, Noah took it upon himself to taste it. He drank too much, becoming drunk. And as many drunks do, he became sleepy, stumbled to his tent, took off his clothes, and fell asleep. While Noah lay naked in a drunken stupor, his ambitious son Ham, who was a homosexual, entered the tent.

In Noah's defense, it should be noted that before the Flood there was no wine, because there was no fermentation. The theory is that the bacteria necessary for fermentation came into existence only after the Flood. Therefore, Noah didn't know he would get drunk. He thought he was drinking grape juice.

The name Ham, when used as an adjective in the Hebrew language, means "hot." As a noun, Ham means "black," and refers to the color of Ham's skin. Because of some genetic variation, Ham had more melanin in his skin than his brothers Shem and Japheth.

The Bible says, "And Ham, the father of Canaan, saw the nakedness of his father, and told his two brothers outside." The word 'saw' refers to homosexual activity, which means that Ham entered Noah's tent, and engaged in homoerotic sex with the stupefied Noah. Precisely what type of homosexual activity took place, the word does not specify. It could have been masturbation, fellatio, or sodomy.

Abba Arika presents a different version of what took place in the tent. He states that Ham castrated Noah. Whereas Rabbi Samuel declares that Ham merely "sexually abused" Noah. The Midrashic tradition attributes the castration story to Ham's son, Canaan, who, knowing full well what he was doing, gelded his drunken grandfather like a horse by cinching a rope around his scrotum, effectively cutting off the blood supply to the testes.

The important point is this: whatever type of sex took place, it was against Noah's will, which makes it rape; it was done by Ham upon his own father, which makes it incest. Both actions are criminal.

Then Ham further exacerbated his crime. He left the tent, found his two brothers, and reported to them what he had just done. In fact, he provided a detailed account of the event.

Shem and Japheth, rather than participate in such lewdness, found a mantle and stretched it across their shoulders. They then backed into their father's tent, using the mantle as a screen, which prevented them from gazing upon Noah's nakedness.

The general principle here is that Shem and Japheth respected their father's authority and his privacy. Ham did neither.

Ham was black.

The story proceeds: Noah awoke suddenly and knew what Ham had done. Ham has manufactured sin out of sexual perversion, by violating his father's privacy. This demonstrated, of course, than Ham did not respect his father's authority and, by implication, had no regard for any authority.

The word 'manufactured' sounds bizarre when used to describe a sinful act. I chose the word carefully, in an attempt to convey the precise meaning of the Hebrew. When you manufacture something, it implies an active choice. You give birth to the idea, then you implement it according to your desires. All of which entails active participation of your mind and your body. This was what Ham did.

In effect, then, Ham was just waiting for the opportunity to sate his sexual lust for Noah.

Noah was aware that Ham had committed the sexual outrage, yet he actually pronounced the curse upon Canaan, Ham's son. By doing so,

Noah indicated the prophetic nature of the curse. For a prophecy was the prediction of the future under divine guidance. Thus, Noah spoke for God. This was a divine curse.

The curse will be projected into the future with definite and dire consequences upon all Ham's descendants – if they choose to follow in his ways, i.e., homosexuality and the rejection of authority. In other words, Ham's progeny will only be culpable, and thus cursed, if they involve themselves in such behavior.

It should be noted that Canaan was white. His father, Ham, was black. His mother was white.

The prophecy that followed – pronounced by Noah – did not make Canaan responsible for Ham's sins, but it did make Canaan liable for his own. And if Canaan's sins resembled his father's, then the terms of the curse went into effect.

Noah's curse, then, was not only divine, it was genetic. It recognized hereditary tendencies among human beings. And sadly, according to the Bible, Canaan and his descendants, who included the inhabitants of Sodom and Gomorrah, willingly embraced the degeneracy percolating through their bodies. Indeed, the Canaanites' sins surpassed their most ardent imitators.

The Canaanites excelled at incest, adultery, idolatry and human sacrifice.

Noah's prophetic curse, called the Law of Culpability by theologians, did not punish children for the sins of their parents. Unless the children became involved in the same sin of their own free will.

Which brings up the idea of the four generation curse, as presented in the Bible. Theologians refer to it as the Doctrine of the Four Generation Curse. Anytime something is important, theologians call it a doctrine.

The mechanics of this four-generation curse are described in Proverbs 30: 11-17. Those coming under this curse are described as being arrogant and rebellious toward their parents, yet in their own eyes they are pure. The cursed ones have teeth like swords and fangs like knives, which means they are psychopathic liars. They kill with words. Selfish and greedy, they are never satisfied with what they have. They desire more, always more. Never do they say, "It is enough."

Of the four things that never say, "It is enough," the cursed ones are contained in number four. First is the grave. Second is the barren womb. Third is the earth that sucks up water. And the fourth is the fires of hell. The cursed ones are destined for Hell, which always has room for one more.

* * * * *

Noah's curse: "being cursed Canaan, a slave of slaves." This indicated that the Hamitic races would be conquered by the Japhetic – white – races. Hamitic races mentioned in the Bible included the Phoenicians, the Hittites and proto-Hittites (Trojans), and the Carthaginians.

Historically, then, Noah's curse meant that after the Flood the lines of Shem and Japheth would dominate. The ramifications of this curse explained (supposedly) why in human history no colored race has made a contribution to progress, and why colored races only succeed within the framework of white-ruled nations. And by extension, it also explained why the colored races were good at arts and crafts, and failed in government.

* * * * *

In the year of our Lord 2009, many Americans believe in the Bible and what it says – literally. The Bible is right, according to eighty percent of all Americans. Not only is it right, it is the divinely inspired Word of God. In other words, God dictated the Bible, and his secretaries – people we call prophets and apostles – wrote it down.

Furthermore, more than thirty percent of Americans believe that God speaks to them directly. Which, when you stop and think about it, means that the Bible has been superseded as far as these favored people are concerned. These chosen people, of course, still believe the Bible is the Word of God. It's just that they get special memos from God when He has something to add or when clarification of some point of doctrine is needed.

What's more, fully (which means more than) ten percent of all Americans believe God speaks to them out loud. They "hear," in a very real sense, the voice of God.

Once this information is digested, it's no wonder that blacks rode in the back of buses, drank from separate water fountains, and went to different schools until the 1960s. Books like *The Bell Curve*, published in 1994, paint people of color as biological idiots. According to this type of thought, not only are people of color intellectually inferior, they are amoral at best and immoral generally speaking. Which means they are criminals.

Exactly what Noah prophesied.

Unsurprising, then, that white supremacist groups pop up everywhere. The Montana Militia, the Nazi Low Riders, WAR (white Aryan resistance) and the Aryan Brotherhood being just a few examples. And while skinhead groups are viewed as the lunatic fringe by many people, there is little doubt that most white people agree that people of color are somehow inferior. Noah said so. Moses said so. The Bible says so. And that means God says so.

Although theologians place the Flood and Noah's curse in the year 6000 B.C., which means racism started about 8000 years ago, the term 'white supremacy' was born in 1902.

'White supremacy' is a racist ideology – a strong belief – that white people are superior to other racial groups. White people are superior not only as a race, but because they are God's chosen. As we saw above, through Noah, God placed a curse on the so-called 'colored races.'

Most white supremacists are ardent racists, desire power over others, and are xenophobic. What they don't understand, they hate. And since they automatically don't understand anything or anyone that is different than they are, they hate almost everything and everyone. The automatic (unthinking) part comes easily to them, as they are usually ignorant, un-educated and violent by disposition. But not always – some are indeed educated. Often their racist attitudes mask ulterior motives or are the product of environmental influences, such as parents, peers or churches.

What is amusing is this: white supremacists can't agree on what "white" means. Which means they can't agree on who is the worst enemy – blacks, Jews, or Hispanics.

According to the Pan European white supremacists, the meaning of "white" includes all native and original European peoples: Swedes, Brit-ons, Germans, Italians, Spaniards, Portuguese and Greeks.

Whereas the Pan Aryanism brand of white supremacism defines peo-ple from continental Europe as white, but also accepts certain Middle Easterners, North Africans and some Asians as white. Even here, though, acceptance is not carte blanche. Syrians, Lebanese, Turks and Iranians are defined as white, but Saudis and Yemenites are not. Neither are Pakistanis and Northern Indians from India. Afghans and Berbers are most definite-ly white; in fact, they are whiter than Spaniards and Italians, according to Pan Aryanism.

Nordicism (also called Germanism), which is another brand of white supremacism, is the most restrictive. To them, white people only come from Scandinavia, Germany or Holland. However, if you have blonde hair and blue eyes they might let you in. Maybe.

Religion plays a major role in white supremacy. Most of the suprema-cy groups are either Protestants or Pagans. The Pagan groups usually call

themselves Odinists, which means they believe in the gods of Norse my-
thology. They claim that the world is composed of "worlds of light," who
are white people, and "worlds of dark," who are non-white people.

The Protestant supremacists usually have links to what is called the
Christian Identity movement. This movement believes that the two lost
tribes of Israel migrated to Great Britain before the birth of Jesus, and that
Jesus was British, having blonde hair and blue eyes. He was not a Jew.

In the Christian Identity movement a person's race is his religion. If
you're white, then your religion is white. These supremacists believe that
there exists a Jewish conspiracy to rule the world. The Jews are trying
to bring about this one-world government through their control of international banking and the media. Supremacists refer to the conspiracy
against which they struggle as ZOG, zionist occupied government.

The struggle will culminate in a Racial Holy War (RAHOWA), which
will eliminate Jews and the "mud races" from the face of the earth. This
holy war explains why supremacists pore over the New Testament book
of Revelation. Especially the final chapters, which deal with Armageddon
– the Racial Holy War.

Taking a cue from the zealous Levitical priest Phineas, who, with a
thrust of his holy spear, dispatched Zimri and his girlfriend – a two for the
price of one special – one group of supremacists calls itself the Phineas
Priesthood.

The Phineas Priesthood is a Christian Identity group in the United
States. They oppose interracial intercourse, mixing of races, homosexuality and abortion. They also hate Jews, any kind of cultural pollution and
paying taxes. And in general, they don't like women much either. In fact,
the Phineas Priesthood is so opposed to everything that they have no gov-
erning body, no meetings, and no membership process. You become a
Phineas Priest by simply adopting the beliefs of the Priesthood and acting
upon them.

Blowing up federal buildings, bombing abortion clinics, robbing banks
and murdering immoral people who participate in interracial relation-
ships are approved methods of acting upon your beliefs.

Chapter 5

The Ballad of Robert Jay Mathews

Robert Jay Mathews was a Phineas Priest, only he didn't refer to himself by that term, because the term wasn't invented until 1990, which was when Richard Kelly Hoskins coined it. More about Richard Hoskins later. Yet the idea of a "solitary warrior" did exist. And that's the way Mathews thought of himself – as a "solitary warrior" for God.

Mathews decided he could "accomplish more for God" – those were his words – if he was a little more organized. If his organization combined violence with a system, the sky was the limit.

If still alive in 2017, Robert Mathews would be 64 years old. Instead, he was dead at the age of 31.

The ballad began in Marfa, Texas. Where, on January 15, 1953, Una Mathews delivered the last of her three boys. She and her husband Johnny named the baby boy Robert Jay Mathews.

As you can tell by the spelling of the name 'Mathews,' they were of Scottish descent. And the Scots are noted for being stubborn and violent and honorable.

Robert came from good stock, which meant his family had some money, owned property and were educated. His father was the mayor of Marfa, the President of the Chamber of Commerce, a businessman and a deacon in the town's Methodist Church. While Una Matthews was a god-fearing woman; a good mother, respectable wife and a den mother for the Boy Scouts.

In 1950s America, "respectable wife" meant Una knew her place. She let her husband wear the pants in the family.

When Robert was five years old, his family moved to Phoenix, Arizona. So his father could pursue business opportunities he'd never have in dinky Marfa, Texas.

Robert began school in Phoenix. He attended public schools where he was an average student as far as academics were concerned. His interests were extraordinary. History and politics. Not just local or national accounts of history and politics, but international alliances and relations. Robert's viewpoint of history was conservative. Very conservative. So conservative it was Orwellian. In fact, he followed the conspiratorial interpretation of history and of politics – Big Brother was out there and he was watching you.

When he was eleven, Robert joined the John Birch Society, which, like McCarthyism, saw communists behind every tree and under every rock. The John Birch Society was definitely a cult. A cult of right-wing, Christian extremists, who believed in honor, duty and one country under God.

While in high school, Robert was sucked into the Mormon Church. The Mormons baptized him into the church, literally. This was not surprising, considering the cultic nature of the Mormons.

People like Robert, that is, young, white, conservative males, sought out fringe groups because they felt emasculated by American society. They didn't fit in. They had high school educations and low-paying jobs in a culture that was moving faster and faster. Technology made them feel like they had lost control of their own lives. Their manhood, their machismo had been taken from them.

Since in the eyes of society they were losers, and since in their own eyes they had failed – in other words, since they were nothing and had nothing to lose – they became angry. The anger of unmet expectations, which is a terrible and frantic anger. Almost a kind of madness.

Hating that which they could not understand, they did the only thing they could. The thing that gave them a sense of control, a sense of dominion.

They fought back.

Mathews started his own cultic group. It would be a group like those he saw around him – the people in charge – people like bankers and lawyers and businessmen. They had money. They had power. They had respect. Mathews would have those, too.

The "Sons of Liberty." That's what he called his group. The name was an obvious rip-off from the American Revolution. In effect, then, Mathews had seceded from the society that had taken his manhood from him.

The Sons of Liberty were an anti-communist, extremist militia group. Made up of mostly Mormons and survivalists, they numbered about thirty men. They didn't really know what to do to regain their manhood. They just knew they were angry. So they decided to revolt against paying taxes, because they felt that would be a good place to start. At least it would make a statement: "they were mad as hell and they weren't going to take it anymore" – to quote the rabid newscaster in the movie *Network*.

Mathews set the example. He claimed ten dependents on his W-4 form. This wretched attempt was his idea of tax resistance. It was more than wretched, it was pathetic. The IRS arrested him for tax fraud. He was tried in a court of law, where, when it was all over, he was found guilty. Even his sentence highlighted his status as a loser: six months probation. He couldn't even get thrown into prison. At least then he could have felt like a martyr and laid claim to a bad-boy image.

Meanwhile, the Sons of Liberty imploded. The Mormon members and the non-Mormon members had a tiff, and the group dissolved due to a lack of interest. This merely proved that it was a loser club for a bunch of losers. They were supposedly all Christians, but none of them could forgive the other members. Typical.

When his probation ended, Mathews decided that what he needed was to get back to the land. So he and his father moved to Metaline Falls, Washington. They purchased 60 acres of land. It was to be a new start on a new manhood. Mathews hoped his back-to-nature-program would give him a sense of worth.

They named their property Mathews Acres. Robert cleared and leveled an area on Mathews Acres, then bought two double-wide trailers to sit on the clearing. He added a chicken coop, a root cellar and a barn. Seeding five acres for pasture, he imported a Galloway bull and three cows. His plan was to raise cattle. And not just any cattle, but Scottish Galloway cattle.

Through tradition and the resurrection of his Scots heritage, Mathews was trying to restore his manhood.

Richie Kemp, who was a member of the Silent Brotherhood, worshipped Mathews. After Kemp's release from federal prison, he wrote about Mathews: "in the evenings, he would read from his extensive library until he could barely hold his eyes open. In the morning, he'd start his day at the crack of dawn with John Philip Sousa marching music, or the Black Watch playing reveille on the pipes, blaring on his phonograph."

Kemp presented Mathews as a renaissance man, a virtuous man with an ascetic lifestyle, who devoted his life to learning. Kemp, of course, had fallen prey to the personality cult of Robert Mathews.

In reality, Robert Mathews was a maladjusted monster, who couldn't win for trying.

He began raising cattle, got married to a woman named Debbie McGarrity, a woman of Scottish descent. When she proved infertile, they adopted a son. Mathews, though, really wanted a child from his own loins. So he started seeing a woman named Zillah Craig. She, too, was of Scottish descent, as Mathews didn't want to taint his bloodline. They had a daughter and his marriage to Debbie went to hell.

He got a job as an electrician at the Bunker Hill Mine Company, which tore raw zinc out of the ground. The mine closed due to poor management and the sagging price of zinc. So Robert got a job at the Portland Lehigh Cement Company. Yet he remained dissatisfied with his life. Something was missing. It was as if he had mislaid his soul.

So he started looking for it in all the wrong places – extreme right wing politics and warped interpretations of history.

Like Solomon in the Bible, Mathews decided that knowledge might make him happy. So he read a lot of politics and history. Most of what he read supported a racist interpretation of history. From this junk, Mathews concluded that he wasn't the problem. He wasn't a loser after all. The real problem was that the white race was being polluted and challenged in its supremacy by the colored races.

So Mathews started another club, a club for white people only. He invited other white supremacist families to Washington State. He called it the "White American Bastion." And to learn more about starting his own country within a country, he visited the Aryan Nations, a group started by a guy named Richard Butler. The Aryan Nations were white power exclusionists. They were white. They wanted power. And everybody who wasn't white and didn't want power was excluded from their club.

Aryan Nations dreamed of a whites-only kingdom, which would be located in Idaho. And of course, Richard Butler would get to be king. They advertised themselves as Christian Nazis.

Then Mathews joined the National Alliance, which was a white supremacist group started by a rabid racist guy named William Luther Pierce. Once upon a time, Pierce had been a physics professor at Oregon State University in Corvallis. Corvallis was a dreary town with only two things to do: drink and watch the rain.

So it was not surprising that Pierce got mixed up with the American Nazi Party. Pierce guided Mathews to two books that completed his white power brainwashing. *Which Way Western Man?*, which divulged the hideous intention of the Jews – to wipe out the "white Christian race." The other book was *The Turner Diaries*, which was written by Pierce himself. This book was the fictionalized story of the salvation of America by white supremacists, who take over the U.S. government by violence. Then they go on and take over the world. After installing their international white power Christian dictatorship, they butcher all Jews and non-whites on the face of the earth. In the book, the white power extremists are called The Order.

Mathews was favorably impressed by both books. To him, the books taught that you had to go out and take your manhood. By power and by violence.

At the National Alliance Convention, in 1983, Mathews gave a rabble rousing speech. It was a call to action. To do what, no one could really say. But it sounded great and got everyone all fired up. They gave him a standing ovation, which made him feel good about himself.

Mathews felt so good about himself that he went back to Metaline Falls and started a secret club. He called it the Silent Brotherhood. Everybody else called it The Order, because it was a semi-religious fraternity. Their bible was *The Turner Diaries*. The Silent Brotherhood had nine members. Up until they joined The Order, none of the nine had ever committed a violent crime or been in prison.

But that changed soon enough.

The nine members consisted of: Robert Mathews, who was the high priest and boss, and Kenneth Loft. Loft was Mathews' best friend. A former Ku Klux Klansman named David Lane; Daniel Bauer; Denver Daw Parmenter II, Randolph Duey, and Bruce Pierce, who came over from the Aryan Nations. Richie Kemp and William "Bill" Soderquist used to be members of the National Alliance. To a man, they were all misfits, anti-social and potentially dangerous.

Mathews determined the first thing the secret club needed was money. Without it, they were a joke. And Mathews couldn't bear being laughed at. So he decided to do what the white power guys in *The Turner Diaries* had done. In the novel – which was now The Bible – the white supremacists had taken whatever they needed. Armed robbery and counterfeiting were the preferred methods. Not only did these crimes bring forth the desired objective – money, but they had the added payoff of capsizing the economy. An economy that was run by the rotten Jewish conspiracy.

As Richie Kemp told it, Mathews brought Loft's infant daughter into the room and turned off the lights. "He placed her on a blanket on the floor in the middle of the circle, lit some candles and dimmed the lights. He told us he wanted us to make a pledge to one another; he said it was just as sacred, if not more so, than a wedding vow. Bob told us that the oath we were about to swear was directed toward all white children, which were represented this night, by this one child. It was a pledge to defend the children at any cost.

"We all raised our right arms as Bob began reading prepared words from a sheet of paper, in a trembling, yet determined voice. As he read a line, we would repeat after him. The moment was so moving I could feel the energy generated by each one of us, fill the room. Tears filled my eyes as I felt a deep connection to each of the men standing in the circle. Like a pebble dropped in a pool of still water, I could feel the energy radiating outward, through space and time, to our brethren not present with us on this evening. We were pledging to give our life for our folk and would use all our resources to protect this child and all White children, to defend their safety and honor. From this moment on, our lives were thoroughly charged."

The Order was aptly named. For it was a religious order, a sect, a denomination, a cult. A cult of terrorism and violence. Mathews required a holy vow, taken over a White child – how Messianic. I wonder if Mathews saw himself as the Messiah of a new world order? One thing was for sure, though, Mathews may have been a psychotic megalomaniac, but he was a brilliant one. For by appealing to something that all the men held as sacred – a white female baby, i.e. life – he had transformed armed robbery from a violent crime into a spiritual crusade. And the nine members of The Silent Brotherhood were the armed saints who would accomplish the holy war.

The Silent Brotherhood also known as The Order. Their goal was a world-wide race war – Armageddon. When it was all over, only white people would remain alive on the face of the earth.

The holy campaign began on October 28, 1983. It was pretty much a miserable failure. Four armed and masked gunmen marched into a porn shop in Spokane, Washington. World Wide Video was the name of the place. It rented and sold XXX-rated movies to sex addicts, perverts and deviants.

Robert Mathews, Bruce Pierce, Randolph Duey and Daniel Bauer were the four armed men. They wore black ski-hoods so their faces wouldn't show up on the security tapes, which were recorded 24 hours a day in the back room.

Pierce, Duey and Bauer fanned out through the small shop. They moved in what they called combat-readiness-mode, holding their guns out, their eyes scanning the room. In reality, they looked like crouching old men, scuttling like crabs.

There were two perverts in the back of the shop, trying to pull the plastic covers off of skin magazines. They wanted to see the pictures of naked women. When confronted by the masked gunmen, the two perverts stood rigid, waiting for whatever would happen next.

"This is a robbery," announced Pierce, pointing his .45 automatic at the two perverts. His voice sounded funny because the mouth hole in the ski mask didn't fit right. It kept shrinking around his lips.

The two perverts glanced at each other. One of them shrugged. "Okay," he said. "Only we ain't got any money."

"We're robbing the store, not you," said Pierce.

"Okay," said the pervert. Then he turned his attention back to the skin magazine.

Pierce described the two men as perverts because to him such behavior – hanging out in porno shops looking at T & A magazines – was immoral and perverted. Actually, the two perverts were just ugly men with no money and no social graces. They were horny, so they sought to gratify their longing with airbrushed tits.

It never entered Pierce's head that what he was doing was immoral and more than a little freakish: standing in a dingy porno shop, wearing a ski-mask, holding a gun as big as a cannon on two social washouts, while his boss robbed the place.

At the cash register, Mathews held his gun on the clerk. "Empty the cash register. Put all the money in this," said Mathews, handing the clerk a black velvet bag.

The clerk, who had his hands up like in the movies, kept them up. He didn't want this masked desperado to shoot him.

"Take it," said Mathews, getting pissed off. He glanced nervously at the front door.

"Don't shoot," said the clerk, slowly extending one hand to the bag.

"Empty the register," repeated Mathews.

The clerk opened the register. Fumbling at the money, some of it dropped to the floor.

"Goddammit," yelled Mathews, jabbing his gun at the man. "Pick it up and put it in the bag."

The clerk bent over and picked up the money. Finally, he got it all in the bag.

Mathews snatched the bag out of his hands. "All clear," he shouted. That was the signal to his men. They crouched, whirled and moved toward the front door.

Mathews was the last one out. Jumping into a 1980 Ford Bronco, the marauders left in a squeal of tires.

Back home, the men discovered that crime doesn't pay – literally. They had netted $369.10 from World Wide Video.

"Shit," said Bauer.

The other three men shook their heads. They were disgusted.

"All that – for this?" said Pierce, pointing his gun at the $369.10. He looked at Mathews. "It ain't worth it, Bob. All that risk for so little money."

Everybody else nodded in agreement.

"You're right," said Mathews. He sat down on a barcalounger and stared at his gun. The other men watched him while he thought.

Mathews looked up. "Okay," he said. "No more of this petty-anti-shit. From now on we focus on armored cars and banks. That's where the money is."

Everybody nodded.

* * * * *

The next day, Mathews started scouting around. He drove to Seattle, looking for a likely bank to rob or an armored car to follow. At a mall in the suburb of Shoreline, he spotted an armored car in front of the Fred Meyer store. He watched, as two fat guards carried canvas bags of money out of Fred Meyer's. They walked toward the armored truck, where two more guards waited. One sat in the driver's seat, the other, in the back of the vehicle, opened the heavy door as the money-toters approached.

Piece of cake, Mathews decided. He and his crew could take them easily, especially if they used big guns and armor-piercing rounds in the big guns.

Meanwhile, the Silent Brotherhood had set up a counterfeiting operation in nearby Hayden Lake. David Lane was running the show. He had a helper named Gary Lee Yarborough, who was a new guy.

The Aryan Nations had a print shop in Hayden Lake. And in the print shop was an offset press. Lane was using the press to print phony 50 dollar bills. It turned out that Lane was not a very good forger.

For on December 3, 1983, Bruce Pierce drove to the Valley Mall in Yakima, Washington. He had a stack of bogus 50's with him. Entering the mall, Pierce randomly selected a store, entered and bought something that cost ten dollars or less. He paid for the item with one of his sham bills. It was easy, and he walked out of the store with about 40 dollars in real money. Plus whatever he bought.

After about five stores, Pierce headed for the Union Gap store. He wandered around the store, shopping for some new shirts. He picked out two and went to the register to pay for them.

As he handed over two of the fake 50s to the clerk, he didn't notice two men coming up behind him. They were cops.

Hallmark had been the first store Pierce shopped in. He bought a pen for $8.95. After he got his change and left, the saleslady took the 50 dollar bill out of the register drawer. It felt funny, like it was too thick and kind of rough. Holding it up to the light, she examined it. She didn't have another 50 to compare it to, but something was wrong.

She called the manager over. Rubbing the bill between their fingers, they decided it was counterfeit. The manager called the police.

"Sir," said one of the cops. Actually, he was a detective. Dressed in Dockers, a green polo shirt and Hush Puppies, he looked like another Christmas shopper.

Pierce jerked around. "Yes?" he said.

The cop with the Hush Puppies flashed a badge. "We'd like to ask you some questions, if you don't mind." He pointed to a door behind the counter. "In there."

Pierce panicked. "What's this about?" he asked. "I haven't done anything wrong."

The two cops pressed close to him. "It's just a few questions, sir."

"You got a warrant or anything?" demanded Pierce. "I'm minding my own business, doing some shopping for my brother. That ain't a crime, is it?"

He made a movement with his right hand. The cops reacted. As fast as snakes they grabbed him and put his hands behind his back. One of them cuffed him.

"What the hell is going on?" shouted Pierce. "I haven't done anything."

Nearby shoppers stopped and stared at the hubbub.

"Sir," said the cop with hush puppies, "we're taking you to the station for some questions." He and his partner pushed Pierce through the door into the back of the store, where boxes of merchandise were stacked.

Pierce stood still while one of the cops searched him. The other cop stood guard. They found his wallet in his back pocket. Then the stack of bogus 50s in his jacket pocket.

Putting his hand under the left side of Pierce's jacket, the cop stopped. He glanced wide-eyed at his partner.

"Well," he said. "What do we have here?"

The cop slowly removed his hand. His partner peered around Pierce's shoulder to see what it was.

A .45 auto, with combat grips.

"Sir," said the cop with Hush Puppies on his feet, "you're under arrest for carrying a concealed weapon."

"Mirandize him," said the other cop. He didn't want this punk getting off on some technicality.

Hush Puppies pulled a small card from his pocket. Reading from the card, he informed Bruce Pierce of his rights.

Then the cops marched him outside where it was starting to snow. They put him in the back of an unmarked, white Chevy Tahoe. There was a heavy screen separating the back seat from the front seats. Pierce sat in the back, with his hands cuffed behind him.

Pierce was scared and pissed off. "I didn't do anything," he screamed through the screen. "You're the pawns of your ZOG masters. You stupid shits. I'm a free white man going about my God-given rights."

Up front, the two cops looked at each other. One of them made a circular motion next to his ear. His partner grinned and nodded.

"Shut up," said the cop with the Hush Puppies on, as he turned of the mall parking lot onto a slushy street.

At the Yakima Police station, the two cops put Pierce in a holding cell. Seven feet by ten feet, it had a steel bunk, steel toilet and steel sink.

A few hours later, the cops hauled Pierce out of his cell. The led him out to a white van, which took him to court, where he was arraigned in record time. Usually criminals sat in jail for three to five days before they were arraigned. But a counterfeiter with a .45 auto concealed under his left armpit was a big deal in Yakima. Counterfeiting was a federal crime. So they made an exception.

The Judge set his bail at $25,000. It would have been higher, but Pierce had no record. This was his first offense. And the Judge didn't know Pierce was part of a terrorist group.

Since Pierce had no money to put up his bail, they took him to the local jail. They put him in administrative segregation, which meant in solitary confinement. Twenty-four hours later, they escorted him to a waiting room, where a Secret Security Agent from Spokane wanted to talk to him.

"Where'd you get the counterfeit bills?" said the agent. "You print them yourself?"

"I got nothing to say," said Pierce. Bruce Pierce remembered the oath he had taken. He was determined to keep it.

The agent shook his head sadly. "You know, if you cooperate, it will go a lot easier on you. In fact, if you help us, you can probably just walk away from all this."

He looked meaningfully at Pierce.

"I got nothing to say," said Pierce.

* * * * *

The Silent Brotherhood knew about Pierce's arrest. Mathews was worried. The longer Pierce sat in jail, the more likely he was to turn snitch and talk to the cops. Or he might say something to another prisoner, who would rat him out. And that meant they would all go to jail.

Mathews knew Pierce. He wasn't too bright and he talked too much. Which explained why Pierce was making phone calls from jail to his pals. Pierce didn't realize the cops could add two and two together and make the connection.

The only thing to do was to get Pierce out of jail. Which meant bail money. But none of the Silent Brotherhood had any money. They needed ten percent of $25,000, which was $2500. Which, in turn, was a lot of money when you were broke.

Mathews decided to get the money. He didn't tell the others. He just did it.

On December 18, 1983, seven days before Christman, Mathews entered the Innis-Arden branch of the Citybank. Innis-Arden was a sleepy little city just north of Seattle.

Wearing his black ski-mask and toting a .45 auto in a shoulder holster, Mathews walked into the bank. He carried a black Browning pump shotgun in his hands.

Strolling nonchalantly up to a teller, he pointed the shotgun at her. "I want all the money in the bank in a bag. Now."

Scared to death, the teller did as she was told. Five minutes later, Robert Mathews walked out of the bank with a bag of money. Getting in his Bronco, he tossed the bag of money on the passenger seat. He had left the Bronco unlocked and the key in the ignition. He turned the key. The engine roared and he drove off.

$25,952. That's how much Mathews took from the bank. More money than he had ever seen.

But he couldn't use it. There was a red-dye pack in the bag. It had exploded. All the green money was now red. If he tried to spend any of it, the cops would be all over him.

Five days later, on December 23, 1983, Pierce bailed himself out of jail. He put up $250 dollars and walked out. His court appointed public defender had argued that the bail of $25,000 dollars was too high. Especially since it was his client's first offense.

The Judge reduced Pierce's bail to $2500.

That night the Silent Brotherhood partied. Beer and Subway sandwiches. They had taken on ZOG and defeated it. Anyway, that's the way they saw it.

* * * * *

The Silent Brotherhood struck again. It was March 1984.

Mathews, Pierce, Duey and Yarborough drove to the Seattle suburb of Shoreline. After casing the Fred Meyer store for three days, they made their move.

On March 16, a Continental Armored Transport truck parked near the curb of the main entrance of Fred Meyer. There were three guards in the truck: the driver, the backup, whose job was lookout and extra gun in case of trouble, and the messenger. Messenger was the nickname the guards had given to the guy who moved the money.

People didn't realize how heavy money was. A lot of money weighed could weigh hundreds of pounds, especially if there were a lot of coins. Not only that, but money was bulky, which made it awkward. To get around these problems, the messenger used a metal cart with sturdy wheels. The cart would be taken out of the armored truck, pushed into the bank or store, loaded with money, and then pushed back to the truck.

Betwixt and between said the old time robbers. That was the best time to steal the money. When it was between the bank or store and the armored car. That was the soft spot in the armor. There was only one guard, and he was busy pushing and steering the cart. The other two guards were out with the truck. The driver was inside behind the wheel. The backup was just inside the truck, ready to open the door when the messenger arrived.

Sometimes the bank or store had their own security there, but they were amateurs, who got paid peanuts. They weren't going to try to hard to protect some rich corporation's money for a lousy $8 an hour, plus uniforms.

* * * * *

The guard pushed the loaded cart out of the manager's office at Fred Meyer. Six large money bags and six coin boxes pressed heavily on their cold steel carriage.

"Messenger on the way," said the guard into his walkie-talkie. A long hallway stretched in front of him. It had the signature Fred Meyer flooring – white and black linoleum.

The expected reply was preceded by a crackling screech. "Roger that," replied the backup, sitting in the truck. He checked his watch. "If you hurry it up, we'll have time for a lunch break."

"Roger," said the messenger. The suggestion made him aware of how hungry he was. He picked up his pace a little as he pushed the cart in front of him.

"Hold up, Bub," said a voice from behind.

The messenger turned his head to see who was there. Later, he told police he saw two things at the same moment: a black ski mask and a big-ass shotgun – which was pointed right at his face.

He put his hands up. The cart rolled another six feet, then bumped into the wall and stopped.

Out of nowhere, two more men in black ski masks appeared. One of them took the messenger's revolver, which hung in a holster on his Sam Browne belt. Then his walkie-talkie was taken.

"Don't move and nothing will happen to you," said the guy with the shotgun, who seemed to be the boss.

"Yes sir," said the messenger. He could tell these guys weren't fucking around. If he moved, he'd get to see what was at the other end of that big-ass shotgun barrel.

"Quick now," said the boss to the other two robbers. "Get it there and get it loaded."

The two men pushed the money cart down the hallway a ways, then turned down a side hall. Followed by the sound of a door opening.

The messenger stood still, waiting, staring at the black hole of that big-ass gun. He noted the size of the guy holding it. Not very tall, really. Slim with wide shoulders. An automatic pistol was stuck into the waistband of his pants. Just the butt was visible, so the messenger couldn't tell what kind it was. But it looked substantial.

Footsteps echoed out of the side hall. A masked face appeared around the corner. He gave the thumbs up sign to the boss. The thumb was blue, because of the blue latex glove on the robber's hand.

"I'm leaving," said the guy with the big-ass shotgun. "Stay here and count to one hundred – slowly."

"Yes sir," said the messenger, nodding once. He licked his lips.

Then the guy walked right by him, holding the shotgun down the side of his leg. The messenger watched the guy's back as he strolled to the side hall and turned into it. Shaking his head with respect, the messenger started counting out loud. "One, two, three…"

When the police arrived, the messenger gave them a description of the robbers. All wore black ski masks, blue jeans and dark jackets. Only one of the robbers said anything. The other two never said a word.

"The one who spoke – the boss – was a little feller. About five foot seven or eight, maybe 140 or 150 pounds. He had wide shoulders and narrow hips. And was cool as a cucumber," said the messenger.

Except for the barrel of that big-ass shotgun, that's all he could tell the police. The other two armored truck guards hadn't seen a thing. They didn't know anything was wrong until the messenger arrived with his empty cart and told them his story.

They missed lunch.

* * * * *

Back home, the Silent Brotherhood counted the stolen money. $43,345. Things were looking up. As criminals, they were improving in leaps and bounds.

Mathews told his crew, "I'm proud of you guys."

They had beer and pizza.

* * * * *

Bruce Pierce stood next to his attorney. It was April 3, 1984, and he was in U.S. District Court in Spokane.

Pierce's attorney had cut a deal with the feds – a plea bargain. Pierce would plead guilty to passing counterfeit money. And he agreed to be cooperative. In other words, he would be forthcoming and answer questions honestly. In return, he would receive a light sentence – under a year – maybe just probation.

It was a good deal. But it fell to pieces because Bruce Pierce was a stupid redneck son of a bitch.

"Mr. Pierce, where did you obtain the counterfeit money you passed?" asked the Prosecutor.

Pierce's face tightened. He glanced down and to the left, then back at the prosecutor. "I don't know," he said.

"You don't know? Or you won't say?"

"I don't know. And if I don't know then I can't say, can I?" said Pierce, a smirk on his lips.

The prosecutor looked at Judge Robert McNichols for help.

"You are instructed to answer the question," ordered the Judge.

Pierce turned his head to look at Judge McNichols. "I don't remember where I got it," he said, lifting his shoulders.

Judge McNichols sighed. "Continue," he said to the prosecutor.

"Mr. Pierce," said the prosecutor, "are you affiliated with a group known as the Aryan Nations? Which is a group of white supremacists – a hate group?"

Pierce squinched his face. "Never heard of such a group."

The prosecutor rolled his eyes and picked up a sheaf of papers. "Mr. Pierce, we have evidence and statements to the effect that you have heard of such a group. And that you are in fact a member of said group. The Aryan Nations." He walked around to the other side of the room.

"Let's try it again, okay?" said the prosecutor, hiking his eyebrows. "Are you affiliated with the Aryan Nations, Mr. Pierce?"

Bruce Pierce hunched his shoulders in complaint. "I told you. I ain't never heard of any Aryan Nations," he said.

The prosecutor turned to Judge McNichols. "Your Honor, this man is not cooperating. Worse yet, he is without remorse. Therefore, I am asking the court to impose the harshest penalty allowed."

As the prosecutor sat down, Pierce glared at him.

Due to a bad attitude, Bruce Pierce was sentenced to two years in federal prison.

"You have three weeks to settle your affairs," said Judge McNichols. "On April 24, you will report to the U.S. Marshals to begin serving your sentence. Report before noon on that date."

After court was adjourned, Bruce Pierce informed the clerk of the court that he would be staying with Robert Mathews in Metaline Falls.

"That's where you'll be for the next three weeks," asked the clerk of the court.

"Yes ma'm," said Pierce.

"Okay. You are fully aware that you must report by noon on April 24, right?"

"Yes ma'm."

As Pierce left the courthouse, he laughed. If these ZOG puppets thought he was really going to turn himself over to ZOG, they had another think coming.

* * * * *

The Magnificent Seven. That's what Mathews called them. Seven freedom fighters. Seven holy knights, fighting for the freedom of the white race. Seven crusaders on a mission for Jesus.

The seven were Mathews, Pierce, Parmenter, Duey, Kemp, Yarborough and Andrew Barnhill, who was a new recruit from the Aryan Nations.

Barnhill came over to the Silent Brotherhood because they were doing things, not just sitting around making pompous speeches. The Silent Brotherhood was actively battling against the evil forces of ZOG.

It was April 19 when the Magnificent Seven – aka The Silent Brotherhood, aka The Order – drove back to Seattle. They were there to hit another armored car. Another Continental Armored Transport truck, this time as it left the Northgate Mall. It would be full of the weekend earnings from the big department stores, like Nordstrom, the Bon Marche', and J.K. Gill, which sold office supplies.

Mathews had already cased it out. To bring it off, they would need a diversion. Mathews asked Yarborough to make a small bomb. One that had a timer.

Yarborough took his bomb to the Embassy Theater on Union Street in the sleazy, downtown part of Seattle. The Embassy was a XXX-rated movie house. Just the kind of place The Silent Brotherhood hated – an immoral fleshpot.

Love Machine was the featured flick. Some non-aryan sat behind the ticket counter.

"The movie she already start," the guy told Yarborough. "No refunds." Yarborough bought a ticket and entered the theater. It was dark and smelled of stale popcorn and steamy sweat.

Finding a seat in the middle of the theater, Yarborough waited till his eyes adjusted to the dim light emanating from the screen, where moaning previews were being shown.

Yarborough bent down and placed his homemade bomb under the seat in front of him. He flipped the switch, activating the timer. He had sixty minutes.

He left immediately, walking past the ticket guy, who didn't even look up. Getting in his rental car, Yarborough drove to a 7-11 five miles away. Parking his car, he went inside and bought a Slurpee. Then walked outside and across the parking lot to the phone booth. He dialed the number of the Embassy Theater.

"Embassy," said a voice on the other end. It was the ticket guy. Yarborough recognized his non-white, un-American accent.

"There's a bomb in the theater," said Yarborough. "It's set to go off at 3 p.m."

"What?"

"I said there's a bomb in the theater. It's set to go off at 3 p.m," repeated Yarborough. He looked at his watch. "In about 40 minutes. You better get everybody out of the place."

"Who is this? Is this a joke?"

"Look stupid shit. A bomb. In the theater. Get everybody out." Yarborough slammed the phone down.

At the Embassy Theater, the ticket guy thought about what he'd just been told by some nut on the phone. Who would want to blow up a porn house? No one. He shrugged and forgot about it.

The timer on Yarborough's makeshift bomb was slow. So it went off at 3:05 p.m. Yarborough was parked just down the block from the Embassy. He wanted to witness his handiwork.

The explosion was pretty impressive. A loud boom, followed by the tinkle of showering glass, followed by geysers of gray smoke.

The fire department arrived and rushed into the theater, dragging heavy hoses and medical gear. After they doused a small fire, the fire marshal determined that it had been a crude bomb. There wasn't much real damage, and only a few patrons got hurt. Mostly cuts and bruises. One guy messed his pants.

Cheering happily, Yarborough drove back to the Motel Six, where The Silent Brotherhood was staying. In an excited voice, he told Mathews and the others about it. Everybody gave him high-fives.

Mathews gave him one of those looks, the one they all lived for. "Good job, Gary Lee," he said, nodding.

Gary Lee Yarborough got goosebumps.

Mathews sat down on a chair and said, "Now, we'll call the Embassy again on Monday, just before we hit the truck at the mall. Tell them there's another bomb in the place. The cops'll be all over the place."

Six heads nodded and smiled. It would be a good diversion. Mathews was a genius.

* * * * *

Seven men walked into the Northgate Mall. Each man came in through a different entrance. Each carried a colorful shopping bag from the Bon Marche'. In the bags were black ski masks and semi-automatic pistols.

All seven of the men were dressed alike. Gray twill work pants, black ankle boots and short gray twill jackets over light blue shirts.

Mathews stopped at a pay phone in the mall and called the Embassy Theater. Janet Garner answered the phone. She was a student at the University of Washington. Desperate for a job, she had reluctantly agreed to work at the porn house. Yesterday – the day the bomb exploded – had been her day off. Today, all the employees were at the theater to help clean up the mess caused by the bomb. The theater was closed, but the owner wanted to re-open as soon as possible.

"Embassy Theater," said Janet.

"There's a bomb in the theater," said Mathews.

"That was yesterday," said Janet. "Today we're closed. Call back in a few days when we're open."

"There's another bomb in the theater," said Mathews. "It's set to go off at 3:00 p.m."

Janet slammed the phone down and started crying. Glancing up at the clock, she saw it was now 2:00 p.m.

She ran into the manager's office, where Joe Showa was sweeping broken glass into a dustpan.

"Joe, Joe," shouted Janet. "I just got off the phone with the bomber. He says there's another bomb in the theater. It's going to explode at 3 o'clock."

Joe stared at her. He knew she wasn't making it up. "Christ!" he said.

He paused for a moment. "Okay, you go call the police. Tell them we have another bomb scare. I'll go get everyone out of the building."

"Yes. Right," gasped Janet. She ran back to the phone and dialed 911.

Within minutes, most of the Seattle Police Department was headed at high speed for the Embassy Theater. Fire trucks and paramedics roared down city streets like giant red bugs, sirens wailing and lights flashing.

The Seattle Bomb Squad saddled up for action, donning huge bomb proof suits that made the men look like the Michelin Tire Man.

* * * * *

Robert Mathews walked up behind the messenger of the Continental Armored Transport truck, who was pushing his cart down the mall. He had just left the Bon Marche,' and was headed for the service corridor which was about ten yards away.

As he approached the door that led into the service corridor, the messenger pulled out his keycard. He parked the cart next to the tan colored door and swiped his keycard. An indicator light changed from red to green as the lock popped with a click.

The messenger pulled the door open, braced it with his right foot and pushed the cart into the doorway. Something poked into his lower back.

"That's a gun you feel," said Mathews, pressing the barrel of his .45 into the man's back. "Just keep going into the corridor."

The messenger hesitated. Then pushed the cart through the door. Mathews followed right behind him. As the door closed, Mathews hit the man on the back of his head with the .45. He dropped like a bag of rocks.

Mathews moved back to the door and opened it two inches. One after another, six men carrying Bon Marche' shopping bags walked to the door, and entered.

When they were all in, Mathews closed the door.

"Masks," he said.

All the men pulled black ski masks from their shopping bags and pulled them over their heads.

"Weapons," said Mathews.

Six slides on six .45 semi-automatic pistols clacked back, then snapped forward again. The guns were stuck into waistbands.

Mathews surveyed his men. "Good. Everybody grab two bags."

Each man took two heavy canvas bags from the cart. The bags were full of money from the Bon Marche'. Each bag weighed twenty-five pounds.

"Remember," said Mathews, "five seconds apart. Move rapidly. Do not stop for any reason."

The others nodded.

Mathews moved to the door, took a deep breath, then opened the door. "Go."

One after another, five seconds apart, the men walked into the mall concourse. Mathews was the last man out. Each man carried two bags, one in each hand. The bags skipped along the floor as the men strode hurriedly down the mall.

Some shoppers stopped and pointed, others kept moving but gawked at the sight. Seven men with black ski masks hustling through the mall with canvas bags.

Five year old John Stiles tugged at his mother's dress. "Mommy! Mommy! Look!"

His mother looked. When she saw the black ski masks, she took her son by the hand. "Let's go, John," she said. Mother and son walked into the nearest store.

Robert Mathews felt alive with power. He and his men were pulling it off. Walking right down the mall in broad daylight, wearing ski masks, with stolen money. What a rush!

The first robber reached the glass doors of the South main entrance to the mall. He turned and bumped the door open with his butt. Then he held the door open, using his boot as a doorstop.

One after another, five seconds apart, six men walked through the open door and across twenty yards of cement to the curb, where a gray panel van sat parked. The first man to the van opened the back doors of the van and tossed in his two bags. Then quickly moved to the driver's side door. He got in and started the engine.

As each man passed the rear of the van, he tossed his bags into the back of the van, pulled off his mask and headed into the parking lot toward a white Cadillac.

After Mathews tossed his bags into the van, he moved to the passenger's side and got in. Once inside he pulled off his ski mask and buckled his seat belt.

The other five men got in the Cadillac. The engine started and the car backed up, then turned and drove slowly out of the lot.

The gray van drove slowly off in the opposite direction.

Back at the Motel 6, the canvas bags were transferred from the gray van to the back of a Ford pick-up truck. A tarp was thrown over the money bags and steel fence poles were laid across the tarp in three separate layers.

Pierce and Kemp, now wearing blue jeans and t-shirts, jumped in the pick-up and drove off.

Mathews returned the white Cadillac to the Hertz car rental at SeaTac, the Seattle airport, where Duey picked him up in a Chevy Blazer. The other three members of the Silent Brotherhood had already left in Mathews' Ford Bronco.

All three vehicles headed for Metaline Falls.

* * * * *

"How much?" said Pierce.

"$536,000," said Parmenter.

"Sweet Jesus!"

"You got that right."

All the men grinned, then started laughing. Pierce pounded his fist into a pillow on the couch.

"Dear God! Dear God!" said Pierce, raising his fist on high. "We are invincible!"

A great cheer went up.

Mathews nodded. "ZOG has met its match," he said.

Of the $536,000 stolen, $301,000 was in checks. Mathews ordered them burned in the fireplace. Which left $235,000 in cash. A pretty good haul for a bunch of losers.

Each man was given $10,000 to spend as he wished.

Mathews and Barnhill drove the Ford Bronco to Missoula, Montana. They checked into the Motel 6, using aliases and paying cash. The cash came from the Northgate Mall.

They went to a local gun shop called Missoula Arms. Missoula Arms catered to outdoorsmen, macho types who lived to fish and hunt. Hundreds of rifles, shotguns, and semi-automatic assault rifles stood at attention on custom built display racks. Beneath them, millions of rounds of ammunition snoozed in cupboards. In front of the cupboards, in glass display cases whose tops served as counters, hundreds of revolvers and pistols exposed themselves to lustful patrons. Some were steel blue, some were feral black, some were chromed.

It was like a porn shop. Only instead of flesh, it offered cold steel. And all the goods could be touched and fondled and caressed before money changed hands.

Mathews and Barnhill felt like they'd gone to heaven.

They shopped for hours, asking the salesman to bring one after another of the guns to them as they stood at the counter. Anything that caught their eyes, they wanted to hold it. See if it fit their hands. Feel the weight, the balance.

In the end, they walked out with two shotguns, three H&K 91s, which were semi-automatic assault rifles, and six pistols. Thousands of rounds of ammunition completed their purchases.

The loaded it all in the back of the Bronco and drove down the street to Comp USA. Comp USA sold computers and accessories. A national chain-store, it had the very latest high-tech gizmos.

A computer was Mathew's idea. He wanted a state-of-the-art computer system so he could access the Internet. That way he could get the latest news, find rental properties to use as hideouts, and interact with other White Supremacist groups.

The Order needed to get progressive and technologically savvy.

* * * * *

Bruce Pierce and Richard Kemp looked at the building. The sign out front said Congregation Ahavath Israel Synagogue. Church for Jews was what it was.

The synagogue sat on the corner of North 27th and West Bannock Street, in Boise, Idaho. Across the street, in a Hertz rental car sat Pierce and Kemp.

After the adrenaline high of the armored car robbery, they couldn't sit still. They needed some action. So they decided to blow up some Jews, Jews who had the gall to build one of their damn temples right in the middle of white aryan Idaho.

"Fucking ZOG Jews," said Pierce.

"Yeah," said Kemp.

"Looks easy enough," said Pierce. "I can get in through the side door there. I'll put the bomb under the floor. It'll be on a timer. When it goes off, there'll be a few less kikes in Idaho."

He laughed.

Kemp grinned. "Yeah."

"Okay," said Pierce. "Let's go. Get over to the Radio Shack so I can get what I need for the timer."

Kemp started the rental car and eased into traffic.

Bruce Pierce had never made a bomb before. Gary Lee Yarborough had told him how to do it. Yarborough had built the bomb they had used as a diversion in the Embassy Theater. It sounded simple enough in theory, but doing it was another thing.

Pierce taped together dynamite, primer caps, a digital clock, a battery and copper wires. It was crude but it should work – he hoped.

Dressed like one of the workers of the janitorial service the synagogue used, Pierce entered the building on Friday, April 27th. No one was around except for one secretary, and she was about to leave.

Pierece pretended to mop the bathroom floors, while he waited for her to leave. Finally she gathered her purse, turned off the lights in the office and walked over to him.

"I'm outta' here," she said. "Please be sure to lock up when you finish."

"Yes ma'm," said Pierce, not looking up from his work.

"Have a nice weekend," she said. Then she walked off.

Pierce waited five minutes. Then he went down the stairs into the basement. Searching the joists, he found a likely spot that he figured was right in the middle of the sanctuary. He super-glued the makeshift bomb between two floor-support beams, where they touched the flooring boards. Then he wrapped duct tape around the whole thing, just to be sure.

He set the timer for 2:00 p.m., April 29, which would be Sunday right in the middle of the afternoon service. The place would be full of kikes. Boom!

Pierce grinned as he imagined it. Then he left.

The bomb exploded right on time. Only the energy of the explosion burst straight down toward the cement floor of the basement. It was supposed to go up and out, hurling shrapnel into a sanctuary full of Jews. So instead of dead and maimed Jews, all it did was pit and scar the cement floor. It also took a chunk out of one of the support beams, and punctured a hot water heater.

Even if the bomb had done what Pierce wanted it to do, it wouldn't have killed anyone. Pierce and Kemp made a mistake. They set the timer for Sunday. Jews go to synagogue on the Sabbath, which is Saturday. They had the right time, but the wrong day.

Together, they had the IQ of a ....

Although no one was hurt, and very little damage was done, the Jews of Boise got the message. Congregation Ahavath Israel immediately hired security guards to patrol the premises. The guards were armed and instructed to question anyone who looked suspicious. Bomb sniffing dogs were brought in on a rotating schedule to check the building.

* * * * *

Robert Mathews sat on a brown couch with blue and white flowers. Bruce Pierce stood in front of him.

"You just drove to Boise and decided to bomb some kike church?" said Mathews.

"Yeah," said Pierce.

"You didn't bother to clear it with anybody?"

"No," said Pierce. He tugged at his earlobe.

"What happened then?" said Mathews.

"The bomb went off right on time, boss," said Pierce.

Mathews stared at Pierce. Something was fishy. "How many Jesus murdering Jews did you kill?"

Pierce looked at the floor.

"None," he said.

"None? Why not?"

"Something went wrong with the dynamite, boss. It didn't go off right or something," said Pierce, tugging at his other ear.

"Shit!" said Mathews.

His eyes bored into Pierce. "I don't mind that you went off on your own, you know? But the least you could have done was used enough dynamite to blow the place to hell and back."

He slapped the couch once. "Dammit!"

Pierce examined his feet. "Sorry, boss," he said.

Mathews took a deep breath. "I know you are, Bruce. I'm just disappointed is all."

Pierce nodded, still examining his feet.

* * * * *

Walter Edward West was 42 years old. A member of the Aryan Nations, he wanted to belong. He wanted to be part of something bigger than he was. He wanted to be respected, too.

But he wasn't.

When he heard about what Mathews and The Order were doing – robbing armored cars and setting off bombs in downtown Seattle – he got jealous. For he wanted to be part of it. He wanted people to talk about him with awe in their voices. He wanted to be one of the guys – The Order – out there doing something to make America free and white.

But he wasn't.

Instead, Walter West got drunk every night in the bars around Hayden Lake. When he got drunk enough, he started gossiping about The Order and their infamous exploits. He told everybody about what The Order had done, how they had done it and, from the way he told it, like he was part of it.

Being a blabber mouth was not a wise thing for any white supremacist, especially not in the Aryan Nations. There were too many feds sneaking around, trying to get information on them. In fact, the feds had classified the Aryan Nations as domestic terrorists. Which meant the feds had undercover agents everywhere. Which meant the white power extremists needed to remember that loose lips sink ships. In other words, keep your fucking mouth shut.

Walter West forgot. He kept getting drunk and kept shooting his mouth off about The Order. Pretty soon, word of Walter's yakkety-yak filtered back to Robert Mathews, who believed in taking care of business – right now.

Mathews called Duey and Kemp and invited them over for a beer. When the two men got there, Mathews tossed them cans of Pabst Blue Ribbon. Then he told them what he had heard about Walter West and his big mouth.

"I want you two to take care of it," said Mathews,

He looked at them to see if they knew what he meant.

Kemp nodded. "Okay, boss," he said. "When?"

"Tomorrow," said Mathews. He tossed back the rest of his beer. "Take the two new guys with you."

Kemp nodded.

Duey showed an ugly grin. "Boss," he said. "I'd like to be the one who actually takes care of him."

Mathews considered for a moment. "Okay," he said.

Duey bared his teeth in a smile. "Thanks," he said.

Randolph Duey was 34 years old. Richard Kemp was 22.

* * * * *

The two new guys were David Charles Tate and James Dye. They were recruits who wanted some action. Tate came from the Aryan Nations and Dye came from the National Alliance. Both groups were supreme white power gangs.

Kemp and Duey told the two recruits what was going to happen. The new guys merely nodded. They were ready to rock and roll.

"You got weapons?" said Kemp.

"Yeah," said Tate.

Dye nodded.

"Okay. Bring 'em along," said Kemp.

He pointed at Duey. "Randy will do the wet work. We're just along as muscle." Kemp loved using tough-guy words like 'wet work' and 'muscle.' It made him feel like he was a professional soldier or something.

The next evening, the four men got in a green Ford Bronco, which had been purchased with cash stolen from the Northgate Mall. They drove to the suburb of Athol, Idaho, just outside Boise. Which was where Walter West lived.

Athol was a dump. The people there hated anybody who wasn't like them.

Parking in front of the small house, the four men walked with quick steps up to the porch. All were compact and wore tight dark garments. Since Tate was formerly from the Aryan Nations, they decided he would do the talking. The plan was simple. Tell Walter West what he wanted to hear. That they had heard good things about him. That he was reliable and could be counted on. So Mathews had sent them around to recruit him. See if he wanted to join The Order and make a difference.

Arrogant as well as stupid, Walter believed the pr puff. He knew Tate a little, anyway he'd seen him around. And he'd heard of Duey and Kemp. Hell, they were famous. When they told him that Mathews himself had sent them, he became intoxicated with self-importance.

"Let's go get a drink," said Kemp. "And celebrate."

"Celebrate what?" said Walter.

"Being white and free and The Order," said Kemp. "And you – our newest member. We'll raise a few to our new comrade."

He clapped Walter on the shoulder. Walter glowed with conceit.

They all piled into the green Ford Bronco and drove to the Red Rooster Bar in Boise. Lots of white supremacists hung out at the Red Rooster. The guy who owned the place was in the Aryan Nations. He had a big confederate flag mounted on one wall. Two fists clenching lightning bolts had been painted on another wall.

Kemp, Duey, Tate, Dye and Walter West came in and found a booth. They ordered Budweisers with whiskey chasers and munched on Planter's party peanuts. When the drinks arrived, they immediately ordered another round. Then they chugged the beers, chased it down with the whiskey, and began talking.

They talked about the weather, women, cars and food. No one mentioned The Order. Twice Walter asked about Mathews, but the others acted like they didn't hear him. Walter shrugged and had another beer. Then two shots of whiskey.

Pretty soon Walter was loaded. The others had been nursing their second rounds, watching Walter suck at the whiskey tit.

"Let's go," said Kemp.

Everyone stood up except Walter. He looked up confused. "Where we going? We just got here," he said.

"We got some business to take care of," said Kemp. "Serious business. Maybe you could come along and help us out."

"Sure, sure," said Walter. "Where we going?"

"Up into the Kaniksu," said Dye. The Kaniksu National Forest was just outside Boise.

"What for?" said Walter.

"We gotta' drop something off for Mathews," said Kemp, staring at Walter.

"Okay," said Walter, hitching at his pants. "Let's go."

The got in the green Ford Bronco and took off. It was 9:00 p.m. An hour later they were deep in the Kaniksu. Walter sat in the back seat of the Bronco with Tate and Dye. He'd been sucking at a whiskey bottle someone had given him.

Kemp pulled the Bronco to the side of the highway, then turned onto a dirt fireroad. After a hundred yards, he stopped the Bronco. Kemp shut the motor off, but left the lights on.

Everyone except Walter got out of the Bronco. Walter was too drunk to even notice they had stopped. Duey had a Black and Decker hammer in his hand. It had a heavy black metal head and a yellow plastic handle.

"Get the little fucker out," ordered Kemp.

Tate and Dye grabbed Walter and dragged him from the vehicle.

Walter could hardly stand on his own, but managed it somehow.

Duey walked around behind Walter. Duey hit him in the head with the hammer. It made a deep thunking noise, like an axe biting in to a tree trunk.

Walter sagged to the ground, like he was sitting down.

Tate, Dye and Kemp watched. Kemp ran the tip of his tongue over the edge of his front teeth.

Duey moved to the back of the Bronco and opened the door. He reached in a pulled a rifle from beneath a tarp. It was one of the H & K 91s that Mathews had bought in Missoula.

As he walked back to where Walter slumped forward, Duey pulled the bolt on the rifle back, then let it snap forward.

Duey put the toe of his boot under Walter's chin and kicked up. Walter's head snapped back and he fell backward. Duey shot him in the face.

The four men stood staring at Walter. Duey held the rifle with one hand, still pointing it at Walter's face. Tate had his hands in the pockets of his jacket. Kemp played his tongue over his teeth.

A minute passed.

Kemp said, "Get the tarp. Roll him up."

Tate and Dye got the tarp from the Bronco and spread it out next to the body. They rolled the body onto the tarp, then rolled it up like a carpet. Tate used two lengths of rope to tie off the ends of the carpet.

Kemp nodded. "Okay. Drag him to the grave."

Tate and Dye grabbed one of the ropes and pulled the stuffed carpet off into the woods, where a long deep hole waited. A mound of dirt roosted next to it. They had dug the grave the day before. It took the two of them three hours to dig. They used picks and shovels.

The shovels leaned against a nearby tree, waiting.

They dumped the carpeted body in the hole. Taking up the shovels, they filled the hole back up. Tate spread pine needles over the grave.

When it was done, Kemp said, "Let's go. Take a look around. Make sure we don't leave any traces."

The men walked around the area, looking for anything they might have left.

They walked back to the Bronco, tossed the rifle and shovels in the back and drove off.

* * * * *

Robert Mathews had a shit list. It was a list of people who deserved to die. At the top of the list was a Jew by the name of Alan Berg. Berg lived in Denver, where he worked for a radio station called KOA 850. He was a talk-show host. And he excelled at pissing people off. He knew how to push their buttons.

Berg was a liberal and enjoyed picking on conservative groups. His favorite targets were right-wing extremist groups, like the Ku Klux Klan or the Aryan Nations.

As far as Mathews was concerned, Berg deserved to die for three reasons: he was a Jew, which meant he was part of ZOG; he was a liberal, who believed people had equal rights; and he was anti-white power.

Jean Margaret Craig was 51 years old. She believed white people needed to keep their race pure. She was a friend of Mathews.

Because she looked like the wicked witch of the West, Jean Craig was perfect for undercover work. No one gave her a second glance.

Mathews sent her to Denver to follow Alan Berg and learn his routine, if he had one. Most people do, they just don't realize it. Jean Craig watched Berg as he went about the business of living his life. She recorded his movements in a notebook she carried in her purse.

After following Berg for a week, Jean Craig called Mathews and told him the Berg would pose no problem. He would be an easy target. His routine rarely varied because he had a methodical personality.

Mathews, Pierce, David Lane and a new guy, whose name was Richard Scutari, sat reviewing their plan for the assassination of Alan Berg. Scutari was 38 years old, handsome in a dark way, and very nervous. Not because of what they were going to do, he was just high-strung.

The color scheme of the room was gold and garish red. More like something one would expect in a whorehouse. But this was not a cathouse in Las Vegas, it was Mathews' room in the Motel 6.

"I want to pull the trigger," said Bruce Pierce. He was sitting on the bed. Next to him were a .45 semi-automatic pistol and an Ingram MAC-10 submachine gun. Energy of extravagance dripped from Pierce.

Mathews gazed at Pierce from his seat on the couch. There was an energy about Mathews, too. His was the dynamism of personality and a decided heart. Whereas Pierce's fervor was clearly that of madness.

Mathews nodded. "Okay, Bruce," he said. "The privilege is yours."

Pierce grinned.

"Let's go over it one more time," said Mathews, looking at the three men.

* * * * *

David Lane parked the green Ford Bronco. Seated in the passenger's seat was Robert Mathews. Pierce and Scutari sat together on the back seat. Pierce cradled the MAC-10 in his hands.

Across the street was a complex of light brown townhouses. Berg lived here. His townhouse was in full view of the men in the Bronco. The four men waited patiently. No one said anything.

At 9:21 p.m, a Volkswagen beetle turned into the driveway of the townhouse. It was Alan Berg. A bag of groceries sat on the passenger's seat.

"Go," said Mathews.

Lane started the Bronco's engine, then drove into the driveway, pulling up behind Berg's car. Berg couldn't see who it was because of the blinding headlights. Mathews leaped out of the Bronco and opened Pierce's door. Pierce moved quickly around the back of the Bronco, holding the MAC-10. Then he ran up the driveway toward the beetle.

Alan Berg got out of his car, holding the bag of groceries. He turned to see who had pulled up behind him. A figure loomed in front of him.

Pierce pulled the trigger on the MAC-10. Twelve rounds slammed into Alan Berg. He was dead before he hit the ground. Groceries spilled all over.

Then the gun jammed. Otherwise, Pierce would have emptied the entire clip into the Jew-boy.

"Come on, come on!" hissed Mathews.

Pierce ran back to the Bronco and jumped in. The Bronco spun its tires as it backed out of the driveway. Once out of the driveway, Lane slammed on the brakes, turned the wheel as he found 'drive,' and the Bronco sped off down the street.

Back at the Motel 6, the four murderers went to their rooms, grabbed their already packed bags and drove west on I-70. It was June 18, 1984.

* * * * *

David Lane had a new batch of counterfeit bills he wanted to try out. He'd been refining his efforts with the use of a computer and a high-definition scanner. Now he was ready to pass the phony bills and see if anyone noticed.

Mathews told him not to pass the funny money anywhere near home. By "near home" Mathews meant anywhere on the West coast of the United States. If the bogus bills attracted attention, he didn't want any of it connected to The Silent Brotherhood, aka The Order.

So Lane got in touch with a guy he knew. The guy lived in Philadelphia. His name was Thomas Martinez. Martinez was half Mexican and half white, but he considered himself all white. He was also a white racist, who hung around with the Klan, the National Alliance and the Aryan Nations. But he never really committed to any of them. He just floated on the edge.

On June 24, 1984 – six days after his part in the Alan Berg assassination – David Lane got off a plane that had just landed in Philadelphia. In his carry on shoulder bag, he had $30,000 in funny money.

Lane took a cab to Martinez's house. There he gave him the money, along with some common sense instructions.

"Don't pass more than one hundred dollars in any store," said Lane. "And don't go back to any store you've already been to. If you do, they can put two and two together and come up with you."

Martinez nodded, but didn't say anything. He didn't really want to be doing this. Funny money wasn't his thing. But he couldn't think of a way to say no without pissing The Order off. And he knew how these guys operated. If you weren't with them, you were against them. And if you were against them, well, they took care of business in a very final way.

"And whatever you do," said Lane, "do not pass the money around here, in your own neighborhood. Go over to Jersey and pass it there. Like in the casinos."

Martinez nodded his understanding, which was as phony as the money.

After Lane went back to the airport, Martinez peeled off $2000 of the money, and stuffed it in his wallet. Then he went out.

Martinez spent $1500 on the first day – in his own neighborhood. At the local liquor store, he bought some beer and whiskey and chips and dip. He paid for it with the bogus money.

He didn't get up until noon the next day, and when he did he had the mother of all hangovers. After coffee and donuts and a shower, Martinez went out and passed another $500 worth of bad bills. On his way home, he stopped at the liquor store again. He bought a lottery ticket, hoping he could win the jackpot, which was now up to $32 million. He paid for the two-dollar ticket with a phony $10 bill.

The guy who owned the liquor store had found the bad bills from the day before when he took them to the bank for deposit. The bank spotted them right away. They told him to keep an eye out for more.

When Martinez handed him the bogus $10 bill, the owner recognized it as counterfeit. He also recognized Martinez from yesterday. The owner didn't say anything. Just gave Martinez his change. Then as Martinez drove off, the guy wrote down his license plate number.

Then he called the feds.

Agents from the U.S. Secret Service showed up at Martinez's door that evening. They knocked on the door. Martinez was watching television and drinking beer.

"Shit," said Martinez, getting up to answer the door. "Who the hell is that, I wonder?"

He opened the door and saw two men with crew cuts standing there.

"Yeah?" said Martinez, taking a big gulp of beer. He was on his fifth beer and not thinking too clearly.

"Robert Martinez?"

"Yeah," said Martinez.

"We'd like to ask you some questions, sir? Mind if we come in?"

"What the hell about?"

One of the men pushed into the room. The other followed right behind him and moved quickly to the side.

"Whaddaya' want? What's going on?" said Martinez, slurring.

Both men produced badges. "You're under arrest, Mr. Martinez," said one of them.

"For what?" said Martinez.

"Passing counterfeit currency, which is against the law. It's also a felony," said the agent, pulling out a set of handcuffs.

They let Martinez put his shoes on. Then they cuffed him, read his rights and took him down to the Federal Building for questioning.

Martinez didn't tell the feds anything. The next day he was arraigned on the charge of passing counterfeit currency. Since it was his first offense and was non-violent, the Judge released him on his own recognizance.

Martinez went home and called Robert Mathews. When he told Mathews that he had been arrested, Mathews got worried.

"You didn't say anything, did you?" said Mathews.

"No. Nothing," said Martinez.

"Good," said Mathews. "What's going to happen now?"

"I'm out on OR," said Martinez. "But I have to go to court next month and I need an attorney or I'm going to end up in jail."

"You got an attorney?"

"Not yet," said Martinez. "I need $1600 for a retainer fee. And probably another 5 or 10 thousand after that. And I don't have that kind of dough."

"Okay," said Mathews. "Don't worry about it. We'll take care of the fees for you. But you'll have to sit tight for a few days. We're going to hit another armored car, then we'll have plenty of cash."

"Okay," said Martinez. "I don't care how you get the money, as long as I have it before I go to court."

"You will. You will," said Mathews. "Just hang tight, okay?"

"Okay."

Mathews knew that Martinez knew too much. In their past conversations, Mathews himself had told Martinez all about The Silent Brotherhood and their crimes. Which included murder, armed robbery and counterfeiting. So they had to take care of his legal expenses. If they didn't, there was always the risk that Martinez could turn snitch to save himself. That would not be good for The Order.

And Mathews had already vowed to himself that he would never let ZOG imprison him.

* * * * *

The driver of the Brink's armored car slowed as he came around a curve on Highway 101. Something was wrong.

A white cadillac was parked in the middle of the highway. The car's left side and left front bumper crumpled and badly scratched. Off to the side of the highway sat a green Ford Bronco. Two men stood next to it.

One of the men spotted the Brink's truck and walked into the roadway, waving his arms.

"Looks like an accident," said the driver to the guard in the passenger's seat.

"Well, duh," said the guard.

The driver chuckled. "Yeah," he said. "Kind of obvious, huh?"

"We'd better see if we can help," said the guard. "Pull it over behind the caddy."

Braking the heavily armored vehicle, the driver steered it onto the shoulder of the road. The rear end of the cadillac was five yards away.

The two men from the Bronco jogged over to the Brink's truck. They both wore dress shirts and ties.

Lowering his window, the Brink's driver said, "What happened?" His forearm, resting on the doorframe, was thick and rippled with muscle.

"I'm not sure," said one of the men. "We're on our way to San Francisco for a business meeting and when we came over the rise back there" – he pointed to the north – "the car was like this."

"Where's the car it hit?" said the driver.

"I don't know," said the businessman. "Must've taken off is all we can figure."

The driver nodded and glanced at his partner. "Hit and run."

"Probably," said the businessman. "You got a radio in there?"

"Yeah," said the driver.

"Well, get on it and call for an ambulance, will ya'? There's a guy in caddy. Unconscious. And we can't get the door open."

"Yeah, sure," said the driver, reaching for the radio. He looked at his partner, "You and Frank better get out there and see if you can help these guys get him out of the car."

"Gotcha," said the guard. He turned and yelled into the compartment of the truck. "Frank! Unlock and unsaddle, will ya'? Gotta' injured man out here and we need some muscle."

A muffled voice came from the compartment. "Right there."

The guard opened the passenger door and stepped out onto the tarmac. At the same time, the back door of the truck swung out and Frank got out. Both men wore revolvers in black leather holsters on their hips.

The two businessmen and the two guards jogged to the cadillac. Inside the armored car, the driver was on his radio talking to a dispatcher.

Frank got to the caddy first. The window on the driver's side was down. Frank could see a man lying on the front seat. His seat belt was still on and blood smeared his face.

Grabbing the door handle of the cadillac, Frank gave it a sharp tug. Nothing.

"Here," said Frank. "A couple of you guys grab the door. Get a good grip. On three we'll all pull like hell."

One of the businessmen crowded next to Frank and grabbed the door. So did the other Brink's guard. The other businessman stood behind them.

"One, two, three!" counted Frank.

Everybody heaved and the door popped open.

Two other things happened at the same moment. The bloody-faced driver of the cadillac sat up, pointing a 9mm Smith and Wesson semi-automatic pistol at the four men. And three men appeared from behind the

Brink's armored car. All three of the men wore black ski masks. Two of them carried vicious looking shotguns. The third man had an Ingram MAC-10.

The man with the MAC-10 moved quickly and silently to the open window of the Brink's truck. He pointed the barrel of the gun at the driver, who stopped talking into his microphone and turned his head to look at the gun. The driver's mouth hung open and he held the mike as if he was trying to talk with his ear.

"Don't move," said the man with the MAC-10.

The driver stared at him stupidly.

"Both hands on the wheel. And don't move," repeated the masked man.

The driver shook his head. Then did as he was told.

With their shotguns pointed waist-high, the other two masked men had moved closer to cadillac, where the four would-be rescuers held their hands up and stared at the driver of the cadillac, who was pointing the 9mm at them.

"Get the guard's pistol," said the man with the 9mm.

The four rescuers jerked their heads around to see whom he was talking to.

"Nobody move," ordered one of the shotgun-toting men.

Staying out of the line of fire, the other masked man walked to Frank. Unsnapping the holster, he took Frank's pistol.

"Move back ten feet," said the man inside the cadillac.

The four rescuers stepped slowly back. Their every movement covered by two shotguns.

Releasing his seatbelt, the man got out of the cadillac. The red substance on his face – the fake blood – screened his features. He looked like something out of a horror movie.

Frank noted that the bloodstained man had brown hair and wide shoulders. Frank guessed him to be five feet eight or nine inches tall.

Frank didn't know it, but he was looking at Robert Jay Mathews.

"Move 'em together over here," said Mathews, turning his head to make sure the man with the MAC-10 heard. "Sit 'em down against the caddy."

Thirty seconds later five figures – the two businessmen and the three Brink's guards – sat on the highway, resting their backs against the white cadillac. Two masked men guarded them. One masked man leveled a shotgun at them. The other masked man held the MAC-10.

Frank stared at the guy with the MAC-10. The man's body language seemed eager. Eager for someone to try something so he could demonstrate the lethality of his weapon.

Mathews and the masked man who carried the other shotgun walked to the back of the Brink's armored car, where Frank had conveniently left the door open.

Leaning against the cadillac, Frank watched as another vehicle came around the curve of the highway – from the south. It was a white Chevy Tahoe that looked brand new. The Tahoe made a u-turn in the middle of the highway, then backed up to the Brink's truck. A masked man got out of the Tahoe. He walked over to Mathews and said something. Mathews laughed and pointed toward the cadillac.

These guys were pros, Frank told himself. All five of them.

The three robbers unloaded heavy canvas bags from the Brink's truck, stacking them carefully in the back of the Tahoe. There were a lot of bags.

When they finished, Mathews strolled over to the caddy.

"Put the Brink's guys in their truck, in the back," he said, waving his 9mm at the Brink's armored car. "Make sure they're secure."

"Then put the two suits in their car. Secure their hands and feet," said Mathews.

The masked men did as they were ordered. Seating the three guards in the back compartment of the armored car, they used yards and yards of duct tape on their hands and feet.

Mathews came over and looked in the compartment. "Thanks for your cooperation," he said. "Someone'll be along sooner or later and will find you."

"Who are you guys?" said Frank. "How'd you know where we'd be at just the right minute?"

Mathews waggled his 9mm. "We're nobody," he said. Then he laughed and shut the door.

He walked over to the green Ford Bronco, where the two businessmen sat waiting. Their hands and feet were not secured. When Mathews got nearer the two men grinned at him.

Mathews smiled back at them. "You guys done good," he said.

"You weren't bad either, boss," said Parmenter.

Mathews nodded. "Okay. Now, you know what to do, but I'm going to repeat it just so there're no mistakes."

Parmenter gave him a thumbs up.

"We all go south to Ukiah, where we'll then head east to Reno. You guys park the Bronco at the mall, where the rental car is waiting. Then take the rental car east to Reno."

"Smooth and easy," said Parementer, gliding his hand out.

"Be sure you leave nothing in the Bronco. And take the plates with you. Got it?"

"Yeah boss, we got it," said Parmenter, looking over at Barnhill, who nodded.

"Okay. Let's go," said Mathews.

Mathews walked over to the Tahoe and got in.

Both vehicles drove south on highway 101.

In the canvas bags, in the back of the Tahoe, was $3.6 million. The Silent Brotherhood had hit the jackpot. And the job had come off without a hitch, just as planned.

Almost.

Once in Reno, they dumped the Tahoe and the rental car driven by Parmenter and Barnhill. They split up again. Four white Hertz rental cars headed north to Boise, Idaho. When they got to Boise, they rendezvoused at Motel 6 and divided the money. Each man got $500,000, except Mathews. He got $600,000.

They made one mistake. At the crime scene, FBI agents found a 9mm semi-automatic in the glove box of the white cadillac. Mathews had forgotten it was there and left it behind. It was registered to Andrew V. Barnhill.

The FBI now had its first real clue. And the Silent Brotherhood didn't know it.

* * * * *

The hijacking was an inside job. Charles E. Ostrout was the insider's name. He was a 50 year old white supremacist. He and Mathews had met two years before when Ostrout had visited Hayden Lake. Ostrout had driven up to "hang out" with fellow white power types.

Ostrout lived in San Francisco, where he worked at the Brink's Armored Car Service depot. While hanging out in Hayden Lake, he had complained to Mathews about all the minorities in San Francisco. How they got all the jobs and promotions where he worked. It was like reverse discrimination or something. The "muds" were taking over. White people needed to defend the job market. If they didn't, pretty soon there wouldn't be decent jobs to be had.

"You're right," said Mathews, nodding. "Where you work? What's the name of your company?"

"Brink's," said Ostrout. "Brink's Armored Car Service."

Mathews stiffened. "Whaddaya' do there?"

"I'm a supervisor," said Ostrout.

Mathews spent the rest of the day pumping Ostrout for information. And Ostrout wanted to be pumped. He was willing to do most anything to punish his employer for its liberal attitude toward minority groups.

Ostrout told Mathews where, when and how to pull the job off. It had been Ostrout who selected the Brink's run to Eureka, which was a small city north of Ukiah.

"It's perfect," said Ostrout. "Not only is it remote, but it's vulnerable." He smiled. "And the truck carries lots of cash."

As they had discovered, Ostrout knew what he was talking about. The hijacking had been a piece of cake.

* * * * *

Success as an armed hijacker suited Mathews. It made him feel good. What the psychologists called "empowered." So he decided to use Ostrout's inside information to do another job. A big one.

Ostrout informed Mathews that the big money was in the vault at Brink's in San Francisco. This was because every so often Brink's handled shipments of money from all the fancy hotels in Hawaii. When that happened, there could be anywhere between $30 million to $50 million in the vault.

Mathews' eyes lit up when he heard the numbers. Electrified, he asked Ostrout if the vault could be robbed.

"Yeah," said Ostrout. "By a group of determined and disciplined men, it's possible." Then he hesitated.

"But?" said Mathews, sensing a problem.

"Well," said Ostrout, rubbing the back of his neck, "you'd need another man on the inside. Somebody in operations. Because I don't have access to the vault."

Mathews thought for a moment. "Then we need to find somebody in operations to help," he told Ostrout.

"Yeah," said Ostrout. "There might be a guy…"

"Talk to him. Recruit him. Blackmail him, if need be. Just get him to go along," said Mathews, leaning forward.

"Okay," said Ostrout.

* * * * *

The guy's name was Ronald Allan King. And he was the Operations Manager at Brink's depot. Bitterness was his problem. Brink's had passed him over twice for promotion.

Ostrout started talking to him, feeding the fires of bitterness one log at a time. Pretty soon, King was on board and Mathews began serious planning. If the Order could pull it off, it would be the biggest robbery in U.S. history. People would sit up and take notice for sure. The Order would be famous.

Meanwhile, the FBI had traced the registration on the 9mm pistol that Mathews had left in the white caddy at the scene of the crime. They set up surveillance on Andrew Barnhill. Following him everywhere, the agents soon knew his habits and whom he hung out with.

Using sophisticated cameras with telephoto lenses, the FBI took pictures of all Barnhill's associates. Identifying the associates was easy enough. Names, addresses, employment records, health records, school records, and social security numbers – along with a host of other information – were fed into the FBI's computers. Within weeks, they had a complete dossier on The Order, aka The Silent Brotherhood.

Robert Mathews was identified as the leader of The Order.

At first, the FBI labeled The Order as a militant racist gang. Pretty soon, though, the FBI changed that. The Order went from a militant racist gang to terrorists.

This reclassification convinced the FBI powers-that-be to stage an offensive against The Order. It was the first step in what would become an all-out war.

Dozens of federal agents descended upon northern Idaho. All of them dressed in Brooks Brothers suits, wearing neat flat-top haircuts. They stood out like sore thumbs. Within hours, most, if not all, of northern Idaho knew that the feds were thick as flies on a dairy farm. And they were asking questions about Bob Mathews.

Mathews heard about it through the grapevine. So did the rest of The Order members.

A hasty meeting was called. The Order decided to leave and go into hiding. They split into two groups. Mathews and his group packed their stuff and drove out of town. When they got up into Washington, they stayed at cheap motels for two weeks. Then they rented houses and moved in.

Bruce Pierce led the other group. This group traveled around in RVs and campers. Mobility made them invisible, they thought. Although they wandered, their general direction was south.

Gary Yarborough went his own way. He packed up everything he owned and moved from Sandpoint, Idaho. He had a friend who had a friend who owned a cabin in the mountains near Samules, Idaho. Yarborough thought he'd be safe there.

An FBI airplane followed him all the way to Samules, circling above him at 5,000 feet.

* * * * *

Meanwhile, Thomas Martinez waited in Philadelphia for his promised money to arrive. It didn't. Which meant Martinez couldn't hire a private attorney for his defense. He would have to go with a Public Defender. Which meant he'd probably go to prison for a long time. Which meant Mathews had lied to him and betrayed him.

Martinez did not want to go to Club Fed because of funny money. So he decided to take action.

The first day of his scheduled trial was October 1, 1984. Martinez asked for a meeting with the feds. The feds asked the Judge to postpone the trial for a few days. The Judge, when he heard the details, agreed.

Martinez and the feds met in a small office. Sitting on a metal folding chair, Martinez gazed at five federal agents.

"My attorney told me that you guys – the FBI – have tied me to The Order," said Martinez.

The head fed was a guy named Smith.

"That's correct," said Smith. He half-sat on the corner of a desk. One leg on the floor, the other dangling over the front of the desk.

Martinez thought about that, studying his shoes.

"He also told me that I'll be named as a co-conspirator in any indictments you guys bring against The Order," said Martinez. "Is that right?"

"It is."

"And that's RICO, isn't it?" said Martinez.

"It is."

"Shit," whispered Martinez to no one in particular.

He leaned back in his chair, putting his hands behind his head. "Okay," he said, looking at Agent Smith. "I want to make a deal."

Smith nodded, swinging his dangling foot like a metronome. "What kind of deal?"

Smith knew exactly what kind of deal Thomas Martinez wanted to make. The feds loved making deals, especially if it meant getting the bad guys. And The Order weren't just bad. They were the baddest of the bad. So Smith was eager to make a deal. But he didn't show it.

"The kind of deal where I give you something. Then you give me something," said Martinez. "What we used to call tit for tat when I was growing up."

Agent Smith stared at Thomas Martinez for a moment. His leg had stopped swinging. Then he said, "Go on."

"I'll tell you everything I know about The Silent Brotherhood – who you call The Order – and their crimes," said Martinez.

He looked down at his shoes. When he looked up at Smith a few seconds later, his eyes were slits.

"In return," Martinez said, "you protect me and my family. And you make a recommendation to the prosecutor and the Judge."

"What kind of recommendation?"

"That they go easy on me – as easy as possible," said Martinez.

Smith raised his eyebrows. "You'll take the stand? Testify in court?"

Martinez hesitated for a beat. "Yeah."

"Okay," said Smith, cracking a smile for the first time.

Then he turned to one of the other agents in the room. Get some recording equipment in here. And a stenographer.

Fifteen minutes later, Thomas Martinez sat in a different room. This one was larger and more comfortable. It had cushioned chairs, a conference table and windows. Over in the corner there was a coffee maker, one of those big metal ones.

Martinez took a sip of his coffee. A box of donuts sat on the conference table. Reaching out, he selected a cake donut – white frosting with sprinkles. He loved sprinkles.

At the other end of the conference table, Agent Smith took a big bite of his glazed donut and chewed. Dabbing at his lips with a napkin, he said, "Tell us about Robert Jay Mathews."

Martinez chuckled. "A schizophrenic psycho, that's what Bob is." He kept talking for three hours.

* * * * *

A green Ford F-150 pickup drove up the dirt road toward a cabin. A brown and white logo was painted on the doors of the truck – U.S. Forest Service. Inside the truck sat three men in Forest Service uniforms. But they weren't rangers. They were FBI agents disguised as rangers.

Their orders were to approach the cabin and check it out. If possible, they were to speak to the person who lived there. Gary Yarborough.

But Yarborough didn't want to talk and was not in the mood to entertain visitors. When the truck got fifty yards from the cabin, Yarborough stuck the barrel of his H & K-91 out of the window and pulled the trigger.

Three bullets slammed into the grill of the truck.

"Jesus Christ!" yelled the driver. He swerved to the left and slammed on the brakes.

"Back it up! Back it the fuck up!" shouted the phony ranger seated next to him.

The driver threw the gear lever into reverse and punched the gas pedal. A cloud of dust puffed up as the tires spun. Bouncing and bucking over ruts the truck retreated at thirty miles an hour.

Yarborough fired three more rounds as the truck vanished around a bend in the road.

"Goddamn feds!" he yelled out the window.

While the three agents drove back to Samules, Yarborough fixed his lunch. He heated a can of pork and beans in a pan. Then sat down to eat.

Back in Samules, the three FBI agents made some phone calls. Then they changed clothes and armed themselves – shoulder holsters with pistols. They also carried Remington 10 gauge shotguns.

Getting into a black Chevy Tahoe, they drove back up to Yarborough's cabin. Along with their weapons, they took two other things: bad attitudes and a warrant.

The Tahoe stopped three hundred yards from the cabin. Three men got out and moved silently up the road. One of the men carried a bullhorn. When they got to the spot where Yarborough had fired at their truck, they spread out.

The agent with the bullhorn pulled the trigger. A piercing screech tore at the silence, followed by an amplified voice.

"This is the FBI. We have warrant. Come out of the cabin with your hands on top of your head."

No response, no movement from the cabin.

"Mr. Yarborough. This is the FBI. Come out of the house with your hands on top of your head. We have a warrant for ----"

Muzzle flashes and angry popping noises interrupted the agent. Yarborough had begun firing from the window at the front of the cabin.

The three agents hit the ground and returned fire, blasting away at the cabin with their shotguns. White scars appeared on the exterior of the cabin as pellets tore at the wood.

Inside the cabin, Gary Yarborough ripped off a thirty round clip and then dashed out the back door of the cabin. He flitted into the woods and disappeared.

Out front, the three agents waited for another barrage of bullets. When none came, one of them said, "Okay. Enough of this shit. Let's close in on this asshole."

His partners nodded, as they fed new shells into their shotguns.

"Ready?"

"Go!"

The three agents jumped up and ran toward the cabin. Two of the agents blasted away with their shotguns, aiming for the window. The third agent – the one in the middle of the formation – had his pistol out. Pointing the weapon at the door of the cabin, he charged the door, hitting it with his shoulder.

The door popped open and the agent fell into the cabin. He rolled and turned, scanning the interior for something to shoot. The other two agents jumped through the doorway, one going left, one going right. All of them were ready to give as good as they got, but nothing happened.

Panting, sweating and twitching from an overload of adrenaline, they realized no one was home.

One of them pointed at the open back door. "The asshole split," he said.

He walked over and peered out into the dim light. "Nothing but trees and more trees," he said. "We'll never catch him in there."

"Okay," said the agent with the bullhorn. "Call it in. Then let's see what the guy had here."

As a result of the call, the local sheriff set up two roadblocks. And two helicopters made a couple of passes over the area. But no one expected to find anything or anyone. It was dark now, and there was just too much area to cover. Even if they'd had 100 agents, and they didn't, the odds were still in Yarborough's favor.

Back at the cabin, a swarm of specialists swarmed over the place. A portable generator was fired up, feeding an array of halogen lamps the FBI had moved in.

Yarborough's cabin was an arsenal. Plastic explosives, dynamite, gas grenades, cases of ammunition, pistols, shotguns, and rifles and two Ingram MAC-10 submachine guns with silencers. They also found gas masks, knives, crossbows, assault vests (body armor), and radio frequency scanners.

Special Agent in charge Art Ransom shook his head as he surveyed the piles of equipment. "Man," he said, "talk about taking care of business. This guy wasn't messing around."

"Like he was getting ready for a war," said one of the technicians.

They boxed it all up, loaded it in trucks and shipped it off to the FBI Laboratory. The lab guys worked their magic and discovered that one of the MAC-10s was used to kill Alan Berg.

When the FBI powers-that-be heard that, they looked at one another and rolled their eyeballs.

One of them said, "Time to round 'em up."

The others nodded.

There was a problem, though. In order to "round 'em up," the FBI had to know where they were.

* * * * *

Mathews and his group were living in rented houses in small towns just outside Mt. Hood, Oregon. Duey and three others had decided they'd feel safer in a more remote area. So they'd gone up to Puget Sound in Washington, where they rented three vacation homes on Whidbey Island. They hoped the feds would not be able to find them.

Gary Yarborough showed up at Mt. Hood. All he had was the clothes on his back and a semi-automatic pistol. He had dumped the H & K-91. It was too risky to be seen walking around with an assault rifle.

Yarborough told Mathews what had happened at the cabin.

"Shit," said Mathews, knowing the feds would now have classified Yarbrogh and The Order as a terrorist organization. All the weapons the feds had found in the cabin would demand a nation-wide manhunt. The FBI would intensify their efforts to locate the members of The Order. Unfortunately for the feds, The Order was living off the grid. The feds had no idea where they were.

That is until Mathews all but told them.

Mathews was worried about Martinez, who was an unknown wild card in the hand The Order was playing. If Martinez started to feel abandoned, he might decide to roll over on The Order, telling the feds what he knew. Mathews needed to talk to Martinez, letting him know they had not tossed him to the wolves. So Mathews made a phone call.

It was a fatal mistake.

On the phone, Mathews asked Martinez to fly to Portland, Oregon, where Mathews would pick him up. Then they could sit down and talk things over. Martinez agreed to do whatever Mathews wanted. What Mathews didn't know was that Martinez had already made a deal with the feds. In fact, the feds were listening in on the phone call.

November 23, 1984. It was Friday evening, which meant rush-hour traffic was heavy. And it was raining. At Portland International Airport, it was business as usual, which meant lots of planes landing and taking off. One of the planes that landed carried a passenger named Thomas Martinez. It also carried two undercover FBI agents, who shadowed Martinez as he walked off the plane.

As Martinez made his way through the terminal to the baggage claim area, he was under constant surveillance. The terminal was crawling with FBI agents. There was no way they were going to blow this opportunity, because they might not get another one.

After collecting his bags from the carousel, Martinez walked outside the terminal to Passenger Pick-up. A line of cars, each with its engine idling and wipers swishing back and forth, sat waiting in the drizzling rain. Martinez scanned the line of vehicles until he spotted the one he was looking for – a white Ford Bronco.

Inside the Bronco were two men – Yarborough and Mathew. Even though they didn't expect anything to happen in such a public place, they weren't taking any chances. Both men were armed with pistols. A shotgun and a MAC-10 were within easy reach.

Yarborough spotted Martinez as he exited the terminal. "There he is."

Mathews shifted in his seat, looking around. He didn't see anything out of the ordinary. Just a lot of travelers who wanted to get out of the rain, get into cars and go home.

Yet as Martinez walked toward the Bronco, a flurry of unseen activity was taking place around him. Federal agents, dressed as businessmen and toting luggage, were getting into cars parked along the same curb as the Bronco. The cars were driven by female agents dressed as housewives. From a distance and hidden from view, two agents with cameras that had the best telephoto lenses money could buy snapped photos of the Bronco and the two men in it. And at each of the airport's exits agents sat in cars waiting to tail the Bronco after it left.

Martinez opened the back door of the Bronco and tossed his bags in. Then he got in. Yarborough twisted around, extending his hand. "Hey, Thomas," he said, as the two men shook hands.

Martinez, pretending as if he was glad to be there, laughed and said, "What's new, Gary?" Then he looked at Mathews, who nodded.

"What's the plan?" asked Martinez, as Mathews steered the car into traffic.

"First the motel," said Yarborough. "Then some dinner. I'm starving."

"We'll talk over dinner," added Mathews, glancing into his rearview mirror, which was angled such that he could see Martinez in it.

Martinez looked at Mathews's eyes in the mirror. "Sounds good," he said.

Mathews took the cross-town freeway and exited at 82nd Avenue, heading west. No one spoke during the short trip. The windshield wipers slapped back and forth. At the corner of 82nd and Halsey, Mathews turned into the parking lot of the Capri Motel. The Capri was one of a dozen cheap, non-descript motels that lined Halsey Street. Which was why Mathews had selected it. He wanted to blend in. He didn't want anyone remembering they had been there or how many men were in the Bronco. For the latter reason, he and Yarborough had rented two rooms earlier in the day. Mathews and Yarborough would double up in one room, leaving the other room to Martinez.

Martinez dropped his bag in his room, while Mathews and Yarborough dropped the weapons in their room. They each kept a pistol, which they carried in shoulder holsters under their jackets. Then the three men walked across the street to a Denny's Restaurant.

After they gave their orders to an overweight and slow-moving waitress, they talked.

"The FBI is looking for us," said Mathews, coming right to the point. He was unaware that two FBI agents had entered the restaurant sixty seconds after them and were now seated at a nearby table, looking at menus.

"What makes you so sure?" asked Martinez.

Mathews glanced at Yarborough, who proceeded to tell Martinez what had happened at his cabin.

"Damn," remarked Martinez, when Yarborough finished his story. Yarborough shrugged, as if shooting it out with federal agents and then escaping was no big deal.

Mathews leaned forward. "We just wanted you to know what was going on. And we wanted you to know that we hadn't forgotten about you. I got the money you need for a lawyer in the room."

Martinez nodded. "Thanks. I have to admit I was beginning to get a little worried. Felt like I might be left hanging."

"Not at all," said Mathews. "It's just that we got our own problems right now. We gotta' lay real low and stay outta' sight for a while." He glanced around. "When things cool off, we can meet up again and decide what to do."

"Okay," replied Martinez. "I understand. I'll just keep playing dumb. The feds won't get anything out of me. So don't worry about that."

Mathews smiled. "Good. We knew we could count on you, didn't we Gary?"

"Never a doubt," declared Yarborough.

The waitress arrived with their food.

Meanwhile, the feds had developed the photos taken at the airport. When they realized the two men in the car were Mathews and Yarborough, they changed their plans. Initially, the feds had planned to follow Mathews to his hideaway after the meeting. But because Yarborough was there, they decided to arrest the two men the next morning. The feds wanted Gary Yarborough real bad. People who shoot at federal agents move to the top of the list real fast.

Early the next morning, on February 24th, in room 223 of the Capri Motel, the phone rang. Startled out of a deep sleep, Martinez rolled out of his bed to answer the phone. "Hello," said Martinez.

"This is the FBI," said a voice. "Listen carefully. No matter what happens or what you hear, stay in your room. Do not, repeat, do not answer the door for any reason. Is that clear?"

"Yes," replied Martinez. The line went dead.

Outside the Capri Motel was surrounded by armed federal agents. They were waiting for Mathews and Yarborough to leave room 224.

At around 7 am, Robert Jay Mathews left his room. He was on his way to get a morning newspaper from one of the vending machines in front of the motel office. As he closed the door behind him, something didn't feel right. His eyes sifted the area. He spotted one of the federal officers. Turning his head, he shouted a warning to Yarborough, who was still in the room. "Gary! Feds! Get out now!"

Mathews ran down the walkway toward the stairs. While he bounded down the stairs, he pulled his pistol from its shoulder holster. When he got to the bottom of the stairs, Mathews dashed into the parking lot, heading for the street. Two FBI agents opened fire. Shooting from the hip, Mathews returned fire as he ran, loosing a rain of bullets. One of his bullets struck an agent in the thigh and the man went down with a yell. More gunfire followed Mathews as he plunged toward the street. Something slapped his right hand. Mathews increased his speed. He was almost to the street. As he turned onto the sidewalk next to the street, Mathews snapped off three more shots. Then he was out of sight and out of the line of fire.

Running down the sidewalk, Mathews cut down an alley, then out onto a side street. He slowed to a steady jog. Lifting his hand, he saw red dripping from it.

Meanwhile, Gary Yarborough was trying to escape from room 224 by climbing out the bathroom window, which overlooked an alley behind the motel. Exiting the window, Yarborough lost his grip and fell fifteen feet. Luckily, he landed in some tall, thick bushes, which broke his fall. Still, he had the wind knocked out of him. Struggling to breathe, Yarborough tried to scramble out of the bushes. When he finally rolled out of the bushes, Yarborough was looking up at four FBI agents with guns pointing at him. As Yarborough caught his breath, the agents handcuffed him.

Despite an intensive search of the surrounding area, the FBI couldn't find Mathews. The man had gotten away. But he had left his car behind, along with a bunch of other important items the FBI found in room 224: semi-automatic pistols, two shotguns, a hand grenade, a MAC-10 machine gun with a silencer, $30,000 in cash, rental agreements for the houses in Mt. Hood, and a little black book written in code. Later, after breaking the code, the FBI discovered the book contained the names and phone numbers of people sympathetic to Mathews.

Mathews got away by sticking out his thumb and hitch-hiking rides to Mt. Hood. He bandaged his hand with his handkerchief, telling the drivers of his rides he had cut his hand while working on his car, which had broken down on the side of the road. Once he got to Mt. Hood, Mathews walked the last remaining miles to his hideout.

When he arrived at the hideout, where his group was waiting, Mathews was tired but ecstatic. He had shot it out with the feds and escaped. Mathews quickly related the story to the members of The Order. He didn't know what had happened to Yarborough or Martinez. Hopefully, Yarborough had either gotten away and would meet up with them or he had gone out in a blaze of glory, giving as good as he got. Either way, they couldn't wait. The feds knew where they were, because he had left the agreements in the room. That meant the feds would be showing up real soon.

"So we need to get out of Dodge right now," instructed Mathews. "Pack everything and everybody up. We need to be out of here in thirty minutes or less."

"Where we going, boss?" asked someone.

"To the safehouses on Whidbey Island," replied Matthews. "The feds don't know about them. Once we get out of Oregon, we'll be okay. So let's move it."

The Order followed orders. Within fifteen minutes the houses in Mt. Hood were empty of all personal items. The Order was on the move.

Whidbey Island was an island 30 miles north of Seattle, Washington. A fairly large island, Whidbey's population in the 1980s was about 50,000, of whom many were artsy-fartsy types. And more than half the island's residents lived in what were described as rural locations. In other words, there were no suburbs or planned communities with row after row of box-like houses.

Whidbey Island was the perfect place for The Order to hide out. For lifestyle on the island was slow and easy and private. There were no nosey neighbors intent on minding other people's business. As long as The Order didn't call attention to themselves, no one would know or care that bunch of heavily armed and violent terrorists were nearby. While Mathews healed up, the group could decide what to do.

Robert Jay Mathews like many fanatics was an eloquent man. He did a lot of deep thinking and afterwards he often felt the need to express himself. All the experiences he had recently passed through stimulated Mathews' mind. So one day he sat down and wrote a four-page epistle. The title Mathews gave it was "Declaration of War." For he considered himself a self-governing nation – a nation at war with the "Zionist Occupational Government (ZOG) of North America." In his epistle or declaration, Mathews demanded the extermination of all government officials – anyone with constituted authority – who denied The Order their sovereignty.

There was no doubt about it. Robert Jay Mathews was at war with the United States government. The last line of his declaration made his stance quite clear. "Let the battle begin."

The battle began sooner than anyone bargained for.

Eleven days after the shootout at the Capri Motel, in the Seattle office of the FBI a phone rang. An agent picked it up and said, "Hello." A voice at the other end stated that Robert Mathews and The Order were on Whidbey Island, where they were hiding out. They were armed to the teeth.

The caller refused to provide his or her identity. And to this day, no one knows who it was. All calls into the FBI's Seattle office were automatically traced. The trace revealed the call was made from a pay telephone.

On the off chance that the information might be true, the FBI dispatched two undercover agents to Whidbey Island to investigate. Within 48 hours the agents reported back. It was true. The Order was holed up on Whidbey Island. The terrorists were living in three houses on the island. Electrified by the confirmation, the FBI went into overdrive. 150 agents – all heavily armed – left for the island.

On Friday morning, December 7, 1984, members of The Order awoke and found themselves facing a whole new reality. For all three of their houses were surrounded by agents of ZOG. Before anyone had time to make a stand, FBI agents moved in on one of the houses, arresting Duey and three other members of The Order.

Mathews, who was in another house, didn't hesitate. He opened fire on the agents around his house. Not wanting to risk a bloodbath, the FBI wisely decided to negotiate. Eventually, the other members of The Order surrendered. But Mathews refused to listen. He was way past the point of no return.

For the next 35-hours the FBI continued its attempts to persuade Mathews to surrender. Mathews' only response was a hail of bullets from his submachine gun. At 6:30 pm on Saturday, the FBI stopped negotiating. It was clear that Mathews would not give up. In an attempt to flush Mathews out of the house, the FBI fired three M-79 Starburst illumination flares into the house. The flares smashed through the glass windows, setting the interior of the house on fire. In minutes the structure resembled an inferno. It was like a scene in a Gothic horror movie. Flames licked up from the house into the dark sky. Smoke billowed out. Even though the house around him was consumed in fire, Mathews refused to yield. Like the mystical warrior he believed he was, Robert Mathews chose immolation over humiliation.

The FBI maintained their vigil all night long, watching in open-mouthed wonder as the house – now a funereal pyre – burned to the ground.

According to legend, Mathews died a Viking's death, with a gun melted into each hand. And his *Bruders Schweigen* (Silent Brotherhood) medallion melted into the Kevlar vest where his chest had been. His ashes were scattered beneath an apple tree on his property in Washington. All this, of course, was in keeping with the mythos of Aryan mystical warriors, who always died majestically.

The reality of the matter was more ordinary.

On Sunday morning, the FBI moved in, sifting through the charred residue. They found what they thought was the scorched body of a man. Bagging it up, they shipped it back to the lab, where forensic specialists, using dental records, confirmed it was Robert Jay Mathews.

When Mathews died so did The Order. When Bruce Pierce and his group heard the news, they were wandering from trailer park to trailer park in the Southwest. They rapidly fell apart. Some went into hiding. Others scattered across the country. One by one, the FBI began hunting them all down.

In the end, none of The Order got away. Most were arrested and placed on trial, where they received sentences of 40 to 60 years in prison. Some elected to plead guilty before going to trial, thereby reducing their sentences. Five members of The Order, including Thomas Martinez, served as government witnesses. Their voluntary testimony sealed the fate of the other conspirators.

* * * * *

Robert Jay Matthews was the first Phineas Priest. And even though he didn't refer to himself by the term, his rationale and his actions were consistent with the Phineas Priesthood. For he was a "lone warrior" doing what he felt was the Will of God. He was protecting the Honor of God and God's Chosen from the sin of defilement. As far as Mathews was concerned, the White Race and the White Way had to remain pure. So like his ancestor – Phineas the Levitical Priest – he had taken up arms in the name of God.

Chapter 6

Vigilante of Christendom: Richard Kelly Hoskins and the Phineas Priesthood

Richard Kelly Hoskins had the dubious honor of introducing the term "Phineas Priesthood" as the designation for Christian vigilantes who took up arms and avenged "race traitors."

Hoskins was born in Lynchburg, Virginia. His parents were religious, strict and insistent upon the superiority of white Southerners. There was never a doubt that young Richard would play his role well. After finishing his elementary education, Richard was packed off to an exclusive military academy in Waynesboro, Virginia. This was in keeping with the grand academic traditions of Southern gentlemen such as Robert E. Lee and Stonewall Jackson.

Naturally, when the Korean War began, cadet Hoskins fulfilled what was expected of him. He joined the Air Force, seeing action in Korea. After his honorable discharge, Hoskins attended Lynchburg College, where he majored in history. As he steeped himself in world history, Hoskins read and admired the works of Julius Evola. Evola's philosophy was rabidly racist and belligerent, and advocated Fascism and Nazism as the only workable forms of government. Under Evola's influence, Hoskins turned neo-Nazism, joining the American Nazi Party.

Southern gentlemen not only served in the military, but were also expected to be prosperous and good at business. So after Hoskins graduated from College, he moved to New York City, where family connections landed him a job in a brokerage firm. Hoskins flourished as an investment broker. He learned the subtle art of advising others on how to invest their money. Which meant Hoskins learned how to make money off of other people's money.

After a few years, Hoskins returned to Lynchburg, going to work for Francis I. Du Pont and Company. Later, he moved his career to Anderson & Strudwick, Inc., where he became a vice president.

By 1960, the civil rights movement was in full swing. Integration became the boogeyman feared by all right-thinking Southerners. To the shock and dismay of many Virginians, the schools of the state of Virginia were integrated. The very idea offended Hoskins. And rather than stand idly by as cataclysm took place, Hoskins looked around and found inspiration. He decided to "to write a short book on the history of our own Saxon race and publish it myself if I had to."

Which was exactly what he did. Hoskins wrote and self-published *Our Nordic Race*, a historical diatribe supposedly proving the superiority of "pure Nordic" races. His thesis was contagious. His style was agreeable. He radiated confidence and impartiality.

Hoskins started his own publishing company. He had to. No right-thinking publisher dared to touch such overtly racist material. Calling it the Virginia Publishing Company, at first Hoskins only published his own books. Later though, he added the works of other anti-Semitic white nationalists.

In *Our Nordic Race*, Hoskins explained why the Roman and Greek empires had faded into the mists of history. There was one reason and it was simple to understand. The Greeks and the Romans had diluted the purity of their races. Purity of race had been destroyed by interbreeding with inferior races, which were people of color, "mud-people." Hoskins made it very clear when he wrote, "When a race which produces original thought breeds with a race which produces little or no original thought, the resulting breed is a failure." In other words, the Romans and the Greeks, who were of the Aryan line, had gone from being bluebloods to being mutts by means of crossbreeding.

Hoskins boldly branded the Greeks and the Romans as racial apostates. Without equivocation or hesitation, he stated "Our Nordic race in these nations was betrayed and destroyed by their own Nordic countrymen who became Race Traitors."

Hoskins didn't know it at the time, but his thunderous, racist spouting was very similar to the doctrines pouring out of the church of Christian Identity. Hoskins had not yet come into contact with Christian Identity. But he soon would.

Our Nordic Race became widely read among die-hard white supremacists. Hoskins achieved a type of quiet fame.

Up to this point, Hoskins had would not have been described as a religious or spiritual or mystical personality. This changed in the mid-1960s. For Hoskins got religion. His spirituality, previously dulled by insufficient stimulation and by a lack of human compassion, emerged and shone in zealous splendor. Hoskins was narrow-minded and saw no need for religion, because to his way of thinking religion was weak. It preached tolerance, love, forgiveness, and turning the other cheek. Hoskins had no tolerance for such namby-pambyism. He wanted the Jesus of the Second Advent, not the whimpy Jesus of the First Advent, which was what religion taught. At the Second Advent, Jesus came back with eyes like fire and a tongue like a sword, with which he killed his enemies.

Hoskins finally found it. And when he did it was transforming, life-changing. For his spiritual awakening nurtured the seeds of a new and fervent vocation: unreasoning religious fanaticism.

It happened like this. Hoskins had descended into the pit of alcoholism. "On April 28, 1965, at 4:00 in the afternoon, in the green rocking chair on the front porch," Jesus showed up. Only this Jesus wasn't a Jew, he was a Nordic from the great Aryan race. As Hoskins said, "When He saved me all He got was a drunk with a nervous breakdown who couldn't work and who had no money."

Hoskins became a devotee of the hell-fire and damnation preaching of Jerry Falwell. Falwell was an old-line fundamentalist, who hated Jews, abortionists, non-whites and government interference. But Falwell was smart too. He didn't want to be stamped as a rightwing nutcase. It was more profitable to be conservative than radical. So he preached a watered-down version of Christian Identity, a version that made it more palatable to the average champion of the status quo Christian.

Falwell's preaching was music to Hoskins' ears. He had found a kindred soul, a fellow warrior of the White Way. Hoskins began attending Thomas Road Baptist Church, where Falwell held sway every Sunday, preaching the truth of God's word. Which in reality had little resemblance to the truth or to God. More accurately, it was the Jerry Falwell show and the word being preached was the Gospel of Jerry Falwell.

Soon enough though, Falwell's message lost its attraction as far as Hoskins was concerned. The message was too bland, too diluted. In a word, Falwell's message was "moderate." Hoskins wanted something raw, something more pure, something unadulterated by mainstream politics and kowtowing to the unenlightened. In other words, Hoskins wanted hate, extremism and a call to action. For to Hoskins' way of thinking, nothing would change without action brought on by conflict. White people needed to confront their enemies and destroy them.

Hoskins decided to go his own way. Falwell's way was okay for those who simply desired to talk about change. But Hoskins didn't want to just talk about change. He wanted to implement change. So Hoskins moved on to the church of Christian Identity. As he told an interviewer from the Aryan Nations' magazine *White Rebels*, "The only political system in which I have complete confidence is theocracy, although the South African government is doing a pretty good job too."

It was at this time he began publishing his financial newsletter *The Hoskins Report*. He began attending Identity gatherings throughout the South. These gatherings were quasi-religious meetings, featuring an assortment of Identity preachers, who proclaimed the superiority of the white race and backed up their belief with carefully selected passages from the Bible. Along with the preachers, there were keynote speakers. The speakers, ranting and raving like little Hitlers, exhorted their listeners to follow the true, white Christian way of life. The white Christian way of life included everything from not paying their taxes to bank robbery and hate-crimes. The gatherings were a combination of religion, politics and cheerleading.

Hoskins became a familiar figure at these meetings, making numerous important connections. He hooked up with Willis Carto. Carto was considered a founding member of the anti-Semitic movement in the United States. Carto published two neo-fascist rags. *Western Destiny* and a newspaper called *The Spotlight*. At the time, *The Spotlight* was the most prominent publication of the extreme right. Widely read by white supremacists, it carried a lot of weight. Hoskins contributed articles and op-eds to both publications.

In 1973, Hoskins added a second newsletter to his propaganda machine. Along with *The Hoskins Report*, he began sending out his *Portfolios Investment Advisory* (PIA). Exclusively for his private clients, PIA offered not only advice on wealth management, but also helpful hints on such varied topics as the Holocaust, integration, and politics.

According to Hoskins, the Holocaust was "Constant lies. Lies, lies, lies. Forty years of lies ... the anti-Christ Holohoax scam." Regarding integration, Hoskins asserted that even Communism was less of an evil. "Better a blood-soaked Joseph Stalin than a smiling Ian Smith or congenial DeKlerk who opens the door to the barbarians. Compromise means death." And as far as politics were concerned, Hoskins wrote "A political candidate need take just 3 simple stands. 1) Abolish usury. 2) Root sodomists from the land. 3) Outlaw racial interbreeding."

Jews, homosexuals and miscegenation – the three cardinal sins. Hoskins went on and on about all three. Utopia was a place that had purged itself of Jews, perverts and race mixing.

Something had happened to Hoskins. He was becoming more and more peculiar. More and more, he was the object of a refined self-admiration. He felt chosen by God to bring enlightenment to a benighted world. A world in which the white race was losing its position of superiority. Prospects seemed good. His newsletters had a steady following, which meant he didn't have to worry about money. And *Our Nordic Race* had bestowed some small measure of fame and glamour upon him. Only it wasn't enough. Hoskins wanted national recognition. He lusted for celebrity.

And so, taking a lesson from his days with Jerry Falwell, Hoskins sat down to pen another book. Only this time, he would write something a little more mainstream. Something that wasn't quite so radical or extremist.

Or so he hoped.

War Cycles, Peace Cycles was Hoskins' next book. He published it in 1985. Supposedly, it was an analysis of banking and economics in Europe and America. Promoted as Christian in perspective, it was neither Christian nor panoramic. It was racist and threadlike. The theme of the book was anti-Semitism. The Jews controlled the Western banks. They were in cahoots with Western political leaders, who were corrupt and thus easily bought off. Together, these two groups formed an elite cluster of rich, powerful men. Their goal was a New World Order. Over which they would rule. In other words, it was a giant conspiracy perpetrated by a few against the many.

By lending money at exorbitant rates, these elites would soon – literally – own all the governments of the world. And none of these elites or the governments they owned gave a tinker's damn about racial purity. In fact, just the opposite was true. The Jewish bankers wanted to dilute the pure white race. If they could accomplish this evil end, God's chosen people would be wiped away. There would be no superior race. All races would be equal because all races would be equally inferior. Such was the product of race-mixing, according to Hoskins.

War Cycles, Peace Cycles electrified its audience. They read it, believed it, and applauded it. Within certain circles – angry, white imperialsts – Hoskins attained a surprising amount of fame. He was invited to speak at Identity gatherings sponsored by America's Promise Ministries and Scriptures for America. Both these groups were Christian Identity churches.

When he spoke, Hoskins tended to focus on the preservation of racial purity. At this point in his religious-philosophical evolution Hoskins was not yet openly advocating violence as the means to achieve a righteous end. But that soon changed.

In the Spring of 1987, Hoskins was speaking at an Identity gathering in Georgia. Sponsored by the Georgia Peach Church of the Last Days, the event was held at a local amusement park. Lakeside Amusement Park was run by one of Georgia's great showmen, David Beck. Of Germanic descent, Beck described himself as "an impresario of the old school." Which meant he had a taste for fountains and fireworks, along with rollercoasters. Beck, who had been married four times, was an ardent believer in Christian Identity. And his park reflected his religious beliefs.

Lakeside had an array of fountains – most of which were topped with water-spouting eagles or mystical warriors – designed by Beck himself. Beck had expanded Lakeside's gardens, turning them into outdoor wonders. There was a huge ballroom. Its ceiling supported by great wooden arches from which dangled Teutonic chandeliers. A platform had been erected at one end and hundreds of chairs sat in neat rows in front of the speaker's podium.

As the event unfolded, Hoskins sat in a chair behind the podium, waiting his turn to speak. There were a total of five guest speakers. Three of who sat near Hoskins. The fourth man was already at the podium, exhorting his listeners in a high-pitched, darting voice.

Thirty minutes later, Hoskins arose and approached the podium. His features were heavily Germanic in structure and provided him with a powerful presence. His voice, deep and sturdy, could rumble easily or roar vehemently. Whichever he did, galvanizing blue eyes gazed steadily, gauging reaction to his words. All in all, Richard Kelly Hoskins was a handsome man and a persuasive orator.

Today, he emphasized the usury practices of banks and the perfidy of bankers, who were Jewish, of course. Whenever he paused – to catch his breath or for effect – the audience applauded. No one would ever accuse Identity adherents of lacking enthusiasm.

When Hoskins finished, he received a standing ovation, piercing whistles and even a few wild rebel yells. After one final bow, Hoskins returned to his chair.

The next speaker was a man no one had heard of before. Introduced by the Pastor of the Georgia Peach Church of the Last Days as "Webster Smith – scholar and author," the man was tall, thin and impeccably dressed in a dark suit and white shirt. The audience bestowed a round of polite, welcoming applause upon Smith. Then sat back to listen.

Smith began slowly. His voice was strong and smooth. His subject matter was the story of Phineas – the Levitical priest in the Old Testament book of Numbers. As he proceeded, Smith's voice grew stronger and stronger. Soon he was caught up in the rapture of his subject. And so was the audience. Smith soared into a hell-fire-and-damnation singsong, holding his listeners spellbound. Hoskins was mesmerized by what he was hearing.

Christian Identity had been serving up the story of Phineas for a long, long time. But always as a side-dish. Never as the main course, as Smith was doing. As Hoskins listened, his mind swirled like a tornado. Here, he knew, was the fulcrum around which the church of Christian Identity should be wheeling.

Smith concluded his fiery sermon by shouting, "The law of the Lord must be sustained – whatever the cost!" Thunderous applause exploded toward the podium. Smith nodded and sat down.

All the preaching and speechifying was followed by food and fellowship. Hot dogs, hamburgers, baked beans, bread, potato salad, ice cream and pies galore. Since it was a religious gathering, beverages consisted of coffee, soda pop, iced tea, lemonade and water. However, many pocket flasks were produced with amazing dexterity. The contents were added to lemonade, making what was called "a Georgia Cadillac."

Hoskins sought out Webster Smith and introduced himself. He then invited Smith to join him at his table. The two men spent the next two hours engaged in intense conversation. Smith did most of the talking. Hoskins interrupted occasionally, asking a question. But for the most part, Hoskins simply listened. He was soaking up information like a sponge.

When he got back to Virginia, Hoskins began to write. He wrote for the next three years. The result of his labors was an almost impenetrable and incomprehensible 469-page monster of a book – *Vigilantes of Christendom*. In his book, Hoskins set out the concept of the Phineas Priesthood, using Numbers 25 as his starting point. From there, Hoskins moved on, tracing the history of famous Phineas Priests. According to Hoskins' interpretation of history, famous Phineas Priests included John Wilkes Booth, Robin Hood, the Waffen SS, and the Ku Klux Klan. And of course, Gordon Kahl, and Robert Mathews and The Order.

Vigilantes asserted that anyone – man or woman – who saw the Law of God being broken was ordained by God to take any action necessary against those breaking the Law. These law-breakers were called "ungodly." Hoskins called such actions "Phineas Acts."

Hoskins provided Scripture to encourage and back up such violent "Phineas Acts." The first was Ehud, whose story was related in Judges 3: 1-30. Ehud led an armed revolt against the Moabite occupation of territory belonging to the Tribe of Benjamin. Ehud asked for and received an audience with the King of the Moabites. Walking into the King's presence, Ehud killed him. Ehud then rallied the Israelites to take advantage of the situation. Thousands of Moabites were slaughtered.

The second example was Jael, who was a female Israelite. Jael offered Sisera – who was a Canaanite – hospitality and safe haven. By ancient custom, hospitality included protection. She murdered Sisera by pounding a tent peg into his head. Hoskins applauded this act of treachery as an example of a "Phineas Act."

Hoskins went on to add that "The thing that Phineas heroes hold in common is their dedication to the word – dedication to enforcing God's Law. Their ends also all read alike. Most are martyrs or are willing to be martyrs to the cause…. There are countless others, some of whom are mentioned in the pages following. The thing all have in common is the fanatical drive to enforce God's Law and to fight the tyrant and lawbreaker of the day."

Because he understood the power of symbols – especially religious symbols – Hoskins designed a logo for the Priesthood. The letter P with a horizontal line though it. In effect, the logo stated that Phineas Priests were fighting for the Cross. The connection to the religious zeal of the Crusades was obvious.

The logo was quickly adopted by white supremacists. It began appearing on bumper-stickers, T-shirts and jewelry. The Phineas Priesthood came to represent the ultimate commitment any white supremacist could make.

This idea of "ultimate commitment" proved to be the true power of Hoskins' book. Not only did the book clearly and dynamically articulate the idea of the Phineas Preisthood, but it also did much more. It injected the idea of religious exclusivity – even a religious aristocracy – into the emotions of fanatical white supremacists everywhere.

In other words, who didn't want to be part of such an elite group?

Vigilantes of Christendom became a bestseller among white supremacists, ranking right up there with *The Turner Diaries*. The natural result was that Hoskins became even more famous. His presence at Identity gatherings was great demand. It was at one such gathering in 1991 that Hoskins hooked up with Byron de la Beckwith. Beckwith was the Klansman who had murdered Medgar Evers. Hoskins and Beckwith hit it off and began corresponding with each other. Hoskins lived in Virginia and Beckwith lived in Mississippi.

Hoskins printed one of Becwith's letters in *The Hoskins Report*. Beckwith signed the letter, adding, "Phineas for President." In fact, Beckwith was so taken by the idea of the Phineas Priesthood – and the latitude it allowed for justifying violence – that he claimed he had been a Phineas Priest when he killed Megar Evers thirty years before.

When Beckwith was finally tried and convicted for murder a few years later, Hoskins distanced himself from Beckwith. This was necessary because Beckwith's trial received national media attention. And the media exposed Beckwith's connection to the Phineas Priesthood. Which made Hoskins look like a rabid nutcase. Hoskins stated he had never met Beckwith and didn't know him.

It was a lie, of course. But to Hoskins' way of thinking it was a necessary lie. For he wanted the celebrity and fame associated with being a savior – the savior of the white way of life. Being branded as a religious madman did not fit with his self-conception. So he simply denied knowing Beckwith.

Currently, Hoskins still lives in Virginia, where he publishes his newletters and oversees his small book publishing empire. Virginia Publishing Company puts out a steady stream of white supremacist books. He occasionally attends Identity gatherings, where he is adulated as a "Rock Star of Racism." In his own mind, he is "an elder statesman" of the white supremacist movement.

He never attained the national celebrity he desired.

Chapter 7

For God's Sake

His name was Byron de la Beckwith, but his friends called him "Delay." A descendant of Southern aristocracy, Byron de la Beckwith was born in Colusa, California in 1920. Delay was only five when his father died. The official cause of death was listed as "pneumonia and alcoholism." After the funeral, Delay's mother took him back home to Greenwood, Mississippi.

Delay's mother was a Yerger, which meant she was a blue-blood, descended from one of the South's elite families. Susan Southworth Yerger was her given name. And in the glory days of the Confederacy, the Yergers moved only in the best social circles. Jefferson Davis's wife was counted among the closest friends of the Yerger family.

Unfortunately, Delay's mother suffered from what were politely called mental ailments. She was hospitalized frequently. And in the end, when Delay was 12 years old, she died of lung cancer at age 47.

Delay moved in with his uncle, William Yerger, who occupied the family's estate, which had seen better days and had had quite a few less good days since then. And so had Uncle William, who was a little off-center. He spent most of his time fishing for catfish. According to *Time* magazine, more often than not, the catfish ended up in a dresser drawer, which was where Uncle William liked to put them. The stench must have been abominable.

In 1942, Delay joined the U.S. Marine Corps and saw action as a machine gunner. When he was discharged in 1946, he was heavily decorated, including the Purple Heart. He got married to Mary Louise Williams, who was a Navy WAVE. They moved to Rhode Island for a while, then back to Mississippi, where Delay sold tobacco.

The marriage had its ups and downs – divorce, reconciliation and remarriage, then separation. Which meant Delay's life resembled the family estate – it had seen better days. Reed Massengill, who was the nephew of Delay's wife, later wrote a book called *Portrait of a Racist*. In it, Delay was described as a brutal and violent husband.

Somewhere in there, Delay joined the Original Knights of the Ku Klux Klan. No one really knew why, but Delay was a die-hard white supremacist. Delay hated blacks, Jews and Roman Catholics. As *Time* magazine later reported, "He tried to inject racism into everything." Delay composed and distributed racist pamphlets. He also took part in anti-integration rallies, where he did things like obstructing non-whites from using public toilet facilities.

At that time – from 1954 until the mid-1960s – the Klan was engaged in open warfare against the Civil Rights movement. The KKK not only bombed churches and homes, but also wreaked a series of ghastly murders. One of those murdered was Medgar Evers. As Leonard Zeskind wrote in *Blood and Politics*, "That same year [1963] a Klan sniper assassinated Mississippi state NAACP leader Medgar Evers on the doorstep of his home."

Delay was that Klan sniper.

It happened like this: In the evening hours of June 12, 1963, Medgar Evers attended a meeting of civil rights workers at a church in Jackson, Mississippi. At the same time, his wife and children were at home, watching as President John F. Kennedy gave a televised speech on civil rights.

When the meeting was over, Medgar Evers drove to his house. He parked the car in his driveway. As Evers got out of his car, Delay was waiting across the way, hidden in a clump of honeysuckle vines. In his hands, Delay held an Enfield 1917 rifle, .303 caliber, as cited in court records. Delay took aim and fired. The bullet smashed into Evers's back, tore through his chest and exited, leaving a gaping wound. Evers dropped like a sack of potatoes.

Subsequent police reports outlined the following scenario: Mortally wounded, yet still alive, Evers dragged himself toward his house. He never made it. His ebbing strength failed him and he stopped just short of the steps to the door, which was where his wife found him a short while later. Rushed to the hospital, Evers died approximately one hour after being shot.

Medgar Evers was a determined man, as his final crawl toward his house indicated. For Evers wanted to be somebody and to make a difference. Inducted into the Army in 1943, Evers saw action in France. Discharged in 1945, Evers went home to Decatur, Mississippi. In a way, Evers's life mirrored that of Byron de la Beckwith. Both were passionate. Both served their country in WWII. It's after their discharges that their stories diverged.

While Delay was selling tobacco, Evers attended Alcorn College, where he majored in business administration. After graduating, Evers got married and moved to Mound Bayou, Mississippi, where he went to work for Magnolia Life Insurance Company. The company was owned by T.R.M. Howard, who was the president of a civil rights group called Regional Council of Negro Leadership. Evers joined the group and worked as an activist.

Evers made application to the University of Mississippi Law School. Because of his skin color, Evers was rejected. The University of Mississippi's enrollment policy did not admit black people as students. Evers filed a lawsuit against the school. At almost the same time, he was appointed first field secretary for the NAACP in Mississippi. In this capacity, Evers participated in a boycott of white merchants and helped to desegregate the University of Mississippi.

As a result of his activities, Evers became well known as a black leader in the civil rights movement. His growing prominence made him a target for the white supremacists of the KKK. On May 28, 1963, someone tossed a Molotov cocktail into his carport. And on June 7, 1963, someone tried to run him down with a car. Both incidents were duly reported to the local police. No suspects were identified.

Five days later, on June 12, Byron de la Beckwith – aka Delay – assassinated Medgar Evers. Eleven days later, Delay was arrested. Witnesses had reported seeing Delay near Evers's house on the evening of the murder. And Delay's car – a white Plymouth Valiant – had been observed driving in the neighborhood. Police had found the murder weapon secreted in the honeysuckle vines and traced it to Delay. The Enfield's telescopic sight had Delay's fingerprints on it.

What most people didn't know was that the rifle was found after the police received an anonymous phone call. The "tipster" told police where the rifle could be found. Many surmised that Delay himself was the tipster. He wanted to be arrested and go on trail because he was confident he would never be convicted. All this information and speculation came out after Delay's 1994 trial, and was based on court records.

After his arrest, the police questioned Delay. He told them the rifle had been stolen and he had forgotten to report it. Three police officers sympathetic to the KKK asserted they had seen Delay in Greenwood, which was 95 miles away, at the time of the murder. In other words, Delay now had an alibi.

Nevertheless, a grand jury decided there was enough circumstantial evidence against Delay to indict him for murder. Delay lawyered up. He was tried for murder at two separate trials in 1964. Both times the jury selection process resulted in all-male, all white juries. And the judge at both trials was Russell Moore, who was a personal friend of Delay.

At the second trial, the former governor of Mississippi – Ross Barnett – interrupted a witness's testimony. The witness was Myrlie Evers, the wife of Medgar Evers. Governor Barnett walked into the courtroom, looked around, and then walked over to Delay and shook his hand.

The implication of the governor's act was clear to everyone: White people in the state of Mississippi were rooting for Delay.

In both trials, the all-white juries refused to convict a white man for the murder of a black man. Delay's alibi – that police officers had seen him at a gas station back home in Greenwood right after the ambush of Evers – gave the juries the excuse they needed. Sufficient doubt, which resulted in deadlock. Because there was no verdict in either trial, both trials ended in mistrials.

After the second mistrial, Delay felt doubly confident, even arrogant. He officially joined the White Knights of the Ku Klux Klan, which was the most violent cadre of the Klan. The mission of the White Knights was to stop talking and start doing. Delay became good friends with Sam Bowers, who was the Imperial Wizard of the White Knights. Bowers came from Southern aristocracy and had attended the University of Southern California and Tulane University. In other words, he was educated.

Described as thin, smart and charismatic, Bowers was also looney-tunes. A neo-Nazi, he had a thing for swastikas. Probably a latent homosexual, Bowers had never been romantically connected to a woman. He lived with his business partner. They owned a vending machine company called Sambo Amusements. The company's name was indicative of their narrow-minded viewpoint.

Sam Bowers was a religious zealot – a "Swiftian," which meant he embraced the teachings of Wesley Swift. Swift was the founder of the Church of Jesus-Christ, Christian, which was just another brand of Christian Identity. Swift's church eventually became the Aryan Nations.

Wesley Swift taught that the Bible commanded white people to protect the Honor of God. In simpler terms, this meant killing the "enemies of God," who were easy to spot because they didn't have white skin. Swift particularly despised Jews. Since Bowers was an ardent Swiftian, he influenced the White Knights to focus their efforts against the Jews rather than the blacks.

Bowers brought Delay into the fold of Christian Identity. Delay loved it. For it was just his kind of church. A mixture of sick hate and vicious racism.

Both the KKK and especially Christian Identity couched their teachings in the garments of propaganda. The propaganda consisted of deliberately biased information. Information that appealed to the emotions. Meaningless information about how Jews and other non-white races were taking over the white man's world. The inescapable conclusion was that white men – white warriors – needed to do something to halt this insidious onslaught of "mud people." The enemies of God had to be destroyed.

In this sense, KKK and Christian Identity propaganda exerted emotional pressure on its members. It was a push to action. In other words, the KKK and Christian Identity were using their disciples as dupes. For both organizations had agendas. To fulfill those agendas, they had to motivate their members to embrace violent means. Death and destruction were the means to the end.

Essentially, in one sense, Byron de la Beckwith was a pawn and a dupe. His lack of education, his upbringing, his insular culture and his psychological make-up conspired against him. He, along with others, responded to the emotional pressure as expected. They became dupes, who were indirectly used by men like Wesley Swift.

* * * * *

Delay, along with his Klansmen, agitated against the Jews and lobbied to have flouride removed from drinking water. Delay believed flouridated water was a Jewish plot to weaken the white race. He also held that The Holocaust was a giant hoax and urged carpet-bombing Israel.

He began bragging at KKK rallies about how he had killed Medgar Evers. A fellow Klansman, whose name was Delmar Dennis, was one of those who overheard Delay crowing over the deed. Delay exhorted his fellow Klansmen to kill anyone "from the President on down." Then Delay bragged about "killing that nigger," an act he compared to childbirth.

Thirty years later, Delmar Dennis would remember Delay's gloating words. And when he did, the jury would not be all male and all white. There would be no sympathetic judge sitting on the bench.

Delay was now famous in Mississippi. His fame went to his head and in 1967 Delay sought to capitalize on his notoriety. He believed his celebrity would translate into votes for a white candidate. So he sought the Democratic Party's nomination for lieutenant governor. A month before the primaries Delay agreed to an interview with the *Review*. Among his "chief qualifications" Delay said was that he "was conscious of a diabolical international conspiracy against states' rights and racial integrity."

He didn't get the nomination. According to the *New York Times*, Delay "got more than 34,000 votes, finishing fifth in a field of six."

By 1970, it became apparent that the murder of Medgar Evers had not hindered the struggle for civil rights in Mississippi. In fact, Evers' death probably accelerated integration. According to the Department of Health, Education and Welfare, 26.4% of black students in Mississippi public schools attended integrated schools. When Evers died in 1963, there were only 28,000 African Americans registered to vote in Mississippi. By 1971, there were 250,000 and by 1982 over 500,000.

African Americans were being elected to public office in Mississippi. In 1973, the state had 145 black elected officials. And black applicants were accepted as students in the state's public and private institutions of higher learning.

Delay had not stopped integration. And based on what he did next, it was fairly certain Delay did not understand what was going on, that the world was changing.

In 1973, believing he was untouchable, Delay plotted to murder the New Orleans director of the Anti-Defamation League, A.I. Botnick, who had – according to Delay's tangled way of thinking – made contemptuous remarks about Southerners and their attitude toward non-whites.

Delay couldn't keep his big mouth shut about what he was planning to do. Delay had always had loose lips. He had boasted about killing Medgar Evers at KKK rallies. And way back in 1956, when making application to the pro-segregation Sovereignty Commission for a job as an operative, Delay had listed his qualifications: "Expert with a pistol, good with a rifle and fair with a shotgun – RABID ON THE SUBJECT OF SEGREGATION!"

So just like Chatty Cathy, he said too much at the wrong time to the wrong people about his plot to murder A. I. Botnick. When they heard what Delay was up to they couldn't wait to do their own imitation of Chatty Cathy, rapping with the FBI about what they knew. Which was exactly what they did.

The FBI believed the informants and moved quickly. They immediately put Delay under surveillance. And after watching him for a few days, they decided it was time to shut him down. And they did.

Delay was driving his car across the Lake Ponchartrain Causeway Bridge, when – as if by magic – a police car slid in behind his vehicle. Delay didn't think anything of it until he noticed lights flashing in his rearview mirror. Out of options, Delay pulled over and stopped. New Orleans police officers approached Delay's car with drawn weapons. Searching

Delay's car, police found three loaded weapons, a map of New Orleans and written directions to the home of the director of the Anti-Defamation League. In the trunk of the car, they discovered a bundle of dynamite with a timer and a detonator.

Delay was arrested and booked. Once more, Delay lawyered up. At his arraignment he was charged with conspiracy to commit murder. It was a federal charge. When the trial took place in federal court, the jury acquitted Delay of conspiracy to commit murder. It is interesting to note that the jury was composed of 10 white men and two white women. After the trial, jurors told newspaper reporters that the evidence against Delay was remote and inconclusive. And once again it looked like Delay had gotten off.

But not so fast this time. The State of Louisiana charged Delay with transporting explosives without a permit. Which meant Delay underwent another trial in a state court. This time Delay lost. The verdict was guilty and he was sentenced to three years in a Louisiana State Prison. Delay described the five people on the jury as "five nigger bitches."

They shipped Delay off to Angola Prison, where he served his time in solitary confinement from May 1977 to January 1980. He was placed in solitary confinement for a couple of reasons. First, many of the black inmates would have enjoyed avenging Medgar Evers. Second, Delay's constant racial slurs would have gotten him killed in no time. For he called blacks "apes" and "beasts of the fields." While there, Delay became ill and spent a few days in the prison infirmary, where a nurse's aide, who just happened to be black, tried to provide Delay with treatment. Delay refused to allow the aide to touch him. According to *The New York Times*, Delay told the aide "If I could get rid of an uppity" Medgar Evers, it would be no problem at all to get rid of "a no-account" aide.

After his release from prison, Delay went home to Greenwood, Mississippi, where he got a job selling fertilizer. Delay continued to attend KKK rallies and also became active in the church of Christian Identity, which held frequent gatherings throughout the South. It was at one of these gatherings that Delay met Richard Kelly Hoskins. Hoskins was the author of *Vigilantes of Christendom: The Story of the Phineas Priesthood*.

In his book, Hoskins introduced the concept of the Phineas Priesthood, which was that "lone warriors" or vigilantes would appear in history every so often. These warrior-priests were sent by God to punish "race traitors." This punishment was necessary to protect the honor of God and His chosen people, who were, of course, white.

As Hoskins made very clear in his book, the Phineas Priesthood was an exclusive clergy. The only way in was by annihilating the enemies of God. God's enemies were defined as blacks, race-mixers, Jews, homosexuals, and abortionists. Any white supremacist who destroyed these enemies was automatically ordained into the Phineas Priesthood.

The book went on to provide historical examples of such lone-warriors: John Wilkes Booth, the Waffen SS, the Ku Klux Klan and The Order, which was also known as The Silent Brotherhood. According to Hoskins, the common dominant trait of these men was a passion to excel – to protect the Honor of God. And in doing so, they had espoused the doctrine of the Phineas Priesthood. A doctrine understood by a chosen few.

Obviously, Delay had read Hoskins' book, because he now claimed – after the fact – that in murdering Medgar Evers, he had been functioning as a Phineas Priest. In other words, Medgar Evers death was God's Will. And when Delay – acting as a Phineas Priest – killed Evers, he was removing one of God's enemies. Anyway, that's what Delay wanted people to think. In reality, it was nothing more than a lame and abject attempt to justify murder.

Delay and Hoskins were kindred souls and began corresponding with each other.

Hoskins published a regular newsletter called "The Hoskins Report." Supposedly, the newsletter provided financial and investment advice. In reality, it trumpeted racist propaganda. In a 1991 issue of the newsletter, Hoskins printed a letter he had received from Delay, who was still famous in white supremacist circles. At the end of the letter, Delay had written "Phineas for president!"

The letter would come back to haunt Delay.

Mississippi had changed since 1963. Things were different. African-Americans no longer sat in the back of the bus or drank from separate drinking fountains. Segregation was a relic of the past. There were no more all-white juries that looked the other way. A new generation of prosecutors with new attitudes began reviewing old cases in which there had been a miscarriage of justice. One of those cases was the murder of Medgar Evers.

The Clarion-Ledger of Jackson, Mississippi, published a series of articles detailing how the Mississippi Sovereignty Commission – which no longer existed – had helped in screening potential jurors in the 1964 trials of Byron de la Beckwith. Back in 1964, the Sovereignty Commission was rabidly pro-segregation and believed in the Great White Way, which meant no white man should ever be put on trial for the murder of a black man.

The articles caused a scandal. Most of Southern society was outraged. And public opinion demanded justice. The case was reopened and an investigation was begun. Some whites didn't want to open that can of worms again. They didn't want to air once again Mississippi's dirty laundry to the national media. Delay told a reporter, "Country-club Mississippi is tired of this crap the Jews, niggers, and Orientals are stirring up."

Delay was arrested and – for a third time – charged with the murder of Medgar Evers. His bail was set at $100,000. A "stranger" gave him $12,000 so he could get out of jail. It later came out that the stranger was a Jewish lawyer named Harry Rosenthal. As Maryanne Vollers wrote in *Ghosts of Mississippi*, Rosenthal "said he couldn't stand to see Beckwith's rights violated." Even though he hated Jews, Delay took the money.

Rosenthal – and a lot of other legal experts – believed Delay's right to a speedy trial was being violated. And, that since Delay's indictment had been open and on the books from 1964 to 1969, he could have been retried during that period, while his previous lawyers were alive and well, memories were fresh, and witnesses were at hand. But the state had failed to do so.

In essence, the issue was whether Delay could be tried again or not. The matter was placed before the Mississippi Supreme Court. Most of the legal experts and most of the media felt the case against Delay would be dismissed. Delay would get off scot-free again.

Delay's luck finally ran out.

The Mississippi Supreme Court decided not to decide whether Delay could be tried again or not until after he was tried. The decision was a stroke of genius. For if Delay was acquitted, there was nothing to decide. If he was convicted, he could appeal. If Delay appealed, the court would merely say a murder case that has been dismissed could be retried in good faith, because there was no statute of limitations on murder.

Delay spent a lot of time shopping for a lawyer. In the end, he decided on Buddy Coxwell and Jim Kitchens as his defense team. The prosecutors were Bobby Delaughter and Ed Peters.

The prosecution introduced new evidence, which was that Delay had boasted of killing Medgar Evers to many people over the course of the last three decades. Klansman Delmar Dennis took the stand and told the jury how Delay had bragged about killing Evers thirty years before. They also introduced Delay's admission to the nurse's aide in prison, that he had killed Evers. And they linked Delay to the letter published in "The Hoskins Report."

Déjà vu. The letter was back.

The background page of the Anti-Defamation League's website states that "Hoskins's writings drew public attention in October 1991, when prosecutors in Mississippi linked white supremacist Byron de la Beckwith to the Phineas Priesthood."

In other words, for the first time, the general public became aware of the existence of a cluster of violent religious bigots, who killed "for God's sake."

The murder weapon – the 1917 Enfield – was still available as evidence. For Delay – at the conclusion of the second trial in 1964 – had simply picked it up and walked away with it. He had given the rifle to Russell Moore, who was a friend and the presiding judge at the 1964 mistrials, as a "souvenir." Everyone who knew Moore knew he had the rifle. It was in the closet of his house. One of the prosecutors, Bobby Delaughter, just went over to Moore's house and got it.

As the trial unfolded, Delay sat in the courtroom wearing a Confederate flag on his lapel. He still didn't believe he would ever be convicted. However, this time there was no all-male, all white jury. This time the jury was composed of eight African-Americans and four white people. And because of the pre-trial publicity, the jurors were not from Jackson, Mississippi. They were from Panola County and arrived on a specially chartered bus.

In his book – *The Ghosts of Medgar Evers*, author Willie Morris described the atmosphere of the trial as full of hate. Delay's supporters sat in the courtroom, glaring. They were "Klansmen, hate-mail publishers, and homegrown Mississippi neo-Nazis." Delay's second and current wife was there too. Thelma de la Beckwith. She wore a blond wig and "told reporters it was Lee Harvey Oswald who really shot Evers."

On February 5, 1994, the jury returned a verdict of guilty. When the verdict was announced, Delay looked as if dazed and confused. This was more than he had ever bargained for.

The sentence was life in prison without the possibility of parole. Byron de la Beckwith was 74 years old. Normally, they would have shipped him off to Mississippi State Penitentiary, which was Mississippi's only maximum security prison. Once upon a time it had been called Parchman Farm. But because of who he was and what he had done, Delay would have been dead in no time at all. So they didn't send him there. Instead, he would be held in the Hinds County Jail for the rest of his life.

Delay filed an appeal. The basis of the appeal was that he had been denied his right to a speedy trial. The contention was that undergoing a third trial for the same murder – thirty-one years later – could in no way be interpreted as speedy. The appeal was overturned, as there was no statute of limitations for the crime of murder.

Seven years later, on January 21, 2001, Delay died. At the time of his death, he was in the University of Mississippi Medical Center in Jackson, Mississippi. He was being treated for heart disease and high blood pressure.

The only legacy Delay left behind was the exaltation of hate.

Medgar Evers left behind a different kind of legacy – one of compassion, tolerance and service.

After the second mistrial, Myrlie Evers – the widow of Medgar Evers – moved her family to Claremont, California, which was just south of Los Angeles. She enrolled in Claremont College. In 1967, she published her memoir *For Us, The Living*. The title came from Abraham Lincoln's Gettysburg Address. Then in 1968, Myrlie Evers graduated with a BA in sociology.

She became the Democratic candidate for a congressional seat from southern California in 1970. Losing heavily in the Republican districts, she still managed to gain 38 percent of the vote. It was not enough to win. She took a job in public relations and later became vice president for advertising and publicity at Atlantic Richfield.

In 1987, Los Angeles mayor Tom Bradley appointed her to the position of commissioner on the Los Angeles Board of Public Works, where she helped supervise 6000 employees and administered half a billion dollars. She served as a commissioner for five years.

She married Walter Williams, who was a union organizer and civil rights activist. Eventually, the couple moved to Oregon. Several months after Byron de la Beckwith was finally convicted and sentenced to life in prison, Myrlie was elected chair of the board of the NAACP.

Medgar Evers' children grew up in southern California and went on to lead triumphant lives. Darrell became a successful artist. Reena married, had children and worked for an airline. Van became a noted photographer.

Chapter 8

An Eye For An Eye

"Whoso sheddeth man's blood, by man shall his blood be shed; for in the image of God made he man." Genesis 9:6

"So ye shall not pollute the land wherein yea are: for blood it defileth the land; and the land cannot be cleansed of the blood that is shed therein, but by the blood of him that shed it." Numbers 35:33

His name was Paul Jennings Hill. He was born in Miami, Florida in February of 1954. Hill grew up in Coral Gables, which was an affluent city with white stucco buildings, red tile roofs, tennis courts and swimming pools. There were very few minorities in Coral Gables. It was pretty much a white enclave for rich people.

Paul Hill was a nice boy, who lived in a nice city. He went to nice schools, where he was an average student. Considered popular, he had a lot of friends. Some of his friends smoked dope, popped bennies and snorted cocaine. They thought it was cool. Like most teenagers, Paul wanted to be cool too. So he started using drugs.

Paul's father – who flew planes for an airline and whose name was Oscar – found out Paul was using drugs. Oscar confronted his 17-year old son. "What the hell are you thinking?" asked Oscar.

Paul looked at the ground and shrugged.

"Don't just shrug. Answer me!" commanded Oscar.

Paul slowly raised his eyes until he was staring into his father's face. Viciousness bubbled inside Paul. His hands clenched into fists.

"Well?" asked Oscar.

Paul hit his father, knocking him down. Stunned and angry, Oscar scrambled to his feet. Paul hit him again and again and again. Then Paul walked away.

A few hours later, the police found Paul walking down the sidewalk in Coral Gables. They arrested him and took him to the police station, where they told him he was charged with assault. Oscar had filed a complaint against his own son. The police put Paul in a cell, where he waited until Oscar arrived.

When Oscar arrived, his face was bruised and swollen. A policeman led Oscar to Paul's cell. Oscar gazed at his son, who was sitting on a bunk, looking at the floor.

"Paul," said Oscar.

Paul didn't move. He kept staring at the floor.

"What's come over you?" asked Oscar. Then he added, "Are you crazy?"

Paul still didn't move.

Oscar turned and walked away. There were tears in his eyes. He told the police he was dropping his complaint. The police asked him if he was sure that's what he wanted to do? Oscar nodded sadly.

The police told Paul he was free to go. They unlocked his cell and gave him back his personal belongings. Paul walked home. As he walked, he was careful not to step on any cracks. He didn't want to break his mother's back.

One week later, Oscar informed Paul that he was being sent to a military school. It was the first time since the police station that Oscar had spoken to his son. "It's for your own good," explained Oscar. "You need self-discipline and balance in your life. Maybe you'll find there."

For the next two years, cadet Paul Hill marched and drilled. He wore a uniform and attended classes, where he sat erect and took notes. He learned how to handle firearms. And every afternoon – whether he wanted to or not – he went to chapel.

It was there, in 1973, right before graduation that Paul found Jesus. He got religion. And with religion he got self-discipline and balance in his life. Exactly as his father wanted.

Paul later wrote, "God graciously converted my proud and rebellious heart when I was seventeen."[1]

Paul enrolled in Bellhaven College, which was a small, private Christian college. The curriculum at Bellhaven had "Jesus at its core." Which meant the administrators and professors were Christians. Everything was presented from the Christian perspective. Bellhaven College and its students were separated from "the World." No one drank alcohol or smoked cigarettes or played cards. Everyone was serious about being serious for Jesus.

Paul met his future wife at Bellhaven. Her name was Karen. Karen was pretty in a plain, pious way common to the females at Bellhaven. Prim

---

1   Hill, Paul. "Defending The Defenseless," 2001.

and proper, Karen knew her place: submitted to Jesus first and her future husband second. She knew and subscribed to the Biblical passages about women being "helpmates."

Paul felt the call. Which meant God had called him to the ministry. Paul would spend his life helping others, exhorting others to be better Christians. To those who weren't Christians already, Paul would present the Gospel. To prepare himself as a shepherd for God's flock, Paul enrolled in Reformed Theological Seminary.

According to Paul's own words, "Though I am a slow learner, I managed to graduate from seminary in 1984. The Lord then opened the door for me to serve as a minister in both the Presbyterian Church in America (PCA), and the Orthodox Presbyterian Church."[2]

Paul's admission to being "a slow learner" demonstrated his adaptability. For he was not a slow learner. In fact, he was at the top of all his classes in seminary. Which meant he was a fast learner. He was quick to assume the expected humility of all wanna-be ministers. Every ministerial candidate was aware that "pride goeth before the fall." So they all exuded the proper meekness of spirit that so impressed other Christians.

Paul entered the ministry. Pastoring at three different churches, he was restless and impatient. He also had a habit of self-righteously confronting church members. After seven years as a pastor he quit because of an "unfruitful ministry." Those words probably reflect unmet expectations. Paul wanted to change the world. He thought he could change the world. When the awful truth became apparent – he wasn't setting the world on fire – he slipped into disillusionment and depression.

* * * * *

After he left the ministry, Paul moved his family to Pensacola and started his own business – auto detailing. His new work gave him great satisfaction. Physical labor made him feel alive, which gave him a sense of meaning and purpose. And the results of his labors were immediate and empirical – the cars were clean and shined. The family moved to Pensacola so they could be near a reformed Presbyterian church Paul wanted to join. This church practiced infant baptism and infant communion. Both these rites were extremely important to Paul, who had developed an extraordinary empathy for the sanctity of new life. Paul believed passionately that 'Life' began at the moment of conception. Which meant he opposed any type of abortion.

---

2   Ibid.

Somewhere in here – no one knew precisely when – Paul hooked up with the Army of God. The Army of God was an extremist anti-abortion association.[3] The group openly advocated violence to stop abortion. Adopting the concept of leaderless resistance, the Army of God encouraged 'lone warriors' to take up the banner of God and do whatever was necessary to halt the mass murder of unborn infants. *Newsday* reported that the Reverend Michael Bray claimed to be "the chaplain of the Army of God."[4]

Michael Bray had strong connections to the church of Christian Identity. Bray believed the Bible was the inerrant Word of God. He held that homosexuals and adulterers should be executed, because that's what the Bible said. Bray introduced Paul Hill to Christian Identity. From that point on, Paul Hill's life was never the same.

Paul became an activist. "In God's amazing providence, I began to engage in pro-life activism at the Ladies Center in Pensacola."[5] A few months later, Michael Griffin – who was a pro-life activist – shot and killed Dr. David Gunn. Dr. Gunn performed abortions in a medical clinic.

Two days after Dr. Gunn's murder, Paul called the *Phil Donhue Show*. He told the show's producers who he was and stated that he upheld the killing of Dr. Gunn. The producers immediately invited Paul to appear on the show. Paul believed this opportunity was made possible by God's intervention. Which meant – as far as Paul was concerned – that God disapproved of abortion and sanctioned such acts of retribution.

Three days later, Paul appeared on the *Phil Donahue Show*, along with Dr. Gunn's son. In front of a national television, Paul defended the killing of Dr. Gunn. Paul stated that the abortion doctor's murder was the equivalent of executing "a Nazi concentration camp doctor."[6] The implication was that the murder was justified.

Shortly thereafter, according to Paul, "the Lord led me to contact Advocates for Life Ministries. They graciously published an article I wrote for their magazine, *Life Advocate*, and provided the contacts necessary for numerous activists to sign a 'Defensive Action' statement justifying Griffin's actions. After this, through another set of amazing providential occurrences, I appeared on ABC's *Nightline*, and justified Shelley Shannon's shooting of an abortionist in Wichita, Kansas in August 1993."[7]

---

3   The term 'association' is used loosely, as the group has no clearly defined organization.
4   The FBI cited the Army of God as domestic terrorists.
5   Ibid.
6   Ibid.
7   Ibid.

Shelley Shannon was part of the Army of God. Shannon shot Dr. George Tiller in Wichita, Kansas. Dr. Tiller was severely wounded but did not die.

On *Nightline*, Paul claimed he was the national spokesperson for defensive action against abortionists. He also stated he was connected to the Army of God. Paul told Nightline's viewers that the Sixth Commandment ("Thou shalt not murder") did not simply forbid murder. God's prohibition of murder also implied the means to stop murder from taking place. In other words, a correct interpretation of the Sixth Commandment allowed for the protection of innocent people who were being murdered by others.

Paul explained what he meant in language everyone could understand. "The scriptures teach that when the government requires sin of its people that they "must obey God rather than men," according to Acts 5:29. When the government will not defend the people's children – as required by the Sixth Commandment – this duty necessarily reverts to the people. Instead of faulting Griffin for going too far, is it possible that people should be accusing themselves of not going far enough? As distasteful as it is to kill a murderer, isn't it infinitely more repulsive to allow him to murder, not just one or two, but hundreds and thousands of unborn children?"[8]

In defense of such violent acts, Paul cited a story from the Old Testament book of Esther. Where King Ahasuerus passed a law that permitted Persians to murder Jews. The Jews' response was to use defensive force – to fight back – to preclude this atrocity. Killing abortionists was comparable to the historical event in Esther. God has provided people with the means to abide by his commandments. "It is presumptuous to neglect these means…"[9]

There was no denying that Paul Hill was articulate and persuasive. He loved being on national television. He enjoyed the limelight. However, his message had the odor of manipulation about it. Two wrongs never make a right.

It should be noted that Paul believed he was doing God's will. He was convinced of it. There was no doubt in Paul's mind. To him, his rationale was beyond refutation. Murdering those he perceived as murderers was right. It was a defensive action.

By this point, Paul Hill was toying with the idea of fighting back.

On July 21, 1994, "taking this defensive action occurred to me. Although at the time my thinking on these things had not crystallized, no

---

8   Ibid.
9   Ibid.

matter how I approached the subject, everything seemed to fall together in an amazing manner. I continued to secretly consider shooting an abortionist, half hoping it would not appear as plausible after I had given it more thought."[10]

The next day was Friday. As usual, Paul went to the abortion clinic – the Ladies Center in Pensacola – to protest. Another protestor arrived. Paul questioned his fellow-protestor, who told him that the abortionist usually arrived at 7:30 am. A police security guard accompanied the abortion doctor. However, the doctor had a habit of arriving a few minutes before the security guard. Which meant there was room for a defensive action to take place. If the matter was timed right, the doctor could be ambushed.

Paul interpreted this as a sign from God. "God had opened a window of opportunity, and it appeared I had been appointed to step through it."[11]

The following week, Paul's wife took their three children on a planned visit to his parents. Before they left, the family enjoyed an outing at the beach. Paul played with his son, who was nine, and his two daughters aged three and six. Paul knew this would probably be the last time he saw his family. To control his emotions, he "lifted my heart to the Lord in praise and faith."[12] God answered him. "I was reminded of God's promise to bless Abraham, and grant him descendants as numerous as he stars in the sky. I claimed that promise as my own…"[13]

Paul believed that what he was about to do would glorify God. And in return, God would reward him. Everything would be okay.

The fateful day – Monday – arrived. Paul encouraged himself by remembering the words of Romans 14:23. "And whatever is not from faith is sin." Paul was certain God wanted him to commit murder.

One final time, Paul prayed and spent time reading his Bible. Then he put his shotgun, along with his protest sign in his truck. He drove to the Ladies Center, which was a small, two-story building surrounded by a wood fence. He parked his truck and carried his sign and his shotgun to the clinic's entrance. He laid the shotgun on the ground between his feet. Covering it with his protestor's sign, he began laying white crosses out in front of the entrance. The crosses represented the deaths and graves of the unknown unborn children.

It was 7:00 am.

---

10   Ibid.
11   Ibid.
12   Ibid.
13   Ibid.

Just before 7:30 am, the doctor arrived. Dr. John Britton was 69 years old. He wore a bulletproof vest and sat in the passenger's seat of a blue pickup truck. The truck was driven by Col. James H. Barrett. Barrett acted as the doctor's unarmed and unpaid escort. He was 74 years old. Barrett's wife was also in the truck.

Paul Hill stood beside the entrance. Barrett recognized Hill, because Hill protested every Friday. As the truck drove by, Barrett said, "Get out of the way, Paul Hill. You know this truck."

The truck passed through the entrance. Paul Hill picked up his shotgun and leveled it at the truck's cabin. He aimed for Dr. Britton's head.

Barrett's wife looked at Hill, who "had something up to his face. I did not realize it was a gun. Then I saw the recoil ... and heard the boom." She dropped to the floor as an explosion ripped through the truck.

"Oh, my God, he's shooting," she screamed.

Hill fired four rounds into the truck. Then he reloaded and fired four more rounds. He calmly laid the shotgun at his feet and walked away. He held his arms out and away from his body. He didn't want the police to think he was still armed. They might shoot him.

Dr. Britton sat like a statue in his seat. Blood gushed from his head. Barrett was covered in blood. Both men were already dead.

Officer Bruce Martin was in his patrol car nearby. When the police dispatcher broadcast a shooting at the Ladies Clinic, Officer Martin whipped a u-turn. With his lights flashing and siren wailing, Officer Martin sped to the clinic. Arriving, Officer Martin saw Paul Hill walking toward him. Behind Hill, a small group of men pointed excitedly at Hill.

Officer Martin stopped his patrol car and got out. Drawing his gun, Officer Martin instructed Hill to lay on the ground. Hill did so. Officer Martin handcuffed him.

In his article 'Defending the Defenseless,' Paul Hill wrote, "Within a couple of minutes the police arrived. I gave a hopeful and non-resisting look to the policeman who ordered me under arrest with his drawn handgun. I was relieved when they cuffed me. I did not want to be shot, and was glad to be safely in police custody."

Officer Martin found three spent shotgun shells near the clinic's entrance. A black pump-action shotgun was found nearby.

The police took Paul to the Pensacola Police Station. Paul was not questioned in the usual manner. A police officer that had been specially trained in criminal psychology sat with Paul. The two men talked quietly about whatever Paul wanted to talk about. Paul did not want to talk about killing two men with a pump-action shotgun. As he put it, "I did not discuss what had just happened. I did not want to aid those who had sinned by swearing to uphold mass murder (as have virtually all those who have sworn to uphold the law of the land)."[14] In other words, to Paul's way of thinking police officers were nothing more than "sinners" who were accomplices to murder.

Paul's reasoning mirrored the reasoning of the church of Christian Identity, which stated that all government officials were the agents of ZOG. ZOG stood for 'zionist occupied government.' Supposedly, the intention of ZOG was to make everyone a slave in the New World Order.

Three hours later, Officer Martin escorted Paul to a squad car. The distance from the police station to the squad car was twenty yards. It was like running a gauntlet made of human flesh and recording devices. Hundreds of reporters, photographers and cameramen filled the twenty-yard span. The national media focused its spotlight on Paul Hill. The cold-blooded murder of an abortion doctor and his escort was sensational stuff.

Paul knew the media would be there. He had prepared for it. "As I came out of the door of the station, I seized the initiative, and raised my voice in a carefully planned declaration: 'Now is the time to defend the unborn in the same way you'd defend slaves about to be murdered!'"[15]

Not only was Paul defending himself and his actions, he was openly inciting others to take up weapons and kill abortionists. This type of manipulation demonstrated how thoroughly Paul had been indoctrinated by Christian Identity doctrine. For Identity dogma championed violent revolt.

Officer Martin and his prisoner pushed their way through the massed media. When they finally reached the squad car, Officer Martin carefully placed Paul in the back. Officer Martin then drove Paul to Escambria County Jail, where Paul was booked and issued jail clothing. Paul was immediately placed in Administrative Segregation for his own protection. Which meant he was placed in a solitary cell under heavy security.

Once in his cell, Paul gave praise to the Lord. "I repeatedly sang a song commonly used at rescues. The first stanza is, 'Our God is an awesome God.'"[16] In his cell, Paul felt as if he was finally free. He had finally escaped what in his mind was "the state's tyranny."[17] Paul believed that by committing murder he had delivered countless unborn children. He felt his act

---

14   Ibid.
15   Ibid.
16   Ibid.
17   Ibid.

merited a "holiday of feasting and rejoicing."[18] In his mind, Paul believed that if he had not killed Dr. Britton, he would have been guilty of a "sin of omission." By failing to murder, he would have sinned before God.

Within days, the prosecutors for Florida stated they would be seeking the death penalty. This was in accordance with the law. Paul Hill had not only murdered two men, he had thought about it and planned it. Which made it premeditated murder. And he had lain in wait to commit the murders. These "special circumstances" made him eligible for death.

Two pro-life attorneys – Michael Hirsh and Vince Heiser – volunteered to orchestrate Paul Hill's defense. The first thing the attorneys did was file a motion arguing that Paul Hill's murder of Dr. Britton and his escort was justifiable homicide. To defend the unborn, Dr. Britton had to die. Paul Hill's actions were necessary to prevent mass murder.

The judge rejected the motion and slapped a gag order on Paul Hill, because – in effect – if Paul was allowed to claim justifiable homicide, it meant Paul was above the law. It would mean Paul decided what was lawful and what was not. In Florida, abortion was legal under certain circumstances. In other words, abortion was not murder. Paul had committed murder twice over. And in the state of Florida, murder was illegal under all circumstances.

Essentially, Paul Hill was an anarcho-syndicalist. He believed he had been chosen to transact for the unborn. Which meant he – Paul Hill – would decide what was to be done. He became lawmaker, judge, jury and executioner – a tyrant. Therefore his proposed defense – justifiable homicide – would not be allowed. For it reflected his tyrannical anarchy.

Paul maintained he was the victim of judicial tyranny. He accused the court of that which he was guilty of. "Since I was denied a truthful defense, I had none. What was I to say? Since I could not tell the truth, I had almost nothing to say. There was no use in offering lame and ineffectual arguments – doing so would only make it appear that I had been given a fair trial."[19]

The jury found him guilty of two counts of murder under special circumstances. The penalty phase lasted two weeks. "During the penalty phase, I addressed the jury for the first time, and made a short statement as my 'closing argument.'"[20]

Looking directly at the jurors, Paul said, "You have a responsibility to protect your neighbor's life, and to use force if necessary to do so. In an

---

18   Ibid.
19   Ibid.
20   Ibid.

effort to suppress this truth, you may mix my blood with the blood of the unborn, and those who have fought to defend the oppressed. However, truth and righteousness will prevail. May God help you to protect the unborn as you would want to be protected."[21]

Paul's oration to the jury was rambling, pseudo-religious nonsense. It was as if he was performing on stage in a melodrama. He made a grand speech full of flamboyant phrases. None of which made any sense. It was not even an appeal for mercy or justice. In the end, it was nothing more than the muddled buzz words of a religious madman.

On December 6, 1994, Paul Hill was sentenced to death by lethal injection under Florida law. Within days, he was shipped off to death row at Florida State Prison.

In Florida, all death sentences were automatically appealed to the Florida State Supreme Court. This was a fail-safe measure. The Florida State Supreme Court found no reason to stay the death sentence. During this appeal process, Paul petitioned the court to dismiss his attorneys. He did not wish to file any further appeals. The court granted his petition.

Nine years later, on September 2, 2003, Paul told reporters he "would be rewarded in heaven for his actions. I was following God's instructions." He was scheduled to die on the following day at 6 p.m.

The next day, September 3, Paul spoke quietly with his wife and his son. Then he spent a few minutes with his parents and his two sisters. After his family members left, Paul spent time with Donald Spitz. Spitz – who was a Pentecostal minister – functioned as Paul's spiritual advisor.

Outside the Florida State Prison, anti-abortion activists gathered. They held up protest signs denouncing the execution of Paul Hill. The signs condemned Florida authorities as the "helpers of baby-killers." Other signs had pictures of unborn fetuses on them. Most of the protestors carried Bibles and rosary beads dangled from the hands of a few. Then they held a prayer vigil, while 100 police officers looked on.

Inside the prison, Paul ate his last meal. He had requested steak, a baked potato, salad, orange sherbert and iced tea. When he finished eating, he and Spitz prayed and read from the Bible. Then prison officials escorted Paul to the death chamber, where he was asked if he had any final words to say.

Paul looked at the two dozen witnesses and said, "The last thing I want to say: If you believe abortion is a lethal force, you should oppose the force and do what you have to do to stop it. May God help you to protect the unborn as you would want to be protected."

---

21   Ibid.

Paul was then strapped to the table and shunts were placed in his veins. The order was given and the injections were made. A few minutes later Paul Hill was pronounced dead.

Donald Spitz later told reporters that Paul "died with joy in his heart. He knew what he did was right, he willingly gave his life for the unborn."[22]

* * * * *

In reality, Paul Jennings Hill was a narcissistic, religious madman. Mentally and emotionally unstable, he found meaning for his inner emptiness in the zealotry of Christian Identity teachings. Since he openly endorsed "Phineas actions," it seemed obvious he had read *Vigilantes of Christendom* and adopted the book's ideas.[23] Only in *doing* something for God could Paul feel worthwhile. Thus he was a prime target for the rabid doctrines of Christian Identity.

The church of Christian Identity didn't instruct Paul to become a murderer. They didn't need to. To psychologically vulnerable individuals such as Paul, once they were indoctrinated, the call to action came from within. Steeped in the idea of "defending God's Law," they took it upon themselves to become priests, not only in thought but also in deed. They were compelled to demonstrate their holiness. By doing so, they gained not only the approval of their fellow-believers, but obtained rewards from God – the ultimate approbation.

In that sense, then, Paul Hill became the willing dupe of Christian Identity and Richard Kelly Hoskins. He believed and then acted upon his belief. He wasn't brainwashed. Instead, he was "faith-washed," which was even worse. For "faith-washing" overrides every human inhibition.

---

22   *Miami Herald*, September 4, 2003.
23   The Anti-Defamation League states that Paul Hill "advocated Phineas actions."

Chapter 9

The Life and Times of Timothy McVeigh

The amount of information available on Timothy McVeigh is mind-boggling. At least a dozen books have been written on the subject. Some of these books present a carefully sanitized account of McVeigh's life and the events surrounding the Oklahoma City bombing. In other words, there was no conspiracy. The bombing of the federal building was simply the work of baneful disaffected die-hards, who lost touch with reality.

On the other hand, hundreds – if not thousands – of online Websites preach and publish the wildest nonsense imaginable. Everything from McVeigh's supposed connection to Middle East terrorist groups to a government conspiracy to blow up one of its own buildings, and then cover it up by laying the blame on a small group of nutcases. The latter theory was concocted by zealots of the paramilitary and white nationalist groups, in order to keep "those already within the movement circles from jumping ship in disgust at the carnage."[1]

The truth lies somewhere in between simple and surreal. There was a conspiracy, but not one by the government. Rather it was a religious/philosophical conspiracy. It happened like this:

Timothy McVeigh and Terry Nichols were misfits. They didn't fit in anywhere in normal society. They felt left behind, disenfranchised by the government and the culture in which they resided. Because of this, black anger bubbled inside them. They were angry because they didn't receive the recognition they believed they deserved. In effect, they felt unloved and unwanted. This led to feelings of shame. And it was the government's fault. According to McVeigh and Nichols, the government was conspiring to take away the rights and freedoms of all Americans. Which meant fear was now added to their shame. They became paranoid.

Paranoia led to their involvement in the paramilitary/survivalist subculture, which was prepared to resist the conspiracy by force of arms, if necessary. As they got deeper and deeper into the paramilitary subculture, McVeigh and Nichols became paranoid, guilt-ridden psychopaths.

---

1   Leonard Zeskind, *Blood and Politics*, page 402.

To get what they craved – recognition – they decided they needed to do something so outrageous that the world would have to notice them. This, in turn, would absolve them of their shame. They would strike back at their oppressors. Only through violence and death could McVeigh and Nichols purge themselves of their demons – shame and fear.

So they decided to blow up the Alfred P. Murrah federal building in Oklahoma City.

In the fall of 1993, both Timothy McVeigh and Terry Nichols were flat broke. Except for what little money he made traveling the gun show circuit, McVeigh was unemployed. Nichols was in hock to his credit card companies, to the tune of $40,000. In short, the two men needed money. Especially if they wanted to continue practicing for their planned bombing of a federal building.

So McVeigh and Nichols hooked up with the Aryan Republican Army.

On October 11, 1993, McVeigh and Nichols registered at a Motel 6 in Fayetteville. The next day, McVeigh got a ticket for making an improper lane change. He was just outside Cedarville, Arkansas, when he got the ticket. Which meant he was 4 miles from Elohim City. In Elohim City, at that exact moment, Nathan Thomas, Kevin McCarthy, and Michael Brescia were being trained in guerilla warfare by Andreas Strassmeir. All three men – Thomas, McCarthy and Brescia – were members of the Aryan Republican Army (ARA).

Three other members of the ARA were also either in Elohim City or staying at a nearby motel. Richard Guthrie, Peter Langan and Shawn Kenney. "It is highly improbable – if not statistically impossible – for nine men with such violent predispositions and such deep connections within the white power movement, all of whom needed money desperately, to randomly come together at the same time in the same geographical region."[2]

All these men were at Elohim City to plan for the Oklahoma City bombing.

Located in the foothills of the Ozark Mountains in eastern Oklahoma, Elohim City was founded in 1973 by Robert Millar. Millar, a former Mennonite preacher from Canada, had converted to Christian Identity. After his conversion, Millar established Elohim City as an Identity compound, where he and his followers could live in keeping with their beliefs.

Essentially, Elohim City was an armed, religious community made up of members of the radical right. At various times, Elohim City housed members of the Aryan Republican Army; the Covenant, Sword, and Arm

---

2   Mark S. Hamm, *In Bad Company*, page 145.

of the Lord; the National Alliance; the KKK; the Aryan Nations; and other neo-Nazi groups. In other words, Elohim City was a bastion for those involved in the militant white power movement.

The Aryan Republican Army – about which much more later – was a small gang of estranged, violent, white supremacists, who had read *The Turner Diaries*, *The Silent Brotherhood* and *Vigilantes for Christendom*. Not only did they read them and believe them, but they adopted the books' teachings as their motivating ideology. The ARA modeled their mode of dress, their actions and their organization after Robert Mathews and The Order.

Supposedly, the ARA was at Elohim City preparing to rob an armored truck in Fayetteville. The robbery never took place. In hindsight, it appears the robbery was camouflage for the ARA's meeting with McVeigh. After the meeting, McVeigh wrote a number of bizarre letters. In one of the letters, he informed his sister that he now had "a network of friends who share [his] beliefs." He also told his sister of his recurring suicidal thoughts. McVeigh then wrote an anonymous letter to the Bureau of Alcohol, Tobacco and Firearms (BATF), railing against the bloody 1993 raid on David Koresh and the Branch Davidians. On a separate note sent with the letter to the BATF, McVeigh wrote, "You motherfuckers are going to hang."

About a month after the first letter to his sister, McVeigh sent her a second letter, which specifically spoke of the Phineas Priesthood and the "need for action." All these letters were written over the course of a four-week period, from October 1993 to November 1993. During this period, McVeigh was bouncing back and forth between the Michigan farm of Terry Nichols and the home of Michael Fortier in Kingman, Arizona. Fortier was an old Army buddy of McVeigh's. And it was at Fortier's home that McVeigh started using crystal meth and became friends with Jack Oliphant.

Oliphant was member of the Arizona Patriots and a self-appointed preacher in the church of Christian Identity. He used his 320-acre ranch to train neo-Nazi terrorists.

At the beginning of 1994, Terry Nichols and his wife – Marife Nichols, who was a Filipina mail-order bride – moved to Las Vegas. From his condo in Las Vegas, Nichols attended gun shows and military surplus auctions in Kansas. Meanwhile, McVeigh was also attending gun shows. Going by the name of Tim Tuttle, he sold rifles and copies of *The Turner Diaries*.

After a few months in Las Vegas, at the beginning of March 1994, Nichols moved to Marion, Kansas. When not on the road traveling from gun show to gun show, McVeigh hung out at the Nichols place in Kansas. Not surprisingly, the ARA's safe house was only 130 miles south and east of the Nichols home in Marion. In fact, the four corners area of Kansas, Missouri, Oklahoma and Arkansas was a hotbed of angry white power groups.

On September 12, 1994, McVeigh stayed at the El Siesta motel in Vian, Oklahoma, which was only twenty minutes from Elohim City. And it was at this time that McVeigh was seen on the gun range at Elohim City. While blasting away with semi-automatic and automatic weapons, McVeigh talked with Denis Mahon. Mahon was an ardent white supremacist and high-ranking member of WAR (White Aryan Resistance), a national hate group run by Tom Metzger.

Mahon knew how to build bombs. Three years before, he had built a 500-pound bomb. Made of ammonium nitrate, the bomb totally obliterated a truck.

Right after McVeigh left Elohim City, he and Nichols sat down and outlined the precise details of the bomb to blow up the Alfred P. Murrah federal building in Oklahoma City. They knew what kind of bomb they wanted to build and started to gather the necessary ingredients. First they bought 5400 pounds of ammonium nitrate fertilizer from the Mid-Kansas Co-op in McPherson, Kansas. They moved the fertilizer into storage lockers they had rented in nearby Herington, Kansas.

In Ennis, Texas, McVeigh and Nichols purchased 162 gallons of nitromethane, along with a siphon pump. They, too, were placed in the storage lockers in Herington.

Next, the two conspirators stole 299 sticks of dynamite, 580 Primadet blasting caps, and 400 pounds of Tovex sausages from a mining company in Marion, Kansas. These items were not placed in the Herington storage lockers. Instead, McVeigh and Nichols took them to Kingman, Arizona, where they rented more storage space to hold the stolen explosives.

McVeigh needed the explosives in Kingman so he and his expert bomb-building consultants could have access to them. For McVeigh intended to build and test some practice bombs.

Money was a necessary ingredient, too. McVeigh decided to run a fundraiser. In 1993, in Fort Lauderdale, he had met a wealthy gun collector named Roger Moore. Moore had a house in Hot Springs, Arkansas, where he kept many valuable items, including firearms, camera equipment, silver bars, gold bullion, jade, precious stones, large amounts of cash and other collectibles. McVeigh had visited Moore's house a number of times. So he knew where the loot was kept.

McVeigh told ARA members Michael Brescia and Richard Guthrie about Moore and his possessions. Guthrie and Brescia liked what they heard. On November 5, 1994, Guthrie and Brescia showed up at Moore's house in Hot Springs. Both men wore heavy diguises and carried loaded guns. Using duct tape, they bound Moore. Then they blindfolded him. Then they took everything they could lay their hands on, loading it into a van. They drove to Council Grove, Kansas, where they rented storage space. They put the firearms from the robbery inside the storage space. The rest of the loot was turned over to Terry Nichols.

On November 16, 1994, Terry Nichols drove to Las Vegas. He rented storage space into which he placed wigs, masks, panty hose, freeze-dried food and $60,000 worth of gold bullion, silver bars, and jade.

Meanwhile, McVeigh had gone to Pendleton, New York, on November 7. His grandfather had died and McVeigh was settling the estate. This required about a month of McVeigh's time. During this month, McVeigh told his sister that he had begun robbing banks. Which meant he was connected to the ARA. He also indicated to his sister that someone who was supposed to have been murdered had not been murdered. Obviously, he was referring to Roger Moore. Guthrie was supposed to have killed Moore after he robbed him. That was part of the deal. Guthrie had not lived up to his end of the bargain.

On December 11, 1994, McVeigh and three members of the ARA – Scott Stedeford, Kevin McCarthy and Peter Langan – were all in Overland Park, Kansas. The only conceivable explanation was that the conspirators were meeting, finalizing their plans for the Oklahoma City bombing.

On December 15, just four days later, McVeigh was back in Kingman, Arizona, where he took some of the explosives from storage and loaded them in the trunk of his car. He then drove to Council Grove, Kansas.

In the middle of January 1995, Terry Nichols took everything out of the Las Vegas storage space and loaded it in the back of his pickup. He then drove to Junction City, Kansas, where he met up with McVeigh. They traveled to gun shows for about ten days. On January 31, 1995, McVeigh arrived at the Belle Art Center motel in Kingman, Arizona. He was alone, but not for long. Soon a steady stream of visitors flowed into McVeigh's room.

During this same time – February 3 to 8 – the ARA was camping in the nearby desert.

On February 16, 1995, McVeigh went to the True Value hardware store in Kingman, Arizona. He bought 100 pounds of ammonium nitrate fertilizer and 600 pounds of ammonium phosphate. Meanwhile, the ARA was staying in Mesa, Arizona for three weeks.

On February 21, 1995, an ammonium nitrate-fuel oil bomb exploded near the house of Francis "Rocky" McPeak, just outside Kingman, Arizona. The explosive device shattered five glass windows in the house, woke up everyone for miles around and caused the ground to lurch. Neighbors immediately called the police, who called the Feds.

The next morning, pissed off, McPeak drove to Vollmer's house. McPeak had no evidence that Clark Vollmer was responsible for the bomb, but there was bad blood between the two men: Vollmer had asked McPeak to mule some meth for him and McPeak declined.

Arriving at Vollmer's house, McPeak banged on the front door, which soon opened. McPeak began shouting in Vollmer's face. Vollmer said he didn't have any idea what McPeak was talking about. Vollmer invited McPeak inside the house to discuss the matter in a civilized manner.

Entering the house, McPeak found himself standing in the living room. Seated on the couch were two men: McVeigh and another man that McPeak had never seen before.

*****

After attending two gun shows, one in St. George and another in Tucson, McVeigh drove to Kingman, passing through the Phoenix area at the exact same time the ARA was there. Whether or not McVeigh had any contact with the ARA while in Phoenix was unknown. However, the happenstance was pregnant with probabilities.

Arriving in Kingman, McVeigh drove to the home of Michael Fortier. The two men took a long walk together, during which, according to Fortier's subsequent court testimony, McVeigh informed Fortier that Terry Nichols had decided not to participate in the bombing of the federal building. In effect, Nichols had either chickened out or come to his senses, depending on one's viewpoint.

McVeigh wanted Fortier to help him with the bomb. Fortier said no. McVeigh then asked Fortier if, after the bombing, he would transport McVeigh from Las Vegas to the desert, where McVeigh planned to stay while the heat was on. Again, Fortier said no.

Disappointed, McVeigh left. March 17 found McVeigh in Las Vegas, where he picked up a television belonging to Terry Nichols. The television was sitting in the garage of Lana Padilla. Leaving Las Vegas, McVeigh drove to LaPorte, Colorado to visit David Hernandez, who, according to some reports, initiated McVeigh into the Order. If true, this would make McVeigh a Phineas priest.

McVeigh then went back to Kingman, where he got rid of anything that could be used as evidence against him. In other words, McVeigh was tying up loose ends. On March 29, drove to a trailer park, where he made a proposal to Jim Rosencrans: McVeigh proposed that Rosencrans drive him to an unnamed location. Then instead of driving back home, Rosencrans would go to the airport, park his car in long-term parking and fly home on a commuter airline. McVeigh offered Rosencrans $400 dollars to perform this service.

Rosencrans said no.

McVeigh went back to Kingman, where he checked into the Imperial Hotel – room 212 – paying in advance for a week. At the time, McVeigh drove a blue Buick Skyhawk. He parked the car combat style at the hotel.

Leaving his room only for food, McVeigh spent most of his time on the phone, making a multitude of phone calls, most of which were long-distance. During this sojourn, McVeigh placed eight phone calls to the National Alliance, William Pierce's white supremacist outfit.

While residing at the Imperial Hotel, McVeigh had two visitors: Michael Fortier visited twice. He was invited to do so by McVeigh, who was trying to turn Fortier to his cause. Fortier's wife, Lori, accompanied her husband during his second visit. Fortier carried a hand gun with him on both visits because McVeigh was becoming openly angry and unstable.

After his second visit with McVeigh, Fortier left with the impression that McVeigh had pretty much given up on his insane scheme to blow up the federal building. Fortier testified to this feeling in court. Either McVeigh was dissembling or in the interim he found someone to help him with his terrorist plot.

According to most published reports, the bomb used by McVeigh was assembled in Kansas. The authors suggest that the bomb was built on April 19, in Oklahoma City. Three pieces of evidence support this proposition: the expert testimony of explosive experts; McVeigh's statements during his subsequent interviews while in jail; and McVeigh's drawing of the bomb.

McVeigh's Ryder truck contained 13 plastic barrels, arranged in a U-configuration. First, each of the barrels was filled with 350 pounds of fertilizer (ammonium nitrate). Then 140 pounds of nitromethane was injected into each barrel. Using paddles, the mixtures were stirred well.

According to McVeigh's testimony, the bomb makers ran out of nitromethane. They had only enough for nine of the thirteen barrels. So they improvised. Instead of adding nitromethane to the last four barrels, the bomb makers substituted diesel fuel. Because time was running out, the barrels containing diesel fuel and fertilizer did not receive proper stirring. According to McVeigh, "The fertilizer in the diesel barrels was not mixed well. There was not time." The statement was made to McVeigh's attorneys, while they interviewed him in jail.

350 pounds of Tovex sausages ribboned around and between the barrels. The Tovex was utilized to augment the explosive force of the fertilizer. Primadet caps were inserted into the Tovex. The Primadet caps were crucial to the success of McVeigh's bomb, for they would detonate it.

Two salient facts become evident at this point: first, McVeigh could not have constructed his bomb without help. Nor did he have the requisite skills to place and synchronize the Primadet caps. And a third fact interjects itself: McVeigh was not stupid. He would never have mixed the bomb, placed the Primadet caps and then driven from Kansas to Oklahoma. One wrong bump and the volatile concoction would have exploded, obliterating not only McVeigh but any chance of success.

Everything was ready. Wearing a white T-shirt that read, "The tree of liberty must be refreshed from time to time by the blood of tyrants and patriots," McVeigh climbed into the cab of his rental truck.

McVeigh was high on crystal meth when he got into the truck.

Various witnesses observed the truck on its way to the Murrah building. All the witnesses stated that two men occupied the cab of the truck: McVeigh and John Doe. John Doe was described as a tanned white male, with black hair.

The truck was parked. The fuses were ignited. McVeigh and John Doe exited the truck, locking the doors behind them.

At precisely 9:02 am, the Primadet caps kicked in. 168 people died instantaneously. Nineteen of those that died were babies and children.

Questions and Theories

The feds dispatched a small army of agents to Oklahoma City (OKC), 2000 agents, who interviewed over 20,000 people and followed up on 43,000 tips. In the end, the investigation revealed that two people carried out the bombing: Timothy McVeigh and Terry Nichols. And since Nichols dropped out prior to the bombing, the entire scenario rested on McVeigh's shoulders. In effect, he was a "lone wolf."

However, since that conclusion – that McVeigh was responsible – a mountain of evidence points to a different and more nefarious conclusion: Elohim City and Andreas Strassmeir were heavily involved in the bombing plot.

Andreas Strassmeir was a German national from a wealthy, elite family with vast connections in the upper echelons of Germany. Ma Strassmeir was a movie actress and Pa Strassmeir was General Secretary of the Berlin Democratic Union. According to reports, Andreas Strassmeir spent 5 to 16 years in the German Army (reports vary on the length of his service). While in the army, Strassmeir was part of the Panzer Grenadiers, an elite intelligence unit. Strassmeir specialized in "disinformation," i.e. spinning believable lies to fit an agenda.

Educated, handsome and intelligent summed up Strassmeir's profile. He spoke fluent Hebrew and was frequently in the company of a beautiful woman identified as a member of the Israeli Army. There was speculation that both Strassmeir and his girlfriend were members of Mossad; but this has never been proven.

Strassmeir first visited the United States in 1987, flying into Washington, D.C. Classified as "AO" by Immigration, Strassmeir had no difficulty entering the country. Precisely what "AO" status was or is remains a mystery. Administrative Officer?

Strassmeir returned to the U.S. in 1991. His entry into the states was massaged by an attorney, Kirk Lyons, who according to the *American Free Press* also functioned as an undercover agent for the feds. Apparently, Lyons wore many hats because he functioned as the attorney for the KKK. Lyons set Strassmeir up with a driver's license and address in Knoxville, TN.

Almost immediately, Strassmeir began hanging out with retired army officers, retired CIA agents and members of the Civil War reenactment crowd. This was where it became interesting. Strassmeir became friendly with Vincent Petruskie, who from 1954 to 1975 was a member of the Air Force Office of Special Investigation. Petruskie lived in Manassas, VA, where he operated Petruskie Associates. Petruskie was a spook and his tentacles reached everywhere.

Strassmeir went to work for Petruskie Associates; his job was to buy used 747s from Lufthansa Airlines. The 747s were to be used as part of a transport operation based in Costa Rica.

After that, Strassmeir aligned himself with the Texas Light Infantry Brigade, a right wing militia group. However, the Brigade never trusted

Strassmeir. According to reports, the Brigade suspected him of being an undercover ATF agent.

In fact, on July 14, 1996, the *McCurtin Gazette* stated that Strassmeir was indeed an undercover agent of the ATF. His job was to infiltrate Elohim City. This assertion was corroborated by Stephen Jones, McVeigh's mercurial attorney, who stated that Strassmeir was an undercover agent for the FBI. And if that's not mysterious enough, there was also an FBI form 302 asserting Strassmeir was a CIA agent.

Strassmeir did infiltrate Elohim City, which, according to *Time* magazine was "the who's who of the radical right." Elohim City was the preferred residence of the Covenant, Sword and Arm of the Lord; the National Alliance; the KKK; the Aryan Nations and the Aryan Republican Army. In effect, Elohim City was neo-Nazi central.

Elohim City was the brainchild of Robert Millar, who was considered the spiritual head or Pope of the radical right. He established Elohim City as a "white" enclave in 1973. Millar was, in reality, an undercover agent for the FBI and the DEA. This explained why Elohim City was allowed to operate. The feds knew who was there and what they were planning to do. Millar kept them informed.

Indeed, Elohim City was rife with undercover agents, including Gary Hunt, who was a mole for the ATF; James Ellison, who later testified against The Order; and Peter Langan, a mole for the U.S. Secret Service.

On October 12, 1993, McVeigh and Nichols left Arkansas and arrived at Elohim City, where they met with Strassmeir. The meeting also included Richard Guthrie and Peter Langan of the Aryan Republican Army. McVeigh also visited Elohim City on other occasions, using the name of Tim Tuttle.

In addition, the FBI suspected McVeigh was part of the crew that robbed a bank in Ohio, in December of 1994. It was during December of 1994 that McVeigh asked his sister to launder some money for him. Presumably, the money that needed laundering came from the bank robbery.

Canada's popular television program *The Fifth Estate*, confirmed that McVeigh, Strassmeir and Michael Brescia appeared on security tape footage at Lady Godiva's, a strip club in Tulsa, on April 8, 1995, just eleven days prior to the OKC bombing.

The fact that McVeigh and Strassmeir were not only acquainted but also hung out together in strip clubs spoke volumes.

At this point in the McVeigh tale, it becomes necessary to insert some information about Carol Howe, a Tulsa debutante that worked as a confidential informant for the ATF. Calling herself Freya, Howe infiltrated Elohim City, becoming a vital cog in the big wheel of white supremacy. Ms. Howe provided more than seventy reports to Karen Finley, who functioned as her ATF handler.

Ms. Howe informed the ATF that Andreas Strassmeir and Dennis Mahon conceived the OKC bombing. Howe also informed the ATF that Mahon and Strassmeir visited OKC three times prior to the bombing. Indeed, on one of the visits, Howe accompanied the two men as they scouted possible sites.

Later, according to the sworn testimonies of both Finley and Howe, it became clear that law enforcement agencies had prior knowledge of the bombing, yet for some reason either failed or refused to take action.

Many analysts believed that Strassmeir was the John Doe in the Ryder truck with McVeigh. And frankly, it probably was Strassmeir; in fact, it now seems reasonable to say that Strassmeir planned and participated in the OKC bombing. McVeigh was an active participant, but he couldn't have pulled off the plan without the direct involvement of Strassmeir and Mahon.

After the bombing, Dennis Mahon said, "If a person wanted to know about the bombing, then they should talk with Andy Strassmeir because he knows everything."

Strassmeir was never arrested and never interrogated. Instead, he remained at Elohim City until January of 1996, when he left the country aboard a private jet. Some believed the CIA had Strassmeir flown out of the U.S.; others maintained that Kirk Lyons made sure his man was removed from the scene; while still others, like Victor Thorn, asserted that Lyons, with the help of Germany's GSG-9, transported Strassmeir to safety.

Once out of the country and back in Germany, Strassmeir was interviewed by various publications. Needless to say, Strassmeir was not forthcoming. In the interviews, Strassmeir mentioned "sting operations" and even suggested that McVeigh was working for the ATF. Presumably, his statements were simply examples of disinformation, which was his specialty.

Along with all this, there remained other questions about the OKC bombing. For example, could a single truck bomb, no matter how large, destroy half of a building? According to explosive experts, no, it could not. This opened the door for the multiple bombs theory, which claimed that explosive devices were placed at strategic points inside the building.

Videos explaining this theory are available on YouTube. Whether or not they are reliable or even true is anyone's guess.

All of the material suggested in this section – Questions and Theories – implies a vast conspiracy to bomb a federal building in OKC, and then cover it up. And for all intents and purposes, such a conspiracy would necessarily include agencies of the federal government. This begs the question: to what end and for what purpose?

Until more information comes to light or Andreas Strassmeir chooses to write his tell-all memoirs, there is no viable answer. What role Strassmeir played, if any, in the OKC bombing, McVeigh still perceived himself as a Phineas Priest. He did what he thought needed to be done. He killed God's enemies.

Chapter 10

The Army of God

The Army of God was not an organized militia. Nor was it anything like an army. And although the Army of God claimed to be doing God's work here on earth, in reality they had nothing to do with God. The Army of God was a collection of nutcases yoked together by a common cause: they believed abortion was a horrible sin and that brutal force was warranted, acceptable and reasonable to protect those still to be born. In fact, the Phineas Priests of the Army of God advocated blowing up abortion clinics and murdering doctors who performed abortions.

The Army of God was concocted by Don Benny Anderson in 1982. Anderson was religious fanatic, a hard core fundamentalist, who, along with two henchmen, drove to Edwardsville, Indiana, where they kidnapped an abortion doctor. They also kidnapped his wife, who was with her husband on that particular day. Prior to the kidnapping, Anderson had placed bombs in abortion clinics; one in Virginia and one in Florida.

Anderson was arrested, tried and convicted. When interrogated by authorities, Anderson confessed he had invented the term – The Army of God – because it sounded good. The term had flair and was memorable. Anderson didn't know it, but when he conceived the name of his fictional group, he created a brand.

The brand took off. Within a few years, an actual Army of God manual was put together by anti-abortionists. The manual included instructions on effective methods for destroying abortion clinics.

* * * * *

Early on the morning of July 27, 1996, the bomb exploded in Centennial Park. The park was crowded with people.

The bomb consisted of three metal pipes. Each pipe was 12 inches long, with a 2 inch diameter. Each pipe was stuffed with 1.3 pounds of Accurate Arms Number 9 powder. The pipes were then capped. The bomb builder had drilled a small hole into each pipe. Electric matches were inserted in the holes. The bomb builder taped 5 pounds of 2.5 inch masonry nails to the pipes. The nails served a lethal purpose: shrapnel.

The electric matches were connected to an Eveready battery. The wires were connected to an old-fashioned wind-up alarm clock. The bomb, along with the battery and the alarm clock was attached to a steel plate. Tape held the contraption together. At this point, the bomb was placed in a backpack that had a foam pad for easier carrying.

The bomb was, by definition, nothing more than a pipe bomb. Simple, easy to make and highly effective.

The bomber's target was Centennial Park in Atlanta, Georgia, where the Centennial Olympic Games were in progress. 197 countries were represented; 3 million people traveled to Atlanta to watch the athletes in action. The opening ceremony occurred July 19, 1996, at the Olympic Stadium, jam-packed with 85,000 onlookers. The Olympic torch was lit; the games were underway.

Centennial Olympic Park was located in the center of the city. Everyone, athletes and spectators, congregated in the park, which featured musical concerts, restaurants and entertainment. It was place where people had a good time and spent money.

It was also a prime target for anyone intent upon terrorism or any other type of mayhem. To preclude such events, the games' organizers surrounded the park with a portable fence, guards at the entrances and video cameras. These so-called security measures were at best inefficient and at worst lackadaisical.

On July 27, the bomber entered the park, carrying a backpack. Locating a bench near the NBC-TV tower, he sat down. Nearby, a group of teenagers were quaffing beer, joking around and laughing. Already half drunk, the group later told police that the man had a dark complexion, average build and was wearing a sweatshirt. The sweatshirt was weird because it was a warm summer's night in Atlanta.

The teenagers paid the man no mind, being too wrapped up in their drinking and partying. Somewhere in there the man left, leaving his backpack behind. It had been shoved under the bench.

A music concert was in full swing. Jack Mack and the Heart Attack played loud rock and roll for the listeners. It was after midnight and police estimated that 50,000 people were in the park; most in party-mode.

An AT&T security guard, Richard Jewell, was on duty at the east entry into the park. Jewell was an adrenaline junky who loved his job because he liked to be in charge. His job was to allow people to have a good time but not let things go too far and get out of hand. One bad apple could spoil everyone's fun.

Jewell noticed the drunken teenagers. Rather than confront the group by himself, he went in search of backup. He found Tom Davis, another guard, told him what was up, and the two headed toward the location. By the time the two guards arrived, the teenagers were gone. Jewell looked around and spotted the backpack. Moving closer, he scrutinized the backpack. There was nothing unusual about it and Jewell didn't give it much thought because lost and found was full of backpacks and other items people forgot.

Still, they had their orders. So Davis placed a call, asking that bomb technicians be dispatched to his location.

At 12:58 a.m. a call came into 911. It was the bomber.

"Atlanta 911," answered the operator.

"There is a bomb in Centennial Park. You have thirty minutes," said the voice. Then he hung up.

The operator immediately placed a call to the Atlanta Police Department. The line was busy. Three minutes later, she got through.

"You know the address to Centennial Park?" the 911 operator asked.

"Girl, don't ask me to lie to you," said the police dispatcher.

"I tried to call ACC, but ain't nobody answering the phone. And I just got this man telling me there's a bomb set to go off in thirty minutes in Centennial Park," said the 911 operator. She was referring to the fact that entering 'Centennial Park' into her database failed to reveal the address of the park.

"Oh Lord, child," said the police dispatcher. "One minute, one minute. Centennial Park. You put it in and it won't go in?"

"No, unless I'm spelling Centennial wrong. How are we spelling Centennial?"

"CENTENNI – how do you spell Centennial?"

"I'm spelling it right. It ain't taking –"

"Wait a minute. That's the regular Olympic Stadium, right?"

The exchange continued for long minutes as the 911 operator and the police dispatcher attempted to figure out why the database would not accept the input.

Finally, the 911 operator located an address for the park. She entered it, informing the Atlanta Police of the possible danger.

Or thought she had. The notification never went through because the system configuration did not include communication with the police department – a ludicrous situation.

It was Woody Allen that said, "Nothing works and nobody cares."

* * * * *

At a little after 1 a.m., fourteen year old Fallon Stubbs and her mother, Alice, were still in the park. Fallon took a photo of her mother standing in front of a statue.

Meanwhile, two bomb technicians were on their knees examining the backpack under the bench. They were looking for booby traps. None were evident. At that point, one of the techs opened the backpack carefully. Utilizing his flashlight, he peered inside. His eyes widened as he saw wires and a pipe. He informed his partner and they backed away.

The techs placed a call to the bomb disposal unit. Then the techs advised security to clear the area.

Tom Davis, along with other security guards, moved to clear the area, asking people to leave immediately. Jewell entered the NBC-TV tower and told the audio-visual techs to clear out.

At precisely 1:18 a.m., the alarm clock triggered the bomb. The pipe bomb exploded, releasing fiery shrapnel at 3300 feet per second. Hot, 2.5 inch masonry nails flew outward.

People near the bomb were literally lifted off their feet and hurled through the air, just like in a Hollywood movie.

Fallon Stubbs watched in eerie disbelief as her mother performed a pirouette and then dropped like a wet sock. The shock wave blew Fallon off her feet. Shrapnel struck her in the leg and hand. Blood flowed from her wounds. Rising to her feet, Fallon started to move to her mother. Someone nearby told her to stay down.

A fleet of ambulances and rescue personnel arrived in minutes. Blood was everywhere. The initial count was 110 injured people. The backpack's buckle had sliced into a jaw. A cameraman died. Many had open wounds and/or broken bones. The moaning and screaming attained Biblical proportions.

Medics loaded Fallon onto a stretcher, then into an ambulance.

Fallon's mother died instantaneously. Part of a masonry nail impacted her temple, penetrating deep into her skull.

The FBI, along with other law enforcement experts arrived. One of those was Tom Mohnal, an FBI explosive expert. Surveying the site, Mohnal immediately knew it was a pipe bomb.

Evidence technicians gathered up every piece of the bomb they could find. Nails were found hundreds of yards from the point of origin.

The FBI, the ATF and the NRT argued over jurisdiction of the site. Each agency felt it should be in charge. This interagency squabbling hindered the investigation process. In the end, the FBI was granted control. All evidence went to the FBI's lab located in Washington, D.C.

After analyzing the evidence, Mohnal determined that four pounds of Accurate Arms powder was used in the bomb. The powder originated in Israel, but after that no one knew where it had gone or who purchased it.

The bomber's use of the steel plate as a base for the bomb indicated knowledge of military explosive devices. In effect, the steel base functioned as a funnel, regulating the direction of the shrapnel.

Richard Jewell was the FBI's primary suspect. The ATF did not concur. Jewell was not the bomber, according to the ATF.

The FBI's focus on Richard Jewell was convenient. The motivation was political. The FBI wanted to look good, solve the case fast. FBI profilers decided that Jewell fit the profile. If that wasn't enough, Jewell's prior employer informed the FBI that Jewell was erratic. Moreover, Jewell was in his early thirties and still lived at home with his mommy. Jewell was pegged as the bomber. His name was conveniently leaked to media outlets.

And just like the media in the movie *Absence of Malice*, the press fell for it hook, line and sinker. The media descended on Jewell's home like a swarm of locusts.

Jewell was transported to FBI headquarters in Atlanta to be interviewed. During the interview, Jewell caught on that he was suspected of being the bomber. Jewell, intelligently, decided to lawyer up.

Meanwhile, the FBI with warrant in hand searched Jewell's house, an apartment. During the search, the FBI boxed up anything and everything in the apartment as possible evidence.

The Jewell witch hunt lasted for three months, until the FBI finally admitted that there was absolutely no evidence pointing to Jewell as the bomber. Jewell's life was destroyed. His reputation was mud. In the end, all he got was a letter informing him that he was no longer under investigation.

Without Jewell, the FBI had no suspects and no leads.

The bomber had gotten away scot free.

The only thing the FBI could hope for was that the bomber would strike again. If he did, perhaps they would catch a break and pinpoint something leading to his capture. Of course, another bombing was the last thing anyone wanted to occur. It was akin to wishing for another holocaust so Hitler could be caught and punished.

The FBI found itself in an unenviable position. To catch the bomber they needed him to build another bomb and use it. That meant more deaths, more destruction, more maiming and more suffering. A nightmare of unimaginable proportions.

* * * * *

Their worst nightmare came true.

On January 16, 1997, the news media reported an abortion clinic had been blown up in Sandy Springs, a suburb in Atlanta. ATF agent Joe Kennedy arrived on the scene shortly after the explosion. A handful of police officers and firemen were already there.

The Sandy Springs Professional Building was a three story structure whose tenants included medical offices, law offices and other professional offices. One of the tenants was Northside Family Planning Services, an abortion clinic. The bomb had been placed near the exterior of the clinic.

Kennedy parked his car and got out. Putting on his ATF jacket for identification, he walked toward the building. When on-scene authorities saw that the ATF was there, they approached Kennedy. In reality, bombs were not their area of expertise and they needed direction. Bombs were what the ATF did. So they figured Kennedy would know what to do.

A police officer directed Kennedy's attention to a deformed piece of metal nearby. Kennedy told the police officer not to touch it or allow anyone else near it. Then Kennedy instructed the police to set up a perimeter. Only forensic techs were to be allowed into the perimeter, when they arrived.

Next to arrive were the vultures – mobile media trucks replete with reporters, cameramen and telescopic antennae. Then the FBI showed up.

Kennedy called ATF headquarters in Atlanta. He wanted the entire ATF on-scene as soon as possible, along with an ATF PR person to handle the media.

As Kennedy consulted with a police officer, a bright white flash impacted his eyes, followed by an explosion. Dirt mushroomed upwards and a car across the parking lot literally jumped into the air. Police personnel and firemen dropped and covered.

Later examination concluded that it was not a car bomb. Instead, the bomb had been concealed in the dirt near the car. The car had actually shielded rescue personnel from the effects of the bomb. Still, six people suffered injuries from the explosion: one FBI agent and one ATF agent were struck by shrapnel.

It was a booby trap, placed to injure and possibly kill rescue personnel. The bomber, whoever he was, was diabolically smart. He knew law enforcement personnel would be swarming the area.

The ATF called for DoJ National Response Team support; the FBI called for explosive experts.

The second bomb, called a secondary device, by law enforcement was a technique utilized by the PLO, the IRA and the U.S. military, especially in counterinsurgency situations.

The ATF dispatched Special Agent in Charge (SAC) Jack Killorin to Sandy Springs. Killorin entered the site's interim command center in a building across the street from the abortion clinic. Inside the command center, Killorin found Woody Johnson, the FBI SAC and Atlanta's U.S. Attorney, Kent Alexander. It appeared inter-agency jockeying for position was already underway.

Johnson approached Killorin. The men shook hands. "Hi, I'm Woody Johnson and I understand we're fighting" said Johnson.

"Hi Woody, it's a pleasure to meet you. Let's make it a fair fight and tell me what it's about.

Both men smiled.

Forensics techs had gathered evidence and preliminary results were already coming in. They bomb had used nitroglycerin, a high-explosive. In addition, the bomb utilized nails. The nails used in the Sandy Springs bomb were different than those used at Centennial Park. But the signature was plain enough for bomb experts to suggest it might be the same bomber.

Johnson and Killorin discussed the findings like pugilists. Johnson held out a couple of the nails for Killorin's inspection. "We've got cut nails in this bomb, just like CENTBOMB (the code name for the Centennial Park bombing). So we think we should take over the investigation," said Johnson.

Killorin replied. "Yeah, but they're different sizes. Four-penny nails, not nine-penny, so you can't say this is the same guy."

"It's still cut nails –"

"And your guy used smokeless powder. This guy used dynamite. Plus this one was a trap, with two devices. And we don't have a target link –"

In the end, the two men agreed to establish a joint task force. They would share information and responsibilities.

TWINBOMB was designated as the name for the Sandy Springs bombing. Kennedy handled the forensics department. Kennedy wanted mockups of the two bombs as soon as possible. Mockups would allow the task force to – maybe – identify the bomb builder.

The task force dug in and began its investigation. A patient at the methadone clinic in the building maintained that he may have seen the bomber. The patient had arrived at the clinic early and noticed a man dressed in a track suit lurking about. Tracksuit guy had a backpack and a shovel.

The car that shielded personnel from the second bomb's blast belonged to young married couple also in the substance abuse program clinic. They had paid $500 for it. Killorin found a way to reimburse them for the car.

Further forensic examination revealed both bombs were constructed of dynamite packed into ammunition cans. Such cans were available at army surplus outlets and were almost impossible to track.

D-cell batteries and an old-fashioned alarm clock functioned as the timer. The first bomb used on the abortion clinic used 10.5 pounds of dynamite sans shrapnel; whereas the second bomb used 5 pounds of dynamite, along with four pounds of four-penny nails. In addition, the second bomb was bound by iron wire.

Forencis experts determined that the funny steel plate had been cut with a torch and resembled the plate used at Centennial Park in size, weight, composition and cutting method.

On February 21, 1996, a bomb exploded at the Otherside Lounge, a gay bar in Atlanta. Joe Kennedy arrived at the Otherside Lounge shortly after the explosion. The Atlanta Police Department had been well-briefed on the Sandy Springs bombing. Because of this foresight, one of the on-scene police officers had carefully inspected the area. He located a secondary device located near the front entrance to the club. Bomb techs used a robot to approach and examine the bomb.

The robot proved to be ineffective. Finally, bomb techs instructed the robot to spray the bomb with water. Discharging a powerful stream of water on the backpack, the bomb exploded. The powerful explosion sent shrapnel flying and felt like a small earthquake. Part of a steel plate – used to focus the explosive force of the bomb – was later located nearly a quarter-mile away from its point of origin.

The steel plate led investigators to believe they were on the trail of the Centennial Park bomber.

If the Centennial Park bomber was the Sandy Springs bomber was the Otherside Lounge bomber, he was not locked into his modus operandi; he was flexible and creative, as demonstrated by the Otherside Lounge bombs, which used plastic containers rather than ammunition cans, along with still another type of battery and wire nails rather than cut nails.

Nitroglycerine dynamite was used once again in the Otherside Lounge bombs.

The task force was engaged in trying to track down the source of the nails, the steel plates and the dynamite. The nitroglycerin dynamite may have come from the Austin Powder Company in Asheville, North Carolina.

Meanwhile, the bomber, like most such individuals, needed attention. He sent envelopes to NBC News, WSB-TV, Reuters and the *Atlanta Journal-Constitution*. All four envelopes were mailed from the same location on February 23 – north Atlanta. All four envelopes carried a non-existent return address.

All four envelopes contained a sheet of paper with a hand-written note: "The bombing's in Sandy Spring's and midtown were carried-out by units of The Army of God. You may confirm with the F.B.I. the Sandy Springs device's gelatin-dynamite-power source 6-volt D-battery box Duracell brand, clock timers. The midtown devices are similar except no ammo cans, Tupperware containers instead. Power source single 6-volt lantern batteries different shrapnel, regular nails instead of cut nails. The abortion was the target of the first device. The murder of 3.5 million children every year will not be "tolerated." Those who participate in anyway in the murder of children may be targeted for attach. The attack therefore serves as a warning: anyone in or around facilities that murder children bay become victims of retribution. The next facility targeted may not be empty. The second device was aimed at agent of the so-called federal government i.e. ATF, FBI, Marshall's e.t.c. We declared and will wage total war on the ungodly communist regime in New York and your legaslative-bureautic lackey's in Washington. It is you who are resposible and preside over the murder of children and issue the polucy on ungodly preversion that's destroying our people. We will target all facilities and personell of the federal government. The attack in midtown was aimed at the sodomite bar (The Otherside). We will target sodomites, there organizations, and all those who push there agenda. In the future where innocent people may become the primary casualties, a warning phone call will be placed to one of the news bureau's or 911. Generally a 40 minute warning will be given. To confirm the authenticity of the warning a code will be given with the warn and statement. The code for our unit is 4 1 9 9 3. "Death to the new world order""

Other than the fact that the bomber was poor speller and used atrocious grammar and syntax, the letters didn't reveal much the task force could follow up on. The letter writer correctly identified the composition of the bombs used at Sandy Springs and the Otherside Lounge.

The letters failed to mention Centennial Park. And since the task force could not connect the Centennial Park bombing to either anti-abortion or sodomy, some members of the task force floated the idea of two bombers. The identification code – obviously – referred to April 19, 1993, the date of the Waco fiasco. And except for the year, the day and month referenced the date McVeigh bombed the Murrah building in Oklahoma City.

"Death to the New World Order" was the rallying cry for any number of extremist groups that believed Jewish bankers and their lackeys controlled the governments of the world.

The task force recruited a forensic psychiatrist, Park Elliott Dietz, to provide a profile of the bomber. Dietz asserted that the bomber was paranoid and likely operating by himself – the classic Lone Wolf or Phineas Priest.

Killorin agreed with Dietz. Neither Dietz nor Killorin gave much credence to The Army of God crap. It was nothing more than a handy buzzword used by nutcases to give validity to their violent agenda.

The investigations – Sandy Springs, Otherside Lounge and Centennial Park – were classified as the same case in September 1997. A new task force was established – the Atlanta Bomb Task Force – under the auspices of the FBI. The problem was the task force had no concrete leads. So a reward was offered: $100,000 for information leading to the capture of the bomber.

In reality, offering a reward was a smart move. A large proportion of crimes were solved because someone decided to drop a dime on someone else.

* * * * *

Then something happened in Birmingham, Alabama. It took place at the New Woman All Women clinic, a clinic that offered abortions.

Robert Sanderson was the guard on duty that morning. The clinic had the usual collection of anti-abortion protestors that showed almost daily. But they never got violent; limiting their protests to shouted slogans and signs stating abortion was murder.

Sanderson was there for visual effect and to maintain order.

On that morning, an SUV arrived at the clinic at 7 a.m. A family of three; mom was there to have an abortion. The whole family was nervous and apprehensive, flooded by guilt. Dad approached Sanderson, who informed him that he was early. The clinic didn't open until 8 a.m.

At just that moment, one of the clinic's nurses arrived – Emily Lyons. She was there to open the clinic. As she walked toward the clinic, she passed Dad. Stopping, she peered at something near the entrance. Catching Sanderson's eye, she pointed to it. Sanderson walked up to the object, nightstick in hand. He couldn't tell what it was, so he leaned closer.

It looked like a flower pot that had been turned upside down. Sanderson lifted it slowly.

The bomb exploded.

Sanderson's body was tossed into the air. His body flew fifteen feet and landed near Dad's SUV.

John Hicks, a trained EMT, was walking in the area. He saw a blink of white light, heard a loud boom and was almost knocked off his feet by the shock wave. Hicks ran toward the explosion figuring he could put his training to use, if anyone was injured. As he ran, a figure appeared in his peripheral vision: the figure carried a backpack and had long hair.

When he arrived at the clinic, Hicks saw Sanderson's body. He looked dead. Emily Lyons was prostrate near the door. Emily's face had been badly burned; her torso took multiple hits from shrapnel and Hicks could see the bones in her lower legs. The skin had been blown off. And she had a gaping stomach wound.

But she was alive.

Police arrived at the clinic. Then an ambulance roared in. Emily was transported immediately to the nearby hospital, where surgeons were ready.

Sanderson, miraculously, was not dead. His uniform had been blown off; shrapnel had pummeled his body; his right arm had been ripped off by the blast; and one of his legs was held in place by a few shreds of skin. He was still breathing, but died within moments.

A battalion chief with the Birmingham Fire Department arrived. His name was Bob Sorrell. Sorrell realized what had happened at once. A bomb. Sorrell, along with the rest of Birmingham's Fire Departments, had been briefed on possible secondary devices at bomb sites. Sorrell immediately advised all rescue personnel in the area of the possibility of another bomb.

Meanwhile, Jermaine Hughes was doing his wash, when he heard the bomb go off. He ran to the window and watched as a cloud of smoke rose into the air. From his vantage point, Hughes saw something else that seemed funny. The people he could see were either running toward the explosion or stopped dead in their tracks, looking in the direction of the explosion. Except for one guy, who was headed in the opposite direction. The guy was white, just over six feet, of average weight and carried a backpack. He had long hair concealed under a baseball cap.

Suspicious, Hughes ran outside. He could see the guy. Hughes got in his car and drove in the guy's direction. There he was, moving rapidly up the hill on 16th Street. The guy entered an alley between two buildings. Hughes drove around the block to the other side of the alley. There he was, only something had changed – no cap, no jacket and his hair wasn't as long. The guy now sported sunglasses and carried a shopping bag instead of a backpack.

Hughes drove by the guy and then pulled over, pretending to have problems with his car. Opening the hood of his car, Hughes pretended to adjust the carb as the guy walked by.

Hughes got back in his car and followed the guy, staying well back. Twice, Hughes attempted to borrow a cell phone to call 911, but since he was black, no one would help. They probably thought he was a mugger.

Hughes lost the guy on 15th Street. He drove around for another ten minutes just in case, but it was useless. The guy was gone.

Doug Jones, the U.S. Attorney for Northern Alabama, arrived at the clinic. Lionel Wilson, a police officer, met Jones.

"What have we got?" asked Jones.

"A police officer down. He's dead. And a nurse who probably won't make it."

An agent from either the ATF or FBI came up to Jones. "We've got to move you back, there could be a secondary device." Jones moved back.

Battalion chief Bob Sorrell was finally satisfied they had found any and all victims, when some guy ran up to him and asked, "Are you in charge?"

The guy pulled out a badge and showed it to Sorrell.

"That's cute but who are you?" demanded Sorrell.

"If you're in charge here I need you to talk to my boss." The guy proffered a cell phone to Sorrell. The voice on the other end was female.

"I have just three questions," said the voice.

"Go ahead," said Sorrell.

"First, was it an explosion?"

"Yes."

"Was it an abortion clinic?"

"Yes."

"Were there injuries or fatalities, including a police officer?"

"Yes, there were."

"Thank you, we'll take it from here," said the voice.

Sorrell began to hand the phone back to the guy, when the voice on the other end said something. Sorrell put the phone back to his ear and heard the voice say, "Mr. President, did you understand that?"

Sorrell gave the guy his phone.

"That was the attorney general," said the guy. "You boys are about to be covered with feds."

* * * * *

Meanwhile, Jermaine Hughes was looking for some place to make a phone call to 911. He headed for McDonald's. After parking, he went inside and asked the manager if he could use the phone to make a 911 call. Of course, said the manager.

The 911 call went like this:

"Hello! This is really important. You know that explosion downtown?" said Hughes.

"Yes."

"I seen a guy walking from that direction and he had a wig on – and I was like, 'what was that explosion?' You know I walked outside –"

"What kind of wig?" asked the 911 operator.

"And this guy – and he was –"

"Long wig, short wig?" asked the operator.

"He had a long wig but –"

"What color?"

"The wig was like brown color. But then he took – I was following him –"

"Was he white or black?" asked the operator.

"He's, he's a white guy."

"What did he have on?"

"Say again?" asked Hughes.

"What did he have on?"

"I, oh, God, I was following him and uh, first he had on flannel or something, I'm not exactly sure –"

"You can't even remember what he had on?"

"Ma'am! Uh –" Hughes was overly excited, which was hindering his ability to think clearly.

"You cannot remember a clothing description?" asked the operator.

"No. I don't remember clothes. I'm kinda exasperated right now."

The connection went dead. Hughes called back. He glanced out the window. There he was!

"I got him! I got him!" he shouted into the phone.

"Where is he?" asked the operator.

"I got him! I think this is him!"

"Is he on foot?"

"Yes, he's on foot. He has black glasses on. He's walking into the woods toward Vulcan."

An attorney named Jeff Tickal was having breakfast at McDonald's. He was seated near the phone and could hear Hughes. Tickal looked out the window and spotted the man. Tickal began relaying a description of the man to Hughes, who polly-parroted it to the operator.

Black and green plaid shirt; jeans; brown boots. He was carrying a black backpack. The man entered the woods.

"I can't see him now," said Hughes. "I can't believe I'm standing here and there's not a cop here by now!"

"They're on the way," said the operator. "They'll be there in just a minute. Don't hang up!"

* * * * *

Tickal decided to do something. Rising, he ran outside to his car and drove around to the other side of the woods. After Tickal left, a cop car arrived. Hughes ran outside and told the cops that the man had gone into the woods. He pointed to the spot. The cops entered the woods and tried to pick up the man's trail. Hughes couldn't just stand there, so he got in is car and drove around looking for the man.

Meanwhile, Tickal was driving along Valley Avenue, looking for the guy. He decided he had missed him and turned around on a side street. Lo and behold, there on the side street he saw the guy. The guy was loading something into the bed of a Nissan truck. The guy climbed into the truck and drove off. Tickal followed behind. When the Nissan stopped at Valley Avenue, Tickal jotted the truck's license plate number on a coffee cup. North Carolina: KND1117.

The Nissan turned east on Valley Avenue and Tickal followed. The guy drove back to Twentieth Street, where he passed the McDonald's. Tickal saw the police cruiser parked and stopped to tell the cops.

At the same moment, Hughes was driving west on Valley Avenue and spotted Tickal following a Nissan truck. Hughes pulled a quick U-turn and pulled up alongside the Nissan. Hughes looked at the guy and knew it was him. Hughes slowed and fell behind the truck. He, too, wrote down the license plate number.

Then Hughes got caught up in traffic and lost the guy.

Tickal and Hughes reported the license plate number to the cops. More cops arrived and Tickal and Hughes had to repeat their tale many times over.

* * * * *

A BOLO went out: Nissan truck, plate number KND1117, along with a description of the driver. A database search revealed the truck was registered to Eric Robert Rudolph. The bomber!

Rudolph lived at 30 Allen Avenue, Asheville, North Carolina. Asheville was home to 69,000 residents; it was a gentrified small city, full of well-to-do young hipsters. Asheville had a small FBI office. Jim Russell was one of the agents. Russell got a call from the Birmingham FBI headquarters. He was to check out Eric Rudolph.

Russell drove to 30 Allen Avenue, an apartment building with the name of Skyland Heights. Russell checked in with the manager of the apartment complex. There was no Eric Rudolph living there. However, once upon a time, a Patricia Rudolph had lived there. Patricia Rudolph had listed Keith Rhodes as a contact number. Rhodes lived in Hendersonville.

Russell called the contact number. He spoke with Keith Rhodes, whose wife, Maura, was related to Eric Rudolph. Maura was Eric's sister.

* * * * *

Russell and Rhodes met in Asheville. Rhodes told Russell that Eric Rudolph was an introvert, who sometimes worked as a carpenter. No one knew where he lived.

Eric Rudolph had been born on Merritt Island, Florida. One of six children, his mother had packed up the kids and moved to Asheville after the death of her husband, Eric's dad. Eric's mother now lived in a trailer park in Florida.

Like McVeigh, Eric Rudolph had joined the army and then tried to get into Special Forces school. When he was rejected, Rudolph, disappointed, left the army. He drove a Nissan truck and Rhodes had seen him about a week ago. He'd just shown up, then left after an hour or so.

The FBI ran a preliminary background on Rudolph. The guy was a ghost, living off the grid. No credit cards, no bank account; he wasn't registered to vote, had never paid any taxes and didn't own anything other than a Nissan truck.

* * * * *

Meanwhile, back in Birmingham, bomb experts were going through the site of the explosion at the New Woman Clinic. The bomb was composed of dynamite and nails. It utilized an alarm clock and an egg timer, along with a radio receiver, which meant it had most likely been detonated remotely. In other words, this bomb was more advanced, more sophisticated, which allowed Rudolph to watch and explode the device on command.

No secondary device was located.

* * * * *

The inter-agency battle to control the case was heating up. The FBI was chomping at the bit to take command.

Another task force was created: SANDBOMB, which was tasked with the New Woman Clinic bombing. Eric Rudolph was their prime suspect, but finding him would not be easy. The task force issued a "material witness" warrant for Eric Robert Rudolph. This would allow them to arrest and hold Rudolph while they questioned him. It also gave them a viable escape plan. They couldn't prove anything yet and they didn't want another Jewell crucifixion on their hands, especially since the media was already nosing around.

* * * * *

On January 30, Jim Russell and another agent, Tom Frye, paid a visit to Randy Cochran, one of the few people that knew Eric Rudolph. Cochran answered the door and said, "I guess you're looking for Eric Rudolph."

"What makes you think that?" asked Frye.

Cochran shrugged. "It's all over the news."

Russell and Frye exchanged a look that said "WTF?"

Cochran told the agents he hadn't any contact with Rudolph recently. He thought Rudolph lived in Murphy now. Cochran and Rudolph became friends in middle school, although they weren't close friends. According to Cochran, Eric Rudolph was hard to get to know. Cochran told the agents that Rudolph was smart and liked to read, especially the Bible. Rudolph was a fundamentalist Christian, which meant women were to be submissive and people of color were to keep their place. An anti-Semitic, Rudolph believed Jewish bankers controlled world governments through money.

While Russell and Cochran talked, Frye called the Sheriff in Murphy and asked about Rudolph. The Sheriff said he'd check it out. Later, the Sheriff called and said Rudolph lived in a trailer on Caney Creek Road in Murphy.

The agents thanked Cochran and left. They drove to Murphy, where they met up with John Felton, an ATF agent. Felton and Russell donned body armor. Reaching for their assault rifles, they were ready.

Frye drove them to the end of Caney Creek Road. The agents got out and moved silently, keeping low, toward Rudolph's trailer. Even though the trailer's windows emanated light, it looked as if no one was home because the Nissan truck was absent. Russell made his way around the trailer, double-checking the area.

Rudolph's landlord was Jonathan Crisp, who rented the trailer for $250 a month. Prior to renting the trailer, Rudolph had rented a house from Susan Roper for $500 a month. Susan Roper described Rudolph, who she knew as "Bob Randolph," as quiet and well-mannered, if perhaps a little bit strange.

Then the FBI got a call from the proprietor of Cal's Mini Storage, Cal Stiles. Stiles told the FBI that Rudolph rented a storage unit. The FBI checked it out, dispatching a K-9 unit with a bomb sniffing dog to the mini storage. The dog smelled explosives outside Rudolph's storage unit. This was sufficient evidence to allow the FBI to obtain a search warrant.

Bomb techs searched the unit for booby traps. Once the area was determined to be clear, the storage unit was opened and a team of forensic techs entered. The place was full of stuff: grow lights, fertilizer, pipes, nails, Rudolph's personal documents (passport, discharge papers, birth certificate), along with a lot of books. Many of the books were about white supremacism.

Next, the agents obtained a search warrant for the trailer on Caney Creek Road. Again, bomb techs cleared the trailer, then the bomb sniffing dog was brought in. The dog – again – smelled explosives. Evidence was gathered and taken to the FBI lab, where it was tested.

The trailer was full of the usual stuff used for living: food, clothes, etc. And a fully loaded H&K 9mm pistol. All the windows in the trailer were obscured by black plastic. In the bedroom, techs discovered an empty rifle case, along with three more pistols, a shotgun and two hunting rifles. Rudolph either liked guns or felt he had need of them for some reason. More books, mostly history books were found in the bedroom. And a Bible, of course.

The Bible, in particular was interesting. Rudolph had annotated the pages in many places. Rudolph had written "Twin Birth two seed lines" near the passages that spoke of Cain and Abel. This indicated Rudolph believed in the dogma promulgated by the Church of Christian Identity. The two seed lines were the white race and the so-called "mud people," i.e. people of color.

There were explicit references in Rudolph's Bible to his homophobia. Eric despised homosexuals, believed they were an abomination and should be killed as a matter of course. Rudolph's homophobia may have stemmed from his recognition of similar feelings toward other men. In other words, Rudolph may have been a latent homosexual. In reality, his sexual proclivity was not the issue, except perhaps to Eric himself. If he had such feelings and recognized them, he was most likely disgusted with himself. Self-repugnance may have indirectly motivated self-destruction.

Most importantly, Rudolph had rubricated Numbers 25, which relates the story of Phineas. Eric Rudolph perceived himself as a Phineas Priest. He was picking up where Phineas and others, like McVeigh, had left off. In his own mind, Eric Rudolph was standing on the shoulders of giants. In effect, he was killing the enemies of God. He was on a mission from God. And the mission was not only "from" God, but was blessed by God.

* * * * *

February 2: Reuters and the *Atlanta Journal-Constitution* received more letters from the bomber, now assumed to be Eric Robert Rudolph by the FBI, although the agency was still standing by the "material witness" narrative.

The handwriting was the same, along with the block lettering. And the grammar and syntax were still deplorable, whether through ignorance or deliberately. Since Rudolph was an intelligent and well-read individual, the errors were probably deliberate. Still, some geniuses were notoriously poor spellers.

The letters went like this:

"The bombing in Birmingham was carried out by The Army of God. Let those who work in the murder mill's around the nation be warned once more – you will be targeted without quarter – you are not immune from retaliation. Your commisar's in Washington can't protect you! With the distribution of the genocidal pill RU-486 it is hoped the resistance will end. We will target anyone who manufactures, market, sells and distrobtes the pill. Death to the New World Order," followed by the code number used in the first letters: 4 1 9 9 3.

The return address on the letters was the street address of the New Woman All Women Clinic; the sender's name was A.O.G. – Army of God.

Analysis of the letters revealed nothing: no prints, no DNA traces. Operating on the assumption that Rudolph was the bomber, the bombing became a federal matter because Rudolph had crossed state lines in the commission of his crimes – from Georgia to North Carolina. Nevertheless, Georgia could indict the bomber on murder, if so inclined.

* * * * *

Eight days later, two local yokels were out coon hunting near Murphy, when they saw something that caught their attention. The headlights on their truck reflected back off another vehicle. The checked it out. It turned out to be a Nissan truck parked halfway in the forest – KND1117.

The two coon hunters called it in to the Sheriff, who called it in to the feds, who sent out an ATF agent, C.J. Hyman. Hyman put together a group of agents to check it out. A baker's dozen set off to the location of the Nissan truck. All the agents wore body armor and carried automatic weapons. Hyman wasn't taking any chances.

Hyman and three others moved carefully to the Nissan, and peered in. Nothing. No Eric Rudolph.

By the following morning, Hyman had obtained a search warrant for the Nissan. Per the established standard operating procedure, bomb techs first cleared the area. The bomb techs attached ropes to the Nissan's door handles and hood. Tugging the ropes, the techs opened the doors and the hood, checking for booby traps. The Nissan was then loaded on a tow truck and transported to Murphy to be examined.

Somehow the media got wind of the Nissan and showed up in Murphy. It was a circus. Mobile broadcast vans, reporters with microphones and cameramen were everywhere, talking to everyone.

Examination of the truck revealed traces of dynamite, Rudolph's prints, a folding shovel, electrical wiring, a metal swastika, condoms, and music tapes, along with a video of Rudolph washing dishes. There were also receipts from Plaza Video, where Rudolph rented movies, and grocery receipts.

It became apparent that somehow Rudolph was aware the FBI considered him a "material witness" and the manhunt was already in progress. According to his receipts, Rudolph had split, stopping at Burger King for a meal and then purchasing supplies at a local grocery store: oatmeal, raisins, tuna, green beans, peanuts, soap and batteries.

The conclusion was that Rudolph was on the run.

Media coverage of the hunt for Eric Rudolph hit the airwaves. The media played it up in spectacular fashion, showing footage of agents dressed in body armor, carrying heavy weapons scouring the countryside. To television viewers, it looked like Nazi Germany.

Bloodhounds were brought in to track Rudolph. Footage of the hounds in action reminded viewers of Hollywood movies: *Cool Hand*

Luke and *Nevada Smith*. Teams of dogs were displayed on TV, foaming at the mouth, hunting down a hapless escapee. In the end, the bloodhounds were useless. They couldn't pick up Rudolph's trail.

So far, the media's portrayal of law enforcement was not awe-inspiring or comforting. The feds appeared to be out of control and confused, running around like chickens with their heads cut off, looking for a "material witness" that may or may not have been the bomber. The phrase "bad PR" didn't begin to cover it.

It got so bad that the media began following investigators from site to site. As soon as the investigators left, the media pounced on those who had been contacted by the agents. The media interviewed everybody who might know the smallest detail. It was total chaos.

Agents interviewed Rudolph's family members, his brothers and sister. Then two agents were sent to Florida to interview Patricia Rudolph, Eric's mother. She lived in a trailer park in Bradenton, Florida. When the agents showed up, it was late in the evening. Patricia told them to go away; it was bedtime. The agents left, returning the next morning. Upon their return, they discovered a truck with North Carolina plates in her driveway.

The agents over-reacted and really screwed up. They called for a SWAT team. The goon squad kicked in her door and entered the trailer with guns waving. Patricia was sitting in her front room. She watched as they ransacked her trailer, looking for something, anything.

The truck did not belong to Eric.

After the invasion of her home by armed men, Patricia refused to speak with the FBI.

The media began reporting that Rudolph was connected to the Aryan Nations in Idaho, and that Rudolph had been part of a Christian Identity church – the Church of Israel – in Missouri.

Meanwhile, Patricia Rudolph moved to Charleston, South Carolina, which was where her son Daniel lived. The FBI kept Daniel's house under surveillance. And the media surrounded his house, pestering him at all hours for interviews. Daniel and his mother lawyered up. Their attorney, James Bell, held a news conference in which he stated that Eric Rudolph was "innocent" and was being hunted merely because he was "deeply religious."

America's Most Wanted (AMW) couldn't pass up the spectacle. A crew from the TV show arrived and filmed an episode. Even though the show was applauded by some for helping to solve crimes, in reality, the program was extremely exploitative. AMW made money off crime, criminals and their victims.

* * * * *

Jim Russell and Tom Frye arranged to meet and speak with Thomas Branham, who supposedly knew Eric Rudolph. Branham lived outside Topton, North Carolina. Branham showed up with a tape recorder to record the interview, just for protection.

Branham told the agents he hadn't seen Eric since 1996. Years before, when Eric's dad got cancer, Eric had lived with Branham for months. Branham was an ultra-conservative fundamentalist Christian, but he maintained that Eric had no interest in any of that. According to Branham, Eric thought for himself. He didn't allow others to influence him.

After his father's death, Eric's mother moved the family around. Eric dropped out of high school, but later finished by getting his GED. After dropping out of college, Eric joined the army, where hoped to become a member of an elite military unit.

While in the army, Eric received SERE (search, escape, reconnaissance, survival) training. Part of his training included booby traps, explosives and shaped explosive devices.

Rudolph, although religious, drank beer and smoked dope while in the army. He loved Hitler and the Nazis, and preached incessantly to anyone that would listen about the Jewish conspiracy. One year after joining the army, at the age of 21, Eric began dating Claire Forrestor, a high school student. She was blond and looked Aryan, according to Eric. When on leave, Claire helped Eric tend his marijuana, which he planted in the woods.

Eric discovered he didn't like the army. He hated taking orders and hated the U.S. government. In the end, he deliberately failed a drug test so he would be discharged.

Once out of the army, Eric focused on his marijuana plants. He sold his product in Nashville. The fact that Eric was a drug dealer surprised the FBI, because it didn't fit the profile. And most interesting, FBI agents learned that Eric was an avid model airplane builder, the kind with engines that flew via remote control.

Eric was successful as a marijuana dealer, making between $70,000 and $100,000 per year.

* * * * *

On March 9, 1998, Eric Rudolph was officially charged with murder. A federal warrant for his arrest was released. The reward for his arrest and conviction was $100,000.

Profilers from the FBI, officially known as the Behavioral Analysis Unit, arrived in Birmingham: Tom Neer and Ron Tunkel. The agents looked like caricatures of Abbott and Costello. Neer was tall and thin; Tunkel was short and plump.

Upon their arrival in Birmingham, the two agents went to work, visiting the bomb site. They located the spot where Rudolph was suspected of having stood prior to detonating the bomb. They walked his supposed route away from the clinic. Finally, they visited the other abortion clinics in Birmingham to understand why Rudolph had selected New Woman clinic. Based on the sites and the settings of the other clinics, the profilers concluded that Rudolph needed to see his bomb go off; see the damage inflicted; see people die.

In other words, Eric Rudolph, according to the profilers, was self-righteous, narcissistic, sadistic, and, like Adam and Eve in the Garden of Eden, believed "Ye shall be as gods." And what do gods do? They judge and, most importantly, they dispense punishment.

* * * * *

The FBI formally recognized psychological profiling around 1970; and by 1975 profiling was taught at Quantico. The FBI categorized the behaviors associated with criminals and used them to aid in the identification of criminal acts. The problem with Rudolph was he was a bomber and the FBI didn't have any concrete information compiled on the behavioral aspects of bombers.

According to FBI profilers, statistically speaking, bombers were around 30 years of age, heterosexual, smart and came from nuclear families where the father figure bailed out of the marriage prior to the bomber graduating high school. The problem was that the statistics were based on a very small sample.

Fortunately, Neer and Tunkel knew this and didn't consider themselves infallible experts. In fact, Neer and Tunkel focused less on Rudolph's psychological profile and more on pattern recognition. They wanted to predict his actions, not simply explain them.

Based on the information available in the SANDBOMB case, the forensic analyses, the victims and interviews, Neer and Tunkel concluded that Rudolph was not an impulsive nutcase with an axe to grind. Rudolph was just the opposite: an architect of bombings who enjoyed blowing up people and buildings. Rudolph's approach was premeditated, systematic and deliberate.

The fact that Rudolph maintained he was part of the nebulous Army of God was nothing more than a convenient label Rudolph employed to justify his murderous activities. He truly believed he was carrying out God's will by killing the enemies of God, but he was not part of any organized or disorganized group. Rudolph was a Phineas Priest, pure and simple.

Neer and Tunkel's final conclusion was that Rudolph's methodical behaviors "suggest more than ideological needs were being met by this act. Needs of which the offender may not even be aware. These need are internal and speak of degrees of anger and pride that have been found in other offenders who use explosives for evil intent. Anti-government, anti-abortion, anti-homosexuality, anti-technology, etc., were simply convenient positions for them to take in order to meet deeper needs."

This conclusion brought up a pregnant question. What deeper needs was Rudolph satisfying? Power, control, some sort of sexual gratification? Or was it merely revenge and the certain misguided belief that he was doing God's work?

* * * * *

Forensics analysts determined all the supplies necessary to build Rudolph's bombs had been purchased at the WalMart in Murphy; everything but the detonators and dynamite. Analysts also determined the nails used in the Sandy Springs bombing came from the batch of nails in Rudolph's storage unit at Cal's Mini Storage. And the analysts were fairly certain that the steel plates utilized in Rudolph's bombs had been stole from the machine shop where Randy Cochran worked. Cochran admitted that Rudolph had visited him at work.

FBI agents, after going through a multitude of money order receipts, determined Rudolph had purchased two books from Loompanics Unlimited: *Kitchen Improvised Fertilizer Explosives*; and *Ragnar's Homemade Detonators*. Both books were purchased under the pseudonym of Z. Randolph.

* * * * *

While all this was taking place, Theodore Kaczynski – the Unabomber – was making headlines across the U.S. He had been arrested in 1996, after his brother dropped a dime on him. The FBI located Kaczynski in Montana, living in a cabin. Kaczynski was, of course, mentally ill. However, he was highly intelligent and managed to continue his bombing spree for eighteen years. Kaczynski's justification for his bombings was the evils of technology. He was little more than a vicious, deranged Luddite.

The FBI agent responsible for Kaczynski's capture was Terry Turchie. In 1998, Turchie was assigned to the San Francisco FBI office. His boss told him that his presence was required in Atlanta, where he was to look into the Atlanta bombing.

When Turchie arrived in Atlanta, the Director of the FBI, Louis Freeh, decided to shake thing up in the Rudolph case. Freeh mobilized more agents, putting them on the case and he put Terry Turchie in charge of the whole kit and caboodle.

* * * * *

The ATF, when they heard about the changes, was pissed beyond belief. They complained all the way to the top. In the end, because of the louds screaming and bitching, SANDBOMB was excluded from Turchie's control. Both groups were nominally under the newly designated Southeast Bomb Task Force, but SANDBOMB would do their own thing.

Turchie's role changed again. Now he was in charge of the group tasked with finding and arresting Rudolph. "In charge" was a moot term; in fact, Turchie, along with the ATF's Don Bell, were co-commanders. The ATF insisted they not be shoved aside. It was inter-agency politics at its worst.

Fortunately, Bell and Turchie decided they could work together. Turchie didn't have the usual arrogant outlook prevalent among most of the FBI. Turchie said to Bell, "Don't worry. We're in charge and we'll work this out together."

Under Bell and Turchie the manhunt changed complexion: agents pulled longer stints on the case rather than rotating out. And Turchie, along with Bell, decided a low-profile was preferable to a high-profile. Agents stopped wearing body armor and strutting around with assault rifles. In effect, it was the same technique the U.S. Army used in Viet Nam: win the hearts and minds of the citizenry, who perceived their presence as a form a Big Brother police state.

The most telling change Turchie and Bell made was to include local law enforcement agencies in the manhunt.

* * * * *

Those who dwell in the mountains of North Carolina were suspicious of outsiders. And doubly suspicious of outsiders associated with the U.S. government. Agents of the U.S. government were viewed as revenuers, out to arrest people for fun and to demonstrate their power over the general populace. In other word, the FBI and ATF agents had their work cut out for them. The locals were more likely to help Rudolph than turn him in.

* * * * *

The FBI's coordinator, Woody Enderson, who oversaw all the task forces from his office in Atlanta, believed the best way to catch Rudolph was to contract the search perimeter as rapidly as possible, while Turchie's methodology relied on encirclement – make sure Rudolph was contained, and then slowly close the circle. Enderson felt his method precluded anyone aiding and abetting Rudolph in his escape. And to make sure that the locals would think twice before aiding Rudolph, Enderson requested the reward for Rudolph's capture and conviction be increased.

The bounty on Rudolph's head went to $1,000,000. In addition, Rudolph now occupied the FBI's vaunted Ten Most Wanted list.

* * * * *

Pat Curry, the head of the homicide unit of the Birmingham Police Department, couldn't figure out why the FBI did not re-approach Patricia Rudolph, Eric's mother. Curry knew that the FBI had botched its first attempt by allowing a goon squad to go busting into her home and waving guns around, scaring the poor woman to death, simultaneously souring her on the FBI and its tendency to overreact. What he didn't understand was why they didn't try a more diplomatic approach. Apologize and tell her they screwed up. Ask for forgiveness and explain that their goal was to apprehend Eric, not kill him.

Curry's take on the manhunt went like this: "It was a monumental effort," he explained. "Anything we wanted in terms of materials, we got. The sure had deep pockets. If the FBI runs out of money, they just print some more."

Curry wanted the FBI to allow local law enforcement to sit down with Patricia Rudolph and simply talk to her like a human being. But the FBI was a monolithic bureaucracy that moved at a glacial pace. Efficiency was not part of the FBI's playbook.

Curry said, "It was like pulling out eyeteeth to get Washington to allow us to go talk to Rudolph's mother. The FBI didn't so much try to prevent the meeting, but they lawyer everything to death."

Finally, though, permission was granted. The FBI gave the okay for Charles Stone, an FBI agent, to talk with Patricia. But Patricia would not have anything to do with the feds. To get around this problem, Stone asked Curry to ride along,

Curry said, "I figured I was window dressing."

Stone and Curry arranged to meet with Patricia at a restaurant in Tampa, Florida. Patricia surprised the cops by not arriving with an attorney in tow. Instead, it was just her and Daniel, one of Eric's brothers.

Patricia Rudolph astonished Curry with her attitude. "She was very matter-of-fact," said Curry. "She told us, 'I raise my children to think for themselves. And if my son wants to come in, that's up to him.'"

Her words left Curry flabbergasted.

* * * * *

Because of the $1,000,000 bounty, Eric Rudolph sightings increased. Everyone claimed they had seen him. Supposedly someone saw Rudolph in Mexico, where he was lounging on the beach. Other sightings were reported as far away as Viet Nam and Ireland. And of course, the FBI followed up on all the sightings, sending agents gallivanting around the world, just in case.

But Eric wasn't in Viet Nam or Mexico or Ireland. In fact, he was camping in the mountains near Topton. In a sense, he was lounging on the beach. The only thing he really did was use his binoculars to surveil the surrounding area. The only problem confronting Eric was dwindling food. He needed help, but was aware of the $1,000,000 bounty, which meant he couldn't trust most people. Most of the people he knew would sell their souls to the "Devil" for that kind of money. They'd shoot him dead and then ask when the money would arrive.

Except George Nordmann.

Nordmann owned a health food store in nearby Andrews, North Carolina. Father of eight kids, Nordmann was old and thin and a committed Catholic. Nordmann favored the Tridentine Mass, not the new-fangled litany that passed for Catholicism in the modern world. A holocaust denier, he believed in his heart that the Illuminati conspiracy was real. According to Nordmann, the Illuminati ran the world from behind the curtain, like the Wizard of Oz.

Moreover, Nordmann believed that the Catholic Church, with all its liberal conveniences, was bringing the world to the "night of screams," as predicted by the visions at San Sebastian de Garabandal, on the Gulf of Biscay. In the second vision, the Virgin Mary appeared to the visionaries, showing them scenes of a great Tribulation that would descend upon the world when the Catholic Church had succumbed to worldly blandishments and was beyond redemption.

God would punish the world horribly. All technological devices would cease to operate, along with all types of machinery. Intense heat would encompass the world, evaporating all water. Rivers would vaporize, and the seas and oceans would boil. Soon flames would engulf the world and everyone, every man, woman and child would expire in the conflagration.

Nordmann believed the world was on the brink of the "night of screams." The Justice of God would implement what the Righteousness of God demanded.

Nordmann knew Eric, but didn't much care for him.

* * * * *

On July 7, 1998 Nordmann was driving up to his house, an old, dilapidated structure in the woods outside Andrews, when he spotted a figure waiting by a tree. Even though the man had a big beard, Nordmann knew who it was.

"What are you doing here?" asked Nordmann. Glancing around, Nordmann said, "You'd better get out of here."

"Why?" asked Rudolph. "I know there's no law around here. I've been watching you for a month."

"George," said Rudolph, "I need you to get some things for me."

"No. I don't want anything to do with you," replied Nordmann.

But his rejection fell on deaf ears. The two talked for thirty minutes. Rudolph claimed he was innocent, that the Feds were setting him up as a patsy. He needed food. And he had money.

Nordmann finally said he would help. Rudolph gave Nordmann a list: food, batteries, a tarp and rosary beads. And oh yeah, Rudolph wanted to use Normann's car.

Rudolph left, carrying the meager food that Nordmann gave him.

* * * * *

The next morning, Nordmann went to see Kenneth "Kenny" Cope, a deputy sheriff.

"Kenny, I might be in trouble," said Nordmann.

"What do you mean, you might be in trouble?" asked Cope.

"Someone stole my truck."

Nordmann's truck was as old as Moses; it couldn't have been worth more than a few hundred dollars on the open market, if that. Cope wondered why anyone would bother stealing such an old beater. Any car thief worth his salt would avoid it like the plague.

"No, you don't understand," said Nordmann. "Someone stole my truck and I know who it is."

"Well, why does that make you in trouble, George?"

"Because it was Eric Rudolph."

Nordmann was selling Eric Rudolph down the river. He had agreed to let Rudolph use his truck. Now he was playing the role of Judas.

Initially, Cope didn't believe what Nordmann was saying. The old coot had finally gone off the deep end.

But the old coot was scared to death. So Cope asked Nordmann to explain what was going on. Nordmann told his tale, explaining that his truck was missing and that food had been stolen from inside his house. Rudolph had left $500 and a note on Nordmann's table.

"But it can't get very far, Kenny," explained Nordmann. "The lights don't work and the radiator overheats. It won't make it more than six or eight miles."

"Okay, stop right there," said Cope.

Cope immediately got on the phone. First, he called his boss, Sheriff Holbrook. Then he called Danny Sindall of the FBI. Sindall immediately called Turchie. Turchie arrived at Cope's house shortly thereafter. Nordmann repeated his tale for Turchie.

Turchie wanted to visit Nordmann's place and check it out. He asked Nordmann if that would be okay. Nordmann said yes.

Over at Nordmann's place, Turchie looked around then called Woody Enderson in Atlanta. He told Enderson what was going on and suggested that they ramp up the manhunt. After talking to Enderson, Turchie called Joel Moss, one of his FBI agents. Turchie charged Moss with questioning Nordmann. Moss excelled at interviewing people. He was smooth, patient and didn't get in people's faces.

Under Moss' probing, Nordmann it became clear that Nordmann's original story wasn't true. The truth finally came out. Nordmann knew a heck of a lot more.

Rudolph, according to Nordmann, had questioned Nordmann in depth about the FBI, specifically where their command headquarter were in Andrews. And Rudolph had taken great pains to inform Nordmann that his hidey-hole was not near Topton. In fact, it was a great distance from Topton.

In all, Nordmann told the FBI three different tales. The truth was sprinkled liberally throughout all three. The variable details were designed to exculpate Nordmann. The old man was trying to protect himself, which Moss understood. In effect, Nordmann was scared. He was scared of Rudolph and what the man was capable of, and he was scared of the FBI. The fact that he agreed to speak to the FBI meant he had decided the FBI was the lesser of the two evils.

* * * * *

Meanwhile, a group of teenagers were out blasting around on Quads and came across a campsite. They reported the campsite to the feds, who immediately checked it out, where forensic analysts were able to lift a print from Rudolph.

Then the Forest Service came across an abandoned truck in the Nantahala Forest. It was Nordmann's beater. Forensic teams discovered traces of dynamite on the truck's steering wheel.

* * * * *

Two days later, the FBI issued a press release, stating that Eric Rudolph was in the Topton area. They had an eye-witness. The news attracted the media like ants to sugar. News trucks, reporters and cameramen swarmed the area. All motels and hotels were booked solid. And parking spaces were all but impossible to find.

The media wasn't the only group to descend on the area. The FBI mobilized and sent waves of agents and equipment to Nantahala Forest, erecting a city of tents almost overnight. K-9 tracking units were called in. FBI helicopters buzzed the sky above. The atmosphere was almost circus-like, except for the fact that the FBI meant business. As far as they were concerned, this was serious stuff.

Because he was familiar with the area, Kenny Cope was included in the tracking unit. They picked up Rudolph's trail at the abandoned Nordmann truck's location. According to Cope, "We got behind Eric's tracks at the truck, and we stayed on it, and stayed on it. We were finding footprints, his footprints. He went right back up the road to Tusquitee Gap. We stayed on it until the track went from walking to running, that's how close we got to him."

They lost the track. Rudolph, almost magically, disappeared.

Two hundred FBI agents were on-scene, with about half of them humping through the mountains at any given time. Turchie put the ATF's C.J. Hyman in charge of the search units. Each search unit contained FBI SWAT members.

Motion detectors and cameras were placed throughout the woods, along with food and water; it was like putting peanut butter on a rat trap.

Two mobile crime labs were established: one at tent city and another at the nearby National Guard Armory. The search teams collected anything and everything in the forest. The crime labs processed literally tons of garbage, seeking evidence of Rudolph. They found nothing.

*****

The manhunt dragged on, from days to weeks. During this time, Rudolph's legend and mystique burgeoned. He was the consummate anti-hero, the man who continued to escape the clutches of an army of federal agents.

Rudolph's growing fame pissed off the FBI, but it attracted the semi-famous, like Randy Weaver, who arrived with bounty hunter Bo Gritz, who was seeking notoriety. Gritz had a talk-radio show he was trying to boost in ratings. The show was named Freedom Call, and catered to right wing nutcases. In effect, Gritz hoped to catch a ride on Rudolph's coat tails.

Gritz and Weaver had a 100-man contingent along with them. Supposedly, the group was going to locate and capture Rudolph. It was ridiculous. Gritz and his group tramped through the woods for a week, then bailed.

Shortly after Gritz's group left, Eric Rudolph was named as the bomber of the Centennial Olympic Park. He was officially charged with the crime of bombing the Park and with murder at the venue.

As Fall turned into Winter, the FBI continued its manhunt.

Then in March 1999, a bomb exploded outside the Femcare Clinic in Asheville. The bomb did little damage and was not as sophisticated as those employed by Rudolph. The FBI concluded it was not Eric Rudolph. At the same time, the FBI presence in the area was halved to 100 agents. The cost of maintaining an army in the area was simply too expensive.

As time passed, the media lost interest in the story. Nothing was happening. The media had more spectacular news to cover. By 2000, the manhunt was all but called off. A few agents remained in the area, but search efforts had virtually halted.

*****

Eric Rudolph was out there, camped at Fires Creek. The campsite reported by the teenagers on Quads was a ruse. Rudolph wasn't camped there. But he did leave his prints there and make the site look as if he had.

Rudolph had a radio that he used to listen to reports about the ongoing manhunt. FBI helicopters passed above him frequently. He was certain they were using infrared radar to try and locate his heat signature.

When he heard them overhead, he disguised his heat signature, hiding under rocks.

Hypothermia was a problem, but he conquered the problem using leaves as insulation from the cold. Other than a wrenched knee that left him with a limp for a while, he remained in perfect health. Hunters and black bears were a nagging problem. He never knew when hunters might show up unexpectedly, whereas the black bears were inveterate foragers, able to smell out food anywhere.

In 1999, Rudolph moved from Fires Creek to a campsite about a mile from Murphy. It was up high, providing him with a great view of the small town. He stole food from the town's inhabitants and, taking a trick from the black bears, rummaged through the dumpsters at McDonald's, where he found plenty of half-eaten burgers and French fries.

A hardcore nicotine whore, Rudolph loved cigarettes. He stole them when he could, and when he couldn't he became a 'snipe-hunter,' picking up used, half-smoked cigarettes.

Rudolph stole two tons of grain from some grain silos. To transport the grain, he stole a truck that ran out of gas. Deputy sheriffs gave the fugitive a lift to the nearest gas station and then took him back to his vehicle.

Then he made a mistake. A bad one. He had more than enough food stored up, but against his better judgment, decided to make one more run into town for food. He was walking through an alley, when out of nowhere a patrol car bolted into the alley. For just an instant, he contemplated fleeing. But he didn't. Eric Rudolph was worn out; tired of living off the land, scrounging for food, snipe-hunting for used butts and freezing through the long winter nights.

Instead of fleeing, he elected to surrender.

* * * * *

The capture of Eric Rudolph happened like this.

It was May 30, 2003. Eric had been living in the mountains for five years. That night, he was dressed in black. He made his way into Murphy, where he waited behind a strip mall. He knew the cop's patrol routine by heart. He was waiting for the patrol car to make its rounds.

Around 3:30 a.m., Jeff Postell drove through the alley behind the strip mall. Postell, a rookie on the police force was just old enough to legally drink alcohol. Turning the police cruiser into the strip mall's parking lot, Postell turned off his headlights and turned around for another pass through the alley. This was one of his tactics for catching thieves, burglars and drunks.

It worked! He saw someone running through the alley. And the guy had what looked like a rifle with him. Surprised at seeing the lightless car, the man took refuge behind some crates. Postell switched on his lights and called for help on the police radio. Postell stopped his cruiser and jumped out with his gun in hand.

"Come out! Put your hands where I can see 'em!" Just like in the movies. The guy stepped out.

"Okay," ordered Postell, "drop to your knees. Now down on the ground. Arms out. Cross your feet."

Once the guy was down, Postell walked over and put handcuffs on him. Postell's call for help resulted in the rapid appearance of three more police cars, which arrived with sirens wailing and rack lights flashing.

Four policemen stood over the prostrate figure. Postell asked the standard questions. Name, why are you here and where did you come from?

Eric replied that his name was "Jerry Wilson," a homeless vagrant. The object that Postell imagined was a rifle was a long flashlight.

One of the other cops kept staring at the guy. Finally, something clicked and he told the other cops, "This looks like Eric Rudolph."

Postell had heard the name, but he'd been in high school when the furor over Eric Rudolph was making headlines. Mr. Wilson was put in the back of Postell's cruiser, which Postell drove to the jail house, followed by the other cruisers.

Once they had Mr. Wilson inside the jail, they began a perfunctory interrogation. Mostly, they were curious. One cop asked, "Just tell us who you really are."

Mr. Wilson laughed. Postell described the laugh as "the coldest laugh I ever heard."

"I'm Eric Rudolph," said Mr. Wilson. "You got me."

* * * * *

The capture of Eric Rudolph was, of course, big news. And like most big news, it was everywhere simultaneously.

The police chief in Murphy, Mark Thigpen, immediately contacted the North Carolina State Bureau of Investigation, which immediately contacted the high muckety-mucks. Sheriff Lovin contacted the FBI in Asheville.

"I'm 99 percent sure it's Rudolph," said Lovin on the phone. "If it was Easter, I'd have your prize egg."

Asheville contacted Jim Russell and informed him Rudolph had been captured and was sitting in the Cherokee County Jail.

156

"That's crazy," blurted out Russell, who was certain Rudolph had died of exposure or fallen off a cliff or been eaten by a bear.

CNN picked up on the story and blasted it over the airwaves.

After the news broke, every FBI agent in the southeastern part of the U.S. converged on the small town of Murphy. The former Southeast Bomb Task Force set up headquarters in the fire station, which was across the street from the jail. Since Rudolph had been captured by the local sheriffs, and was now residing in the county jail, the ball was in the Sheriff's court.

A deputy was in Rudolph's cell at all times, with two deputies stationed just outside. Per the Sheriff's orders, none of the deputies were allowed to interrogate Rudolph. If Rudolph spoke to them, they could reply. But no questions.

On his part, Rudolph was in one sense relieved. He rested and requested lots of vegetables and fruits to eat. He ate like a pig, stuffing himself with good food.

Rudolph requested a lawyer. He was informed he would receive a lawyer when he arrived in federal court. He had been Mirandized on his first morning in jail. Rudolph elected to remain silent. The Sheriff replied that was okay with him because it was his right to do so. However, added the Sheriff, he didn't want anyone stumbling across Rudolph's camp and accidentally setting off a bomb.

Since Rudolph didn't want to harm innocents, he provided the Sheriff with a map. Rudolph emphasized the camps – Fires Creek and the outside of town – contained no explosives. But there were weapons.

Two agents and a veteran guide from the Resource Commission were dispatched to locate the camps. The first camp, outside Murphy, was easily located. The second camp, at Fires Creek, was 12 miles away. The Fires Creek camp was harder to get to, located at the top of an extremely steep hillside. Everything at both sites was soon collected and analyzed by forensic techs. There were no traces of explosives at either site.

Eventually, Rudolph opened up to the deputies guarding him, telling stories of how he survived in the woods so long. Even Sheriff Keith Lovin found himself beguiled by Rudolph's charm and intelligence. The two men – sheriff and outlaw – had long discussions about religion, politics and the Civil War, which was a favorite topic of Rudolph's.

Rudolph talked because he was starved for human conversation and companionship. Rudolph was opinionated: he was a hardcore conservative, despised liberalism, hated Jews because they controlled the banks and the media; he didn't approve of miscegenation or gays. Rudolph also maintained the belief that there was no solid evidence he was a bomber. But he was realistic about it. He maintained that the prosecutors would make sure he was found guilty, by hook or by crook.

When he topic of abortion was broached, Rudolph's visage transformed from a good old boy into some kind of demon. Abortion, to Eric Rudolph, was the sin of sins, from which there was no salvation. Abortionists deserved to die, according to Rudolph.

Deputy Crisp was talking with Rudolph in his cell one day, when Rudolph went off on the media's characterization of him.

"They paint me like a terrorist! But that other bomber –" Rudolph couldn't recall the guy's name.

"Tim McVeigh?" asked Crisp.

"No, no the other one, the one that mailed his bombs."

"You mean Kaczynski?"

"Yeah that's the one! He was just a misunderstood intellectual environmentalist according to the media. But they labeled McVeigh a terrorist."

Rudolph paused.

"Of course, the FBI and the media will put their spin on things. The world only hears one side of the story."

"Maybe this would be a good chance for you to tell your side of things," said Crisp.

"I think I'll want a lawyer before I do that. In fact, I'd like an attorney right now if it's possible."

Enter Sean Devereaux, who immediately told Rudolph to keep his mouth shut. No statements of any type.

Devereaux, an attorney, hailed from Asheville. He would only handle Rudolph's case until Rudolph made his initial appearance in federal court. Where any subsequent court appearances would take place was anybody's guess. The problem was the same as during the manhunt: everybody wanted the glory. Birmingham wanted the case, and so did Atlanta. And neither would hear anything otherwise.

Birmingham won round one of the battle. They would try him first. Then Atlanta would get a shot at him.

Rudolph appeared in federal court in Asheville. Then he was immediately transported by helicopter to Birmingham, where he was booked into the Jefferson County Jail. Rudolph was placed in PC (protective custody); his cell, which was 8 feet by 10 feet, was the only occupied cell on that block of cells. At least it wasn't the Hole. They weren't taking any chances.

Rudolph was a "red man," which meant he wore red-colored jail clothing. A red man was recognized as either in danger or dangerous. In other words, Rudolph was violent and capable of mayhem.

Ironically, Rudolph's primary CO (correction officer) was a deputy sheriff, one Cedric Cole, who was African-American. Even more ironically, Rudolph's attorney was a Jew, Richard Jaffe. Jaffe, a respected death penalty attorney, was a bulldog who relished what he did. Jaffe knew what he was getting into by agreeing to defend Rudolph. Death penalty cases became all-consuming, requiring a massive commitment of time and resources.

Defending Eric Rudolph was the chance of a lifetime for any criminal attorney.

Rudolph met Jaffe on the day of his arraignment in federal court. Bill Bowen played Sancho to Jaffe's Don Quixote, meaning that Bowen drafted and filed motions with the court, while Jaffe did his thing in the courtroom.

After shaking Rudolph's hand, Jaffe took it upon himself to immediately inform Rudolph that he had been appointed as his attorney and that he was a Jew.

"Why are you telling me that?" asked Rudolph. "Why would it matter?"

"Well," replied Jaffe, "I thought you needed to know my beliefs. And if you have any reservations about me, it's plenty early enough for another competent lawyer to take over."

In his present predicament, Rudolph didn't care about Jew or non-Jew. The only think Eric wanted to know was this: was Jaffe any good? Eric was also very interested in why Jaffe did what he did.

Jaffe told Eric about his experience in death penalty cases, explaining that his only goal was to save Rudolph's life.

Rudolph finally got around to asking the $64,000 question: "If you knew someone was guilty, how could you defend them?"

Jaffe's reply went like this: "I think there are multiple answers," including the fact that Jaffe felt the death penalty was tantamount to legalized murder. Jaffe also believed people changed, and that redemption was available to all God's creatures.

The two hit it off, at least enough for Rudolph to acquiesce to Jaffe's role as his defense attorney.

* * * * *

The courthouse, where the arraignment would be held, was ten blocks from the jail. Rudolph was searched and shackled, then transported to the courthouse. The courthouse, as expected, was packed to the rafters with spectators, including the media and law enforcement officers. Everyone wanted to see the Rudolph Show.

Rudolph was escorted in by U.S. Marshals. His handcuffs had been removed, but not the ankle shackles. Eric took a chair between Bowen and Jaffe. Tension and anticipation crackled through the air like electricity.

Chief U.S. Magistrate Michael Putnam walked in and everyone rose in respect. Once he sat down, Putnam recited the charges against Rudolph. Putnam then asked Rudolph how he wanted to plea.

"Yes," said Eric. "I enter a plea of not guilty."

Putnam set the date for the trial: August 4. Putnam and all the other court officers knew the trial would not begin on that date. Setting a date was a mere formality. Jaffe and Bowen would undoubtedly request a continuance, which would be granted without a second thought. Death penalty cases took forever, as they should. A man's life was at stake.

Eric was escorted out and transported back to jail by the U.S. Marshals.

Outside the courthouse, Jaffe made his appearance before the media. This was a conventional tactic. Both prosecutors and defense attorneys wanted the opportunity to present their case to the public. On his part, Jaffe wanted to neutralize the current media portrayal of Eric Rudolph, which in a word was "guilty."

Indeed, CNN focused almost exclusively on Eric Rudolph. Experts and talking heads appeared in rapid succession asserting that Eric Rudolph was undeniably guilty and should be executed. In effect, CNN had already tried, convicted, sentenced and executed Eric Rudolph.

Jaffe said, "It is only fair, I think, to suspend judgment and allow the courtroom to test whether the proof is really proof or speculation and hearsay." In other words, the criminal justice system exists for a reason. We don't take people out and hang them just because we feel they are guilty.

As Jaffe put it, "We are really not Salem, Massachusetts, in the 1600s. We are in Birmingham, Alabama, where people get fair trials."

The defense team went to work. Literally hundreds of thousands of documents had to be read and categorized. A team of attorneys were assigned the task.

The prosecutors' case against Eric Rudolph appeared to be rock solid; they even had Jermaine Hughes as a witness. But there was a flaw: three of the five search warrants utilized to initially search Rudolph's property were vague. In essence, the warrants weren't worth the paper they were written on. The feds a had confiscated as evidence items they were not authorized to confiscate.

The defense team planned on challenging the evidence based on faulty warrants. If the judge sided with them, the evidence would be excluded, thus weakening the prosecutors' case substantially. They also considered pleading justifiable homicide, but that defense admitted that Rudolph had, in fact, perpetrated the bombings. Besides, justifiable homicide would, in effect, be a trial about the right or wrong of abortion. No court was prepared to take on that subject.

The defense team devised a strategy to negate the testimony of Jermaine Hughes. Put simply, based on Hughes' own words, he could have been following any number of men after the bombing, because the person he named as the bomber kept altering his appearance. This tactic would, perhaps, negate the prosecutors' evidence by introducing the jurors to doubt.

Basically, Jaffe wanted the jury to entertain the possibility that another person, or persons, could have carried out the bombings. The Army of God letter did just that, with its wording: "We will target –" Who was to say the Army of God didn't actually exist? Plus, there was another salient factor: other than being personally and vehemently against abortion, Eric Rudolph was not part of any organized anti-abortion group and, most telling, he had never protested at any abortion clinic, anywhere.

Essentially, the prosecutors would depict Eric Rudolph as a vicious, embittered, violent, murderous terrorist; whereas Jaffe and his crew would depict Eric Rudolph as a person. If the jury perceived Eric Rudolph as a real, live person – with a mother and brothers, service in the army, etc. – Eric might avoid the death penalty, simply because people are reluctant to execute other people. Terrorists were a whole different matter. Terrorists were not human, not people; they were some sort of quasi-animal in human form. Terrorist deserved to die.

* * * * *

In his jail cell, Eric received a torrent of fan mail, along with hate mail, along with well-intentioned religious people worried about his eternal soul and its final resting place. Eric was a celebrity.

Meanwhile, the slow moving wheels of justice ground on. In 2004, Jaffe and his team of attorneys filed a motion to move the location of the trial. The motion contended that Eric Rudolph could not and would not receive a fair trial in Birmingham. In June 2004, the hearing regarding the relocation occurred. The prosecution, naturally, disagreed.

As usual, the hearing was window dressing. The prosecutors and the defense had concluded an agreement prior to the hearing. In effect, the trial would take place in Birmingham, but the jury would be selected from the Northern District of Alabama.

The hearing also covered the defense's motion to postpone the trial. Jaffe maintained the defense couldn't be ready in six weeks. In the end, a new trial date was set – May 2005.

Jury selection criterion was vital to any trial. In fact, it is the most important single factor of any trial because, in the end, the jury makes the final decision. According to Jaffe, "Eric wrote this brilliant, detailed twenty-three-page analysis of the type of juror that we wanted or didn't want. I was blown away."

According to Eric's analysis, the perfect juror was female, around 30 years of age, single and overweight. Basically, a youngish woman with abandonment issues, the kind of woman who read romance novels to spice up her non-existent sex life. Without a doubt, the defense did not want to allow any pro-lifers on the jury.

Male jurors, according to Eric, ideally would be what he called "bubbas," red-necked conservatives, the kind with the American or Confederate flag flapping from the bed of their trucks.

One of Eric's juror questions was: "Do you like Neil Diamond music? Explain."

Unfortunately, Eric's team of defense attorneys was struggling with internal friction. Essentially, Judy Clarke, one of the attorney's Jaffe had brought in, wanted to take control and be the head honcho. She wanted Jaffe gone. So much so that she presented her case to the judge, which meant a hearing regarding representation was necessary. The judge allowed Eric to make the final choice. This made sense since it was Eric's ass that was on the line.

Eric chose Jaffe and his crew. But the judge intervened and fired Jaffe from the case. However, the judge allowed Jaffe and his crew the consideration of voluntarily withdrawing from the case, in order to save face.

Judy Clarke won. She was now the Big Cheese.

Under Clarke, the defense changed dramatically. Eric was now much more involved in his case. In fact, they made it possible for Eric to have access to a laptop computer so he could go through the documents in his case.

Clarke's team filed a motion to exclude any and all evidence gathered in the searches of Eric's belongings. According to the motion, the warrants were not explicit and therefore the evidence was inadmissible. They also filed a motion asserting Eric's arrest and detention was illegal.

The court denied the motions, admitting that the warrants were unconstitutional in nature. However, the court maintained that the property was "abandoned," which meant it could be searched sans warrants.

Clarke's team responded by filing a Daubert motion, which basically asserted that the ATF and FBI labs had not properly processed the evidence.

Meanwhile, Henry Schuster's book, *Hunting Eric Rudolph*, came out just before the trial was to begin, which was an excellent marketing ploy. Schuster's book maintained Eric Rudolph was guilty as hell.

What most people didn't know was that the prosecutors were open to a plea bargain because, even though on the surface they believed their case against Eric was flawless, juries were unknown quantities. If the jury failed to impose the death penalty, in effect, the prosecutors had lost. And they didn't want to lose and look like fools.

For a matter of fact, the prosecutors went through two mock trials and both were dismal failures.

The focal point of the plea deal was that the prosecutors wanted tit for tat, quid pro quo. If the death penalty was removed, they wanted Eric to reveal the location of his explosives, which the prosecutors were certain existed. By the calculations of the eggheads in forensics, Eric's bombs had used about thirty pounds of dynamite. Yet they believed he had stolen 340 pounds of the stuff from Asheville, North Carolina.

Eric was asked. And he told them where his dynamite was located. Eric told them he had 200 pounds of dynamite stored at various locations, along with another bomb, which was not yet functional.

Meanwhile, while all this was going on, the Daubert hearing occurred. Eric enjoyed the hearing, thought it was interesting. Finally, though, he decided to take the plea bargain.

Eric aided the searchers in locating his caches of explosives. He had two caches in Cherokee County, two more in the forest (almost in Tennessee) and yet another two caches near Unaka. There was one more site, near Murphy; located at this site was a bomb, ready to go, except it had no detonator.

The FBI and the ATF sent agents to the locations, along with bomb techs.

The ready to go bomb, just on the outskirts of Murphy, was in a five-gallon bucket with a lid. It comprised 25 pounds of dynamite – a big bomb – and was set up to be remotely detonated. When the bomb techs checked it, they decided it was too volatile to transport; the dynamite had liquefied.

They decided to move it a short distance from the highway and explode it. When it went off, it left a sizable crater.

One of the other sites had a bomb 'under construction.' It was in a Lil' Playmate, kid's cooler with a snap top. In all, the agents found 270 pounds of dynamite. Rudolph had enough explosives to wage a war.

The media finally discovered what was going on. But before the media could release their big story, the FBI beat them to the punch, releasing their own announcement about the plea bargain.

* * * * *

Eric Rudolph's final hearing was a three-ring circus. The media was out in full force; all the primary players from the FBI and the ATF were in attendance. The courthouse was packed like sardines.

Again, Eric was escorted in by U.S. Marshals. Dressed in his red man jail couture, he wore ankle shackles. He greeted and shook hands with his defense team, and then looked roguishly at the prosecutors.

Judge C. Lynwood Smith made his entrance and things got underway. The judge asked Rudolph a series of preliminary questions. Then the charges against Eric were read.

"How do you plead?" asked Judge Smith.

"Guilty, your honor."

Judge Smith asked Eric if he was satisfied with his legal counsel.

"More than satisfied," Eric said. "They are very, very good, superlative lawyers."

One of the prosecutors cited the evidence in the case.

Then Judge Smith asked Eric if the prosecution's evidence was enough to prove him guilty.

"Just barely, your honor," replied Eric.

Eric's reply pissed off Judge Smith. Leaning forward, the judge said, "Let me just cut to the chase. Did you plant the bomb that exploded at the New Woman All Women clinic?"

"I did, your honor."

"And did you cause that bomb to detonate?"

"I certainly did, your honor."

Eric's words dripped with gratified pleasure. His smug arrogance was unmistakable.

* * * * *

In Atlanta, Eric pled guilty. After the Atlanta hearing concluded, his lawyers handed out copies of Eric's "statement," which explained, among other things, why he had pled guilty and taken the plea bargain: "I have deprived the government of its goal of sentencing me to death."

The media, of course, publicized that quote, but failed to comprehend the rest of Eric's lengthy statement, which stated that Eric accepted the plea bargain as "a tactical choice." It also set forth Eric's position on abortion, which Eric stated thusly: "Abortion is murder." He then went on to assert that "force is justified" to stop abortion. In other words, Eric's words substantiated his role as a Phineas Priest.

Another section of Eric's statement propounded his perspective of homosexuality, which he described as "an aberrant sexual behavior." In Eric's opinion, homosexuals had damned themselves by attempting to force the general public to accept and condone their aberrant behavior. And again, according to Eric's thinking, force was justified against homosexuals and their agenda.

In his statement, Eric explained that he had planted a bomb in Centennial Park, in effect, to punish the U.S. government for its "sanctioning of abortion on demand."

During the Summer of 2005, Eric Rudolph composed a 135-page essay justifying the use of force in pursuit of right. Entitled "Pacifism," it was essentially the philosophical defense of the Phineas Priesthood.

* * * * *

On July 18, 2005, Eric Rudolph was sentenced: two life sentences to run consecutively, without parole. His restitution exceeded $1 million; and there was $200 court fee.

Rudolph's victims had their day on that day. Each was allowed to make a statement to Rudolph, who was seated in the courtroom.

And then it Eric's turn to speak. It was less of a statement than a sermon on the evils presently besetting the U.S., primarily abortion, along with porn and homosexuals. He referred to it as "this black night of barbarism." He maintained that his actions – blowing shit and people up – would be vindicated by history. And then he concluded by quoting/paraphrasing St. Paul: "I know that I have fought a good fight, I have finished my course. I have kept the faith."

At the end of his haranguing homily, the courtroom, which was packed to the rafters, was dead silent, as was usual when some nutcase finished his oratorical fulminations.

* * * * *

In Atlanta, the same routine occurred. Rudolph got to listen as his victims sprayed him with hatred and invective. However, this time, when it was his turn to speak, Eric acknowledged his remorse for the Centennial Park bombing.

In the Atlanta hearing, Eric Rudolph was not the star of the show. Fallon Stubbs was. When it was her turn to speak, she told Eric: "My message is not of hate. My message is of forgiveness and acceptance."

Eric Rudolph was incarcerated at the ADMAX – the U.S. maximum security prison – in Florence, Colorado. In effect, he was buried alive. The prison is home to 400 prisoners, all extremely violent. Many of the prisoners are bombers and reside on what is humorously referred to as "Bomber's Row."

Eric's cell is eight feet by ten feet. The interior of the cell – everything – is made of concrete. The food is excellent. Eric is fed in his cell, always. He is allowed a black and white TV, books and writing materials.

Despite all his claims maintaining that his use of violence against abortion clinics was justified, in the end, Eric Rudolph suffered a moral vacuity, which led to an insensate passion for new sensations and experiences – a form of fatuous credulity, wherein he believed he was a demi-god. This belief meant he could do what gods do: judge others and, most importantly, dole out punishment to those he perceived as failing to meet his standards.

This "I am a god illusion" used to be referred to as "hubris." The ancient Greeks expended great amounts of time discussing the concept and traced its path with withering accuracy, watching it lead to what they called "ate" – the point at which evil was mistakenly perceived to be good.

Chapter 11

The Aryan Republican Army

The Aryan Republican Army (ARA) was also known as the Midwest Bank Robbers. The latter name was used by the media and thus became the group's nickname. But make no mistake: the ARA was a white supremacist group that referred to themselves as Phineas Priests.

The ARA was composed of: Michael William Brescia, Mark William Thomas, Richard Lee Guthrie Jr., Peter Kevin Langan, Kevin McCarthy, and Scott Stedeford. Essentially, they were skinheads initiated into the Church of Christian Identity by Mark William Thomas, who was a pastor in the church, an adherent of the founding principles of the Aryan Nations, and the head honcho of the Posse Comitatus.

The Church of Christian Identity was and still is a separatist religion that provided two attractions to alienated skinheads: one, a cultural foundation and, two, a connection or identity. The appeal was magnetic, as even skinheads want to belong and find rapport with other like-minded individuals. In fact, the ARA consisted of alienated losers frantically searching for connection to other human beings.

Kevin McCarthy's life was a shithole: no love, no direction, no sense of belonging to anyone or anything. McCarthy's mom passed away when he was seven years old. Dad split, wanting nothing to do with the boy. So he went to live with his grandmother. Kicked out of school in the eighth grade, McCarthy attended two other schools, both of which booted him out. By this point, McCarthy had had enough. His answer to the problem was running away and self-medication: cigarettes and alcohol, which quickly led to marijuana, LSD and coke.

His grandmother didn't know what to do. So she committed him – twice – to drug rehab programs. Naturally, McCarthy ran away. Then his grandmother moved to New Jersey, taking the punk with her. She felt responsible for the boy.

McCarthy hung out on the Atlantic City boardwalk, home to a variety of cultural subgroups, like gangs, skater dudes and other disaffected youths. And skinheads, of course. The skinheads assimilated McCarthy, who began wearing the classic skinhead style of clothing: combat boots and leather jackets. And of course, he shaved his head; the badge or mark of skinheads. He was fourteen years old.

McCarthy met a skinhead named Frank Meeink, who indoctrinated him into the beliefs of the Church of Christian Identity. He joined the Atlantic City Skinheads, a gang of neo-Nazis. He felt like he belonged. Mostly, the gang drank until blotto. They were all alcoholics.

Meeink and McCarthy decided to have some fun. They went around stealing money or whatever from homeless people and little old ladies.

Then in 1993, McCarthy and his grandmother moved back to Philadelphia. Changing locations didn't solve any of his problems.

* * * * *

Over in nearby Ardmore, Scott Stedeford was growing up in a nice, middle-class family. He was a nice, normal child; attended Haverford High School, where he was an average student. During high school, he fell under the influence of hard rock music, idolizing the rock stars. He grew his hair long and found himself attracted to the opposite sex.

After high school, Stedeford found work at a print shop, but still lived at home. A few years later, he moved out, residing in Germantown, where he formed a rock band – Cyanide. Stedeford, as part of his rock star look, wore combat boots, a leather jacket and shaved his head. At this point, it was just 'a look,' he wasn't a skinhead. But Cyanide appealed to skinheads because the band played kick ass, hardcore rock n' roll.

He got a job at Sound Under, a recording studio. Still part of Cyanide, Stedeford relished his work at the studio, recording, producing and playing. Somewhere in here, he became romantically involved with Susan Palilonis, who was a walking, talking female nightmare. Susan always had multiple lovers, playing one against the other; she was a master manipulator. And she was a neo-Nazi from way back.

Susan's house was white power central. Stedeford came into contact with many skinheads, one of which was Matthew Brescia, the brother of Michael Brescia. Matthew hooked Stedeford up with Michael.

* * * * *

Michael Brescia grew up in an upper middle-class family. He was another nice, normal kid. Only he was bored. After high school, Michael Brescia was accepted to La Salle University, majoring in of all things accounting. While in college, he joined the band Cyanide and began wearing the typical skinhead couture.

Meanwhile, Kevin McCarthy was trying to stop drinking. He decided that Jesus might hold the key to sobriety and began going to a Bible study group. Mark William Thomas was part of the Bible study. The two hit it off and before long were roommates on a farm that Thomas owned.

Although he came from a staid middle-class family, Mark Thomas was a high school dropout, who worked various jobs. The seminal point in Mark Thomas' life – supposedly – was a conversation he had with Jim Morrison of The Doors. Ostensibly, the conversation concerned the "meaning of life."

Later, he joined the U.S. Army and then went AWOL, fleeing to Canada. Why someone like Thomas would join the U.S. Army was a mystery. Anyway, eventually he was arrested and given a dishonorable discharge from the army. He got married and moved onto the farm in Pennsylvania.

A religious eclectic, Mark Thomas was attracted to Odinism, Jung's theory of Aryanism and the end-of-the-world gloom and doom of Jim Morrison. End-of-the-world stuff really turned on Mark Thomas. And since the Church of Christian Identity had one of the best end-of-the-world doctrines around, he added Identity religion to his repertoire.

Identity dogma soon hooked Mark Thomas; he became a member of both the Aryan Nations and the Ku Klux Klan and, eventually, became the Big Cheese of the Posse Comitatus.

Mark Thomas' wife didn't buy into all this shit, so she bailed, taking the kids with her. She divorced him and then Mark Thomas remarried. A woman named Donna Marzoff.

Mark Thomas lost his job, which was driving trucks. Now he was poor. So he traveled to Coeur d'Alene, Idaho, where he was tutored by Richard Butler. Mark Thomas made Richard Butler seem normal by comparison. Mark Thomas' ideas were really out there: spaceships flown by blacks; holistic healing; and massive government conspiracies, including weather manipulation by gigantic weather machines.

As a featured speaker at the Aryan World Congress, Mark Thomas met the other big wheels of the white power movement, along with a menagerie of wannabe big wheels, like Richard Guthrie.

After two years under Butler's tutelage, Mark Thomas went back to Pennsylvania and began preaching. He was good at, gaining national attention, showing up on Fox TV and *Geraldo*, along with other news shows. His rhetoric advocated a violent upheaval. He stated on national TV that "our God commanded us to exterminate them." Then, in this case, was Jews.

* * * * *

Kevin McCarthy was now living with Mark Thomas, a man on the brink of total insanity, a religious nutcase and an advocate of hardcore violence.

At this point, Donna Marzoff, Mark Thomas' second wife, made the decision to get the heck out of Dodge. She bailed, taking her kids with her. Mark Thomas threatened to kill her and the kids if she remarried. Donna got a restraining order against Mark Thomas, who countered by suing for full-custody of the kids.

Mark Thomas' farm was frequented by large groups of white power dudes. He had a cache of weapons on the farm and the local police were beginning to take note of the rattling gun fire coming from the farm.

By this time, Kevin McCarthy had been fully converted to Christian Identity. Mark Thomas decided that he and Kevin needed further training for the day of the coming Armageddon. The only place to receive such advanced training was Elohim City, Oklahoma.

Off they went.

The City of God or Elohim City was an Identity compound where around one-hundred white power fanatics lived. Robert Millar was the founder of Elohim City. Millar received a vision from God that told him what he had to do. Millar's brand of Identity doctrine was watered-down compared to Butler's Aryan Nations' doctrine. According to Millar, Elohim City was not a white supremacist group; they were, instead, "racialists." Millar's peaceful approach to Identity teachings earned him the nickname of "Grandpa."

It was all a front, a sham, camouflage. In reality, Millar was paranoid, scared to death that the government would abolish freedom of any type. Because of this paranoia, quasi-military training was part and parcel of Elohim City's daily routine. Guns attracted violence, and violence in conjunction with guns attracted extremely violent personality types to Elohim City. In other words, neo-Nazis and skinheads began arriving in groups. Almost immediately, the skinheads set up a methamphetamine lab near the compound. They tried to keep it quiet, but everyone knew it was there.

Mark Thomas and Kevin McCarthy arrived. Ostensibly, Kevin was going to attend the compound's private school, called Bethel Christian. But school wasn't Kevin's thing. He dropped it almost immediately and spent most of his time in learing how to shoot, build bombs and engage in tactical maneuvers.

Millar liked Kevin, but thought the kid needed to go to school. If he didn't, he needed to leave Elohim City. So Kevin moved back to Pennsylvania, where he lived once again with his grandmother. Kevin spent his nights "clubbing," hanging out in the clubs that catered to skinheads and neo-Nazis. In one of the clubs, he came across Cyanide and Scott Stedeford.

So now McCarthy, Stedeford and Michael Brescia were pals. They all started hanging out at Mark Thomas' farm, where they got the full treatment – lots of indoctrination in Identity beliefs.

Before long, the brainwashing was complete.

Brescia was still attending La Salle University, where, when not in class or at the Thomas farm, he passed out tracts outlining the joy and empowerment provided by white supremacism. Eventually, college got to be too boring and Brescia simply stopped going. Mark Thomas, nobody's fool, realized his opportunity. He suggested Elohim City as the perfect remedy for boredom. Brescia didn't need to be told twice. He was off to Oklahoma.

1993: Millar made Brescia feel right at home. To Brescia, Elohim City was part paradise part action movie. Brescia roomed with Andreas Strassmeir, who functioned as head of security for Elohim City. Strassmeir (see Timothy McVeigh) was one of those random, contradictory individuals that most people never come across; he seemed to be in constant camouflage. Rumor had it that Strassmeir was a former German spook. No one knew for sure what he was. But there were layers to the guy, lots of layers.

Strassmeir and Brescia hit it off. As Millar said, "Strassmeir and Brescia were buddies."

A few months later, Stedeford and Kevin McCarthy joined Brescia at Elohim City. They were there for military/guerilla training under Strassmeir. Stedeford wasn't there long. He went back to Philadelphia to take care of some business at Sound Under studios. He stayed at Mark Thomas' farm. While at the farm, he met Richard Guthrie and Peter Langan.

Peter Langan was character straight out of *National Lampoon*. An ex-con with no job skills per se, who was confused as to whether he was male or female – gender dysfunction. Just out of prison and on parole, Langan submersed himself in subculture of outlaw bikers, who called themselves "one-percenters." Mostly, Langan went clubbing with other bikers, where they drank, did weed and snorted coke. It was during this period that Langan hooked up with Richard Guthrie, who was highly intelligent, extremely bizarre and loved to demolish shit.

After a brief stint as a thief, Guthrie joined the Navy, where, because of his intelligence (based on Naval testing), he was trained in advanced weapons and explosives. Guthrie applied to become a Navy SEAL. Unfortunately, he couldn't cut the mustard physically; part way through the course, he dropped out.

Still in the Navy, Guthrie came across and read *The Turner Diaries*, which proved to be the turning point in his life, a fascist *point vierge*. Guthrie was court-martialed and dishonorably discharged from the Navy for painting a swastika on the hull of a naval ship.

After getting kicked out of the Navy, Guthrie went back to his former profession: thief, adding con-man to his repertoire. Guthrie's crimes became more and more violent, resulting in multiple arrests. Somehow, he always got off.

By this time, both Guthrie and Langan were attending services at Identity churches.

They took a trip to see Richard Butler, who, once upon a time, had been on good terms with Robert Matthews and his group, the Order. Langan was not impressed. "They were losers," said Langan. "They were nowhere near ready to start the so-called second American Revolution. Aryan Nations had more security leaks than just about anything. And the skinheads? Just a bunch of greasers. They were there to get high. It was an outlet for their frustration and rage."

They left reinvigorated, ready to make a difference, to get the ball rolling. During this period, Langan was getting more and more into cross-dressing. He believed he was a woman trapped in a man's body.

At this point, Langan, Guthrie and newbie Shawn Kenney read and reread *The Silent Brotherhood* and the *Vigilantes of Christendom: The History of the Phineas Priesthood*. In the latter, the author asserts violence, robbery and murder are condoned by the Bible. Such acts were merely men restoring balance to God's divine plan for mankind. The Phineas Priests were God's chosen vessels, those selected by God to perform His work on earth.

Their grand conspiracy against Jews, blacks and the U.S. government started out pretty lamely. On October 11, 1992 they robbed a Pizza Hut. The score was $2300. Hardly a princely sum.

Meanwhile, the inside man on the Pizza Hut robbery, James Stewart, found himself in jail. He wanted out so he snitched on Guthrie and Langan, informing the local Sheriff that Guthrie and Langan had conceived and carried out the Pizza Hut job. Moreover, and even more importantly, Stewart asserted that Guthrie and Langdon were conspiring to assassinate President George H.W. Bush in Georgia. Stewart didn't know Langan's real name; he only knew him as Pedro Gomez, Langan's preferred alias.

Naturally, the Secret Service got involved, escalating a search for the two men. Locating Guthrie's apartment, the Secret Service busted in the door and stormed in. Guthrie was gone.

In fact, Guthrie and Langan aka Pedro Gomez were in Cincinnati, trying their hand at arson. They tried to torch a Masonic Lodge. This foray into arson was a dismal failure. The lodge didn't burn to the ground. The fire department arrived and quickly extinguished the small flames. Little damage was done.

Meanwhile, the Secret Service discovered Pedro Gomez's real name and located his house in Cincinnati. By means of a ruse, they got Langan out of the house. Cuffing him, they ransacked his house, where they discovered weapons, hand grenades, tons of ammunition, explosives and detonators.

They tossed Langan in jail. Langan's arrest and association with the Aryan Nations movement came out. This put unwanted heat on the Aryan Nations, which made Langan very unpopular inside the white power movement. The Aryan Nations believed Langan had squealed to save his own bacon.

Langdon planned assassinating George Bush and Bill Clinton, along with blowing up a federal building in protest against the government. The first rule of jail was keep your mouth shut, which Langan failed to do. So of course his cellie dropped a dime on him. The Secret Service converged on his cell and interrogated him. After determining he was just a big-mouthed braggart, the Secret Service left.

Langan grew tired of jail. So he started making noises about helping the Secret Service locate and capture Guthrie. The Secret Service gave him a deal: they would let him out of jail if he helped them find Guthrie and testified against him at trial. Langan agreed.

In effect, Langan was now a confidential informant charged with betraying his friends. Back in Cincinnati, Langan looked up Shawn Kenney, who informed him that Guthrie was planning another bank robbery. Guthrie had already successfully robbed two banks.

Unbeknown to the Secret Service, Langan met with Guthrie. But he didn't squeal. He kept it secret. Phineas Priests didn't give up other Priests to the feds. Instead, Langan informed Guthrie of the deal. During this meeting the two discussed the formation of the ARA – the Aryan Republican Army. However, to fund the ARA they needed money.

To raise cash, they would rob an armored car. But they needed help. Robbing an armored car required guts, determination, planning and a crew of experienced outlaws.

According to Langan, Guthrie knew Timothy McVeigh, whom he had met on the gun show circuit. Guthrie recruited Terry Nichols and McVeigh for the heist. All the players in the armored car robbery converged on Fayetteville, Arkansas. The crew was to consist of: McVeigh, Nichols, Langan, Guthrie, Kenney, McCarthy, Thomas, Brescia and Strassmeir.

It never happened. The armored car robbery didn't take place. No one knows why.

Meanwhile, Langan gave the Secret Service the slip. He met up with Guthrie in Ohio, at a Park and Ride. The Secret Service agents, when they realized they'd been duped, were way beyond pissed. Partly because they looked like fools, and partly because the FBI now entered the case. The FBI didn't suffer fools gladly.

No one had a clue where Langan and Guthrie were.

They were in Ames, Iowa. On January 25, 1994, they hit the First-Star Bank, located at the mall in Ames. Langan, wearing a ski mask, baseball cap and black trench coat, walked into the bank just prior to closing. Guthrie, wearing a similar get up, pulled guard duty, just outside the bank. Langan exited the bank sixty seconds later. He carried a bag. Langan had left a fake bomb in the bank, telling the bank's employees it was a bomb. The two robbers took off their ski masks and walked through the mall like anyone else. Walking out of the mall, they climbed in their getaway car and drove off.

Their destination was Rochester, Minnesota. When the counted the money from the bank robbery, they had $11,000. From Rochester, they drove to Cincinnati, where they bought the Bitzenvagon, a Ford van. Then they went to gun show and bought weapons.

Now out of money, they needed another score. So they drove back to Iowa, this time they would hit the Brenton First National Bank in Davenport, Iowa. Brenton First National was also located at a mall. Using the same methodology, just prior to closing, Guthrie entered the bank. The bank's tellers handed over the money; and once again, they left a fake bomb. They drove to Lincoln, Illinois and counted their profits -- $4,400.

During the next half year, they hit five banks throughout the Mid-West, utilizing the same tactics each time; all the banks were located at malls. The Aryan Republican Army was in business and business was good.

In April, Langan rented a house in Pittsburg, Kansas. The two bank robbers were full of themselves by this time. Arrogance pervaded them; they thought they were invincible. They'd seen the movie *Point Break* and decided to adopt similar disguises. In June of 1994, "Richard Nixon" and "Jimmy Carter" entered the Society National Bank in Springdale, Ohio. Guns out, the two ex-Presidents also wore body armor. Nixon shouted, "Get down! Get down! No alarms! No hostages!" While Nixon was thus engaged, Carter spoke loudly in what sounded like Arabic.

As always, sixty seconds and gone. They jumped into their getaway car and sped off. Only this time, they made a mistake. The money had a dye-pack in it. It exploded, staining the money red. Of the $12,000 they stole, only $4,000 was untainted by the red dye.

By now, Langan and Guthrie were referring to the ARA by another nickname – "the Company." This was nothing more than a rip-off of The Order, which Robert Mathews had called "the Company." At this point, Langan and Guthrie began actively recruiting new members for "the Company."

So far, they had stolen around $58,000 from various banks. But they wanted a big score, and that meant an armored car. To do that, they needed a crew. Part of their recruiting process was notoriety. Langan began recording *Notes From the Underground*, starring himself as Commander Pedro. The videos were sent to various powerful and influential members of white supremacist groups.

The next step was personal recruitment. Guthrie recruited Shawn Kenney to ask Mark Thomas to become "the Company's" recruiting officer. Mark Thomas agreed.

In September, while all this was going on, Langan and Guthrie hit the Boatman's Bank in Overland Park, Kansa, netting $13,000. Shortly after the robbery, they drove to Mark Thomas' farm in Pennsylvania.

Langan, Guthrie and Thomas sat at Thomas' kitchen table, talking about pulling off a Phineas-like feat.

At this point in his fanatical Identity ministry, Mark Thomas appropriated the symbol of the Phineas Priesthood as his own. The symbol looked like this: #25:6 (Numbers 25:6). In addition, Mark Thomas still had his doubts about Langan's fidelity to the Phineas cause. Frankly, Langan had fucked up in the past and Mark Thomas had reservations: was Langan reliable?

Mark Thomas introduced Langan and Guthrie to Scott Stedeford. Stedeford would become part of the ARA or "the Company." And he would serve a dual function: Phineas Priest/Warrior and spy for Mark Thomas. Stedeford would be Thomas' eyes and ears and report back on Langan's constancy.

Stedeford was hardcore. He was not only a true believer, but he lived it. To that end, he insisted that the ARA function like a true terrorist group: no one knew more than they needed to know about the others, and everyone would use aliases at all times. Stedeford was Tuco; Guthrie was Wild Bill; and Langan was Commander Pedro.

The gang's first job would be to hit the Society Bank in Columbus, Ohio. Arriving in Columbus, the gang surveilled the bank and, disappointed, decided not to hit it. Getting in and stealing the money was no problem. The problem was getting out and away safely. So they switched targets. They would hit the Columbus National Bank instead. It was located on Livingston Avenue.

Guthrie purchased a junker for $500 – an old Ford Galaxy. It would be what they called their "drop car." In other words, they would use it to pull off the robbery, then as their getaway car. It would be the car witnesses would see and describe to police. Later, they would dump the car and drive away in another.

On October 25, the drop car parked outside the bank. It was parked nose out, or what was called "combat style" for a quick getaway. Stedeford (Tuco) and Langan (Commander Pedro), dressed in quasi-combat gear – jungle boots and body armor, along with ski masks – and carrying semi-automatic pistols, burst into the bank.

Commander Pedro shouted, "Everybody get down! Everybody get down on the floor! Lay down!" While Commander Pedro waved his gun and covered the bank's employees and patrons, Tuco walked over to a side entrance and set down a lunchbox, which contained the fake bomb. He then joined Commander Pedro. Both men waved their guns around menacingly. Tuco shouted, "Andale! Andale!"

Commander Pedro went from teller station to teller station, removing the cash from each drawer and placing in a bag he carried.

When they first burst into the bank, Commander Pedro for some stupid reason had taken off his ski mask. A female loan officer – Lisa Copley – got a good look at his face.

Commander Pedro didn't think he was getting enough money. He wanted a big score. So he trundled over to the drive through teller's station, but the drawers were locked.

Meanwhile, Tuco was getting antsy. They'd been there too long. He shouted at Commander Pedro: "Andale! Andale! Come on, man, we gotta get out of here, now!"

As Commander Pedro scrambled over the counter, he shouted, "We didn't get shit!"

Racing out of the bank, they entered the getaway car, where Wild Bill waited, motor running. They drove to an apartment complex, where they had previously parked the Blitzenvagon. Dumping the getaway car, they leaped into the Blitzenvagon. This was where Stedeford made a mistake: he left part of his disguise in the getaway car. Pumped on adrenaline, he simply forgot.

The Blitzenvagon entered the freeway. Arriving in Wheeling, West Virginia, they stopped for gas. Commander Pedro checked the take: $3,400.

From there, they drove to Mark Thomas' farm, where the concluded that the robbery was a success, even though the take was shit. Then they discussed hitting an armored car, which was where the real money was. To pull it off, they agreed, they'd need more dedicated men, serious players.

Later, Guthrie and Langan retired to their house in Pittsburg, Kansas, while Stedeford and Mark Thomas drove to Elohim City, where they met up with honchos of the white power movement: Dennis Mahon and Tom Metzger, along with Strassmeir.

* * * * *

On November 7, Langan and Guthrie arrived outside the East Des Moines National Bank, located in Des Moines, Iowa. They spent a few days casing the bank and twiddling their thumbs in their motel room. On November 11, they hit the bank, scoring $29,000. Easy pickings and no problems. They drove back to the house in Kansas.

While this was going on, the feds were busy gathering forensic evidence. The bomb left at the Columbus National bank was not a fake. In fact, it was a fully functional pipe bomb.

On November 14, Stedeford, Thomas and McCarthy met Langan and Guthrie at a Waffle House in Arkansas. By this time, Langan had taken over as the honcho of the gang. Commander Pedro was not just a nickname. It was his title.

Kevin McCarthy received the usual recruiting patter. Essentially, it was the same old crap about being on a Mission from God, fighting a Holy War against big government, which was exploiting the average Joe and Sally. After listening attentively, McCarthy decided he was in, all the way. He would be called Newt, after Newt Gingrich.

Even gangs take a break for national holidays. Thanksgiving was right around the corner, so they took some downtime, agreeing to meet up in Joplin, Missouri, on December 1. The meeting place was the Northbrook Mall. From there, they all drove to Akron, Ohio. Their next planned hit was the Third Federal Savings & Loan in Cleveland.

On December 9, Langan and McCarthy walked into the bank. Langan was dressed like Santa Claus and McCarthy wore an Elf's outfit. The gang had added communications to their modus operandi: each man carried a two-way radio.

Langan shoued, "Get down! Get down on the floor, now! No alarms! No hostages!" Then he and McCarthy began ransacking the tellers' drawers. At this point, Stedeford came in through the back entrance; he carried the fake bomb and a semi-automatic pistol. Waving the gun, Stedeford shouted, "Andale! Andale! Get down! Get down!"

Langan and McCarthy worked quickly and efficiently. In one minute, they cleaned out the drawers. Just as they finished, Guthrie, who was waiting outside in the getaway car, radioed, "Time's up, Santa."

Time to go.

Santa and his elves walked out of the bank and jumped in the getaway car. The take was $7,400.

A few days later, on December 13, 1994, Langan and McCarthy arrived in St. Louis to scout out potential banks. The Commercial Bank of Westport fit the bill. On December 27, the gang hit the bank. Langan and McCarthy, dressed in blue FBI jackets, body armor, wigs and ski masks, walked into the bank. McCarthy carried the fake bomb and his pistol, along with a smoke grenade, which was something new.

Langan scrambled over the counter, shouting his predictable warning: "Get down! Lay down on the floor! No alarms! No hostages!"

Langan cleaned out the drawers. Then McCarthy lobbed the smoke grenade to cover their exit. The two bank robbers walked out, jumped in the getaway car driven by Guthrie and headed toward Illinois. When they finally stopped, they were in Pittsburg. The take was $32,000.

Each man took his share of the spoils and they split up. Langan went to Kansas City, where he went to a New Year's Eve party hosted by the Kansas City Cross Dressers and Friends. Using the name Donna McClure, Langan arrived in full drag: dress, jewelry, heels and glossy nails and lips. He hit it off with another drag queen named Cheryl.

Langan was walking on the wild side.

January 1995, the gang gathered at the house in Kansas, where they produced a video entitled *The Aryan Republican Army Presents: The Armed Struggle Underground*. Essentially, the video had two purposes: first, to recruit new members; second, to explain the gang's purpose and rationale. It can be argued there was a third purpose: simply to show off, because the gang now considered themselves to be akin to rock stars.

Naturally, Langan as Commander Pedro was the star of the show. He asserted that they – the ARA – took its orders from God, for whom they were "zealous," comparing them to Phineas in the Biblical book of Numbers. Guthrie made an appearance, fulminating against Jews, whom he obviously despised with deep passion. He referred to paper money as "Jewish toilet paper," a reference to Jewish bankers, who, according to Guthrie, controlled the world's economies.

The video was replete with tons of weapons, and seemed to announce that guns were not only useful but a heck of a lot of fun. Much later, in what he called his "memoir," but was more like a rambling manifesto, Guthrie confessed that during the making of the video, they were all drunk, totally blotto.

In the end, the video was nothing more than self-indulgent, self-aggrandizing tripe. It was a self-produced production about how invincible and how right the ARA was. Self-justification at its worst.

* * * * *

The ARA was now ready to take the next big step: robbing an armored car.

They left the house in Kansas in two vehicles, both brimming with weapons, including ammo, pipe bombs and a TOW missile. Dragging along the TOW missile was Guthrie's idea. Their destination was Phoenix, Arizona, where upon arrival they checked into a motel.

On February 17, the four ARA gang members ate breakfast, like many other people, at Denny's. After breakfast, they headed for Mesa, Arizona. Parking at the Fiesta Mall, Langan and Guthrie surveilled the nearby banks, while Stedeford and McCarthy drove around looking for armored cars. Apparently, at this point, the plan was in the early stages because they seemed surprisingly disorganized.

The next day, February 18, Stedeford and McCarthy lucked out, coming across a Wells Fargo armored car making its pickups. They followed it over the next two days, identifying the truck's routine. The truck stopped like clockwork at movie theaters in the area.

They held a preliminary planning meeting and Langan decided they should hit the armored car when it stopped at the theater across from the mall. Guthrie purchased a drop car that he parked at an apartment complex.

No one knew exactly why, but somewhere in there Guthrie developed and nursed doubts about Scott Stedeford. For some reason, Guthrie had a chip on his shoulder where Stedeford was concerned. It bugged him enough that he spoke to Langan about it. Langan listened and then told Guthrie to cut it out. Langan's opinion was that Stedeford was a true believer and could be counted on.

Langan came up with a plan for robbing the armored car. When the armored car parked at the theater, while the gun-toting guards were in the theater collecting the money, Langan ascend to the truck's roof. When the guards reappeared with the money bags in hand, he would drop off the roof, wave his pistol in their faces and force them to open the back compartment of the truck. At that moment, according to the plan, Stedeford and McCarthy would pop up and relieve of the money bags. While this was taking place, Guthrie would be parking the drop car in front of the armored car, thus preventing the driver from trying to take off. Once the drop car was in place, Guthrie would exit the vehicle and provide backup from that position. As soon as they had the money, Guthrie's job was to place two fake bombs near the truck.

Then they would pile the money bags and the robbers into the getaway car and drive off. They'd transfer the money bags to the Blitzenvagon, dump the drop car and jump on the freeway.

However, before going ahead with the plan, they agreed they needed to practice their movements many times. Just to be sure. So while continuing to surveil the armored car, they also practiced the robbery.

Guthrie was antsy. The waiting around seemingly doing nothing was driving him crazy. Adding to his irritability was the fact that he was – most of the time – tweaking. Guthrie had a jones for meth, which made him paranoid, which probably explained his qualms about Stedeford.

* * * * *

March 13 was the day. They parked their vehicles and reviewed the plan. The heist was imminent, when they noticed a construction crew working on the roof of the building next to the theater. They would be exposed to view. So very reluctantly, Langan called it off. Instead, they decided to rob a bank. So they scouted the area and finally decided on Bank

One, located in Phoenix. But as luck would have it, the cops were swarming around the bank. Someone had mistakenly deposited an envelope full of coke instead of money.

The gang decided that Phoenix was full of bad juju and left.

Back at the house in Kansas, the ARA had a financial crisis on their hands. They were broke. So to gain the sorely needed operating funds they decided to hit a bank in Des Moines, which had been lucky for them. The target was Boatman's Bank, located next door to the police academy. This fact – the police academy – particularly pleased Guthrie, who found it immensely humorous. It would be akin to raising his middle-finger to the government.

Stedeford purchased a drop car for $560. When purchasing the car, Stedeford used the same I.D. he had used before. Bad move. Langan told him to dump the car. Guthrie purchased another car of the same make and model. He thought this would confuse the police.

Guthrie explained it to Langan like this: "This is the kind of ruse the IRA uses. Throws the cops off. One we used; the other is a decoy, like duck hunters." He grinned.

"Good thinking," said Langan.

* * * * *

On March 29, the ARA hit the Boatman's Bank. This time Langan, Guthrie and McCarthy dressed like construction workers. Only most construction workers don't utilize body armor and camouflage ski masks. McCarthy toted the fake bomb in an Easter Basket, along with a .45 caliber Glock.

As they stood outside the bank, Langan looked at the others. He nodded and they walked into the bank, guns out.

"Get down! Get down on the floor, now!" bellowed Langan.

Located in the center of the lobby was a high table, with pens and deposit slips. McCarthy placed the fake bomb on it, then turned and waved his gun menacingly at the patrons and employees. His job was to scare the shit out of everyone.

While McCarthy did his intimidation thing, Langan and Guthrie scrambled over the counter and grabbed the money from the tellers' drawers.

At the forty-five second mark, McCarthy shouted, "Andale! Andale!"
Time was up.

Guthrie and Langan stopped immediately and the three robbers walked out of the bank. Stedeford sat behind the wheel of the getaway car.

They jumped in and Stedeford punched it, heading for the Blitzenvagon, which was parked at an apartment complex.

"Almost there," shouted Stedeford, riding an excellent adrenaline high. He glanced at McCarthy, who nodded back. McCarthy pulled out a live grenade, pulled the pin, and stuffed the grenade into the crease between the seat and back cushion.

"Good to go," said McCarthy.

Stedeford pulled to a stop next to the Blitzenvagon and the first drop car, the decoy car. Everybody jumped out and climbed in the Blitzenvagon. Langan was driving now.

"Go, go, go!" sang out Guthrie.

Langan punched it and shot out of the parking lot.

Stedeford and McCarthy exchanged a look, then began laughing with giddy glee.

"Fucking perfect!" said Stedeford.

McCarthy nodded. "Damn right, man!"

Hours later, after a long drive, they were back at the house in Kansas.

Once inside, Langan immediately wanted to count the take.

"Dump it on the table," he said. The bags were upended and the cash tumbled out. Langan began the count, separating the money according to denominations.

"We should get one of those money counting machines, like in Vegas," said Stedeford, who liked gizmos.

Guthrie scowled. "Fuck that shit! We don't need no money machine."

Langan paid no attention, concentrating on the count.

Finished, he leaned back in his chair and smiled. "$28,255," he announced.

Stedeford and McCarthy whooped. Guthrie just nodded in grim satisfaction.

* * * * *

On the 31st of March, the gang divided up the spoils. Then they discussed taking another break.

"I believe it's time for a vacation," said Langan. He looked around at the others.

Guthrie shrugged. He didn't care one way or the other.

"If there are no objections, we'll take a break," continued Langan.

"How long?" asked McCarthy, who was already planning how to spend his loot.

"Three or four months," said Langan. "We need to rest up and think about what's next."

"Armored car," suggested Stedeford, who wanted a big score.

"Let me think about it," said Langan. "In the meantime, we'll split up. Meet back here the end of July."

In his memoir, Guthrie stated that Langan drove off on April 1, heading for Kansas City. Stedeford and McCarthy drove off the same day, heading for Elohim City. And supposedly, according to his memoir, Guthrie remained at the house in Kansas.

In his excellent book *In Bad Company*, author Mark S. Hamm speculated that the ARA decided to take a break for another reason than simply time to rest and plan. Hamm asserted that the ARA participated in the Oklahoma City bombing. In other words, the ARA, along with Strassmeir and Mahon, helped Timothy McVeigh construct and deliver the bomb that destroyed the Murrah building.

* * * * *

On April 25, Stedeford and McCarthy were back in Philadelphia, recording their white power band's CD. The band was called Day of the Sword and the CD carried the same name.

Langan was living in the apartment of his cross dressing lover, Cheryl, in Kansas City. While there, he got a phone call from Guthrie at the house in Kansas.

"What's up?" asked Langan.

"We're almost out of money again, that's what's up," stated Guthrie.

"Fuck."

"Second that. Just over three grand left," said Guthrie.

"Okay. We need to do something about that."

"No shit, man."

"Okay," said Langan. "I'll head back and we can do some business."

* * * * *

Back in the house in Kansas, Langan and Guthrie came up with a plan – another bank. Only this time it would be out of their normal operating area.

"I been thinking," said Langan. "To reduce some of the heat, we should go outside the Midwest. A place completely unexpected."

"Good thinking," said Guthrie. "Where?"

"Down south someplace," suggested Langan. "By now the feds are probably seeing a pattern and this will throw a monkey wrench into the pattern."

Guthrie chuckled. "I like it, man."

* * * * *

The next day, they took off for Louisville, Kentucky. After scouting the area, they decided to hit the Great Financial Bank. It was near a freeway, which met their ease of exit need. Guthrie purchased a drop car for $495. At the used car dealership, he used the name Oliver Revell and presented himself as a former FBI agent. Revell was the actual name of an actual FBI agent that Guthrie had seen on TV. He had been involved in the hunt for Robert Mathews and The Order years before.

On May 23, the two bank robbers arrived at the bank. Guthrie parked the junker combat style and left the motor running. Once again, they decided to disguise themselves as construction workers. Only this time instead of ski masks they used bandannas to cover the lower half of their faces, like Mexican bandits.

Guns drawn, they hustled into the bank.

Langan shouted, "Get down! Everybody on the floor, now! No alarms! No hostages!"

Guthrie carried the fake bomb and a gun. Placing the bomb on a table in the lobby, he then waved his gun, keeping the frightened people in place on the floor.

"We're here to confiscate money for the Mexican Revolution," yelled Guthrie. "Viva la Lapatista!"

By now, Langan had scrambled over the counter and was grabbing the money out of the drawers. He finished quickly and the bank robbers bolted.

Outside, they jumped in the drop car and took off. As they drove away, the dye packs exploded. Guthrie, who was driving, almost crashed the car when the dye packs exploded. They pulled up to the Blitzenvagon and jumped in, abandoning the drop car.

Heading north, they entered Indiana, then headed west toward Kansas. Once back in the house in Kansas, they washed the ruined money. Guthrie had read that the red stain could be washed out by means of water and rubbing alcohol. Langan was in a bad mood because he had a bad tooth.

In fact, a life of crime was taking a severe toll on Langan's health.

The money washing system wasn't very effective. They only saved $2,400, which pissed off Guthrie. The ARA was having a bad day.

The ARA had other problems, too. *Newsweek* had just run a big story that fingered the ARA as part of the Oklahoma City bombing. So now they were running on empty: strapped for cash, declining physical health and the objects of a nationwide manhunt. Things weren't going well, at all.

Guthrie's paranoia was now more intense than ever and it was catching. Langan became more and more paranoid as time passed. He kept looking over his shoulder, waiting for something to happen. Something bad.

Still, they were determined to keep on keeping on.

* * * * *

On June 22, Langan and Guthrie hit the Guaranty Bank in Glendale, Wisconsin. Attired as construction workers – again – the two bank robbers strolled into the bank and went through the usual routine. Guthrie carried the fake bomb, which he placed on a table in the lobby. Langan was pillaging the tellers' drawers behind the counter.

While waving his gun around, scaring everyone to death, Guthrie looked around and noted the vault was open. The ARA had always gone for the easy score, the teller drawers, because trying to get into the vault was too time-consuming. Vaults raised the risk factor exponentially. By the time they managed to get a vault open, the bank would be surrounded by cops.

But this was different. The vault was already open, just waiting to be plucked clean. So Guthrie decided to improvise. He raced into the vault, snatching as many bags as he could carry. Adrenaline pumped through him, filling him with high-voltage energy.

Exiting the vault, he watched as Langan clawed at the money in the drawers.

"Andale! Andale!" yelled Guthrie.

Langan stopped immediately. Time to go!

They dashed to the bank's entrance, where Guthrie stopped, turned and lobbed a smoke grenade back into the lobby. Smoke billowed everywhere. The people on the floor began coughing. It wasn't poisonous, but it sure wasn't pleasant to breathe.

Langan was out the door heading toward the getaway car, followed by the heavily laden Guthrie. "Go, go!" sang out Guthrie.

They reached the car and started throwing the bags of money into it. About ten feet away, a passing motorist stopped right in front of them, staring. Langan looked right at the motorist. He pulled up his shirt, revealing the 9mm semi-automatic pistol jammed in his pants.

"Move it! Fast!" hissed Langan. The motorist didn't have to be told twice. He punched it and drove on.

Guthrie jumped into the driver's seat, as Langan clambered into the passenger's seat. The engine roared and they shot off. On the way, to the Blitzenvagon a dye pack exploded in one of the bags.

"Goddammit!" shouted Langan.

Langan grabbed the offending bag and shoved it out his window, holding it with one hand. Red smoke plumed from the bag.

Arriving at the Blitzenvagon, they transferred the money and left the drop car.

Back in the house in Kansas, they sorted through the money, separating the ruined money from the unspoiled money. In the end, they ended up burning thousands of dollars of cash. But they still had $30,000 of clean money. It was a good score.

* * * * *

The ARA idolized Robert Mathews and The Order, which had once upon a time planned to take out an electrical power station in Los Angeles, effectively cutting the power of millions of people. It never happened, but the ARA thought it was a great idea. They wanted to actually pull it off. If they did so, it would mean they were as good as or even better than The Order.

To that end, at the beginning of July 1995, Mark Thomas and Guthrie scouted out a power station located outside Allentown. The power station provided electrical power to a vast portion of the highly-populated Northeastern states. If they could take it with explosives, they would deny electricity to tens of millions of residents and businesses.

On the following day, they were back at Mark Thomas' farm, where, sitting at Thomas' kitchen table they talked for hours. During this time, Guthrie waxed eloquent, telling Thomas about his exploits as a Phineas Priest. He went into detail about all the hits he and Langan had done. Guthrie, like most criminals, was arrogant and wanted attention. He wanted people to know who he was – a badass. He needed the respect of those he associated with.

What he forgot was that most criminals came to ignominious ends not through stellar police work, but through someone dropping a dime on them. Guthrie forgot the old adage that "loose lips sink ships." Chatty Cathies were their own worst enemies.

A week later, Guthrie was back at the house in Kansas. Langan was not there. He was in Kansas City living on the wild side. Dressed in full drag, Donna McClure, aka Pete Langan, along with other members of the Kansas City cross dressing community, which was referred to as the transsexual community spoke to a class of psychology students at the University of Missouri.

Donna was a powerful speaker. She told the class, "Being a transsexual is not a lifestyle choice. It is not something anyone would choose or wish for. It is just the way one truly feels inside."

No one remotely suspected that the eloquent, cross dressing woman stuck in a man's body was a bank robbing, gun-toting Phineas Priest bent on killing God's enemies.

After the presentation, the cross dressers changed clothes and attended a transsexual party. At the party Donna hooked up with Cheri Roberts, aka Bob, who was a man trapped in a woman's body. Cheri was undergoing hormone therapy preparatory to her sex change operation. The two – Donna and Cheri – engaged in an intense sexual relationship, one that must have been trippy. Yet Donna went both ways, too. During her romance with Cheri, Donna was also romantically and sexually involved with other male cross dressers, who, like Donna, were women trapped in men's bodies.

In one reality, Donna was Commander Pedro, the honcho of the ARA; in another reality, Donna was a cross dressing bi-sexual who wanted to be someone else – a woman. Langan's grip on reality was split and dysfunctional. From any perspective, Langan's neurotic psychosis did not bode well for the ARA.

Langan's mental and physical confusion served to exacerbate his paranoia. He was certain that Guthrie knew about his identity crisis. And Guthrie was, according to anyone who knew him, a complete and total psychopath. Guthrie, by his own admission and actions, despised any type of sexual deviancy. Guthrie believed all perverts deserved to die. Thus, Langan began to fear for his own life, if indeed Guthrie was aware of Commander Pedro's secret life.

A psychological analysis of Guthrie would have revealed he was not only paranoid and amoral, but that he may well have been a latent homosexual, who substituted food and alcohol for the release of sexual desire.

The fact that the members of the ARA were "gear queers" was most telling. Their penchant for camouflaged clothing, combat boots, ski masks, baseball caps and body armor, along with their preference for male companionship, was an overt symbolic manifestation of their latent homosexual tendencies.

It seems reasonable to assert that the other members of the ARA were well-aware of Langan's "walk on the wild side." Stedeford, McCarthy, Mark Thomas and, later, Brescia had no problem with it. For either consciously or unconsciously they realized and accepted it as a normal fixture of the Neo-Nazi, white power movement. For that matter, most skinheads exhibited homosexual tendencies. The skinhead 'costume' had been borrowed directly from the dress code of the homosexual community. It wasn't a coincidence.

* * * * *

While these psycho-sexual undercurrents swirled around the ARA, Donna McClure, aka Peter Langan, was falling in love. The object of his lust and affection was Cheri Roberts. The couple had reached the point of discussing marriage. Of course, Cheri had no clue about Donna's other identity – Commander Pedro. Each of Donna's lives was separate and distinct.

Because of his love for Cheri, Donna finally took the plunge. He began a course of hormone therapy designed to transform him into the woman he was. Estrogen worked its magic on Donna – Pete Langan no longer had to shave and he developed female breasts, called gynecomastia.

At the same time, Langan distanced himself from the ARA and the white power movement. The testosterone-fueled anger and violence of Commander Pedro receded into the background. Now Langan was more concerned with becoming all he was meant to be – a real woman. He talked to Cheri about becoming an interior decorator.

* * * * *

Meanwhile, on August 16, 1995, two men walked into a bank located in St. Louis, Missouri – the Magna Bank. This time the modus operandi was just different enough to notice. The men wore FBI caps and used bandannas to disguise their faces. Instead of climbing over the counter to ransack the tellers' drawers, they threatened the tellers with their guns, until the tellers forked over the cash. Thus, the robbery consumed minutes, rather than sixty seconds and gone – the earmark of the ARA.

One of the robbers carried a fake bomb that was left behind. And the signal to leave was shouted out: "Andale! Andale!"

A smoke grenade was tossed. Thick smoke hissed. The two robbers bolted out of the bank and climbed into an older model orange Ford; the engine was running, as the driver waited.

"Go!" shouted the second robber, slapping the dashboard.

The orange Ford pulled out into traffic, moving rapidly toward a pre-designated point – an apartment complex. The three robbers dropped the Ford and drove away in another vehicle.

It didn't take the FBI long to locate the drop car. When they ran the numbers, they learned the car had been bought with cash by a former

FBI agent, Wayne Manis. Manis was one of the feds featured in *The Silent Brotherhood*, which related the tale of The Order.

Using the name of a former FBI agent to purchase a getaway car was the trademark of Guthrie, who saw the humor in such antics. It was Guthrie's way of thumbing his nose at the FBI, like a little kid saying, "Catch me if you!" Or put another way, Guthrie was double-dog daring the feds.

But Guthrie didn't plan the robbery. Stedeford and McCarthy picked the bank, bought the car, planned the heist, and pulled it off. Guthrie's only role was that of getaway driver. In effect, the young guns, who had formerly followed orders, were now giving the orders, taking matters into their own hands.

Stedeford and McCarthy had discussed the matter prior to, basically, committing mutiny and going solo.

"Pete's absent – again," said Stedeford. "Nothin's happening. Where's the vaunted Commander Pedro when you need him?"

"Fuck it," said McCarthy. "Pete's lost interest. He's got better things to do. He needs to grow a pair. But it's not happening. So fuck it. We'll do it our own selves."

Stedeford nodded.

"We know the routine, how it's done, what to do when. And most of all, we know how to get in, get out and get away. Shit, we did it with Pete enough times."

"Damn right, my man! Let's do it. Commander Pedro has just been demoted." Stedeford laughed.

And that's what they did.

* * * * *

The Magna Bank robbery take was $17,000, which meant it was successful. In, out and away without a problem. Or so it appeared. What looked like a brilliant bank robbery in mid-day wasn't all that brilliant. There had been problems galore: first, the getaway driver was blotto on Tequila; second, when Stedeford and McCarthy dashed from the bank, the getaway car wasn't there. Guthrie had moved it for some reason. So, third, McCarthy and Stedeford stood out front of the bank they had just robbed, with the money they had just stolen, twiddling their thumbs. Finally, Guthrie had driven up and picked them up.

Climbing into the getaway car, Stedeford went all Lord of the Flies on Guthrie.

"Jesus Christ, asshole! What the fuck? Where the fuck were you?" For a second, Stedeford considered whacking the old fart over the head with his gun, pistol-whipping him.

"We came out and you weren't there!" screamed McCarthy, shaking his head in disbelief. "Like fucking amateur day."

Guthrie tried to defend himself, mumbling some drunken spiel about the car standing out and looking suspicious.

"Fuck!" screamed Stedeford. "No fucking excuses. You're drunk! Inept and incapable! It's a goddamned bank robbery, motherfucker! Not a sightseeing tour." Stedeford collapsed back in his seat. "Fuck me."

* * * * *

While this fiasco was transpiring, Donna, aka Commander Pedro, aka Pete Langan was in Colorado with Cheri. They were frolicking at a resort in the Rocky Mountains.

* * * * *

Two days later, on August 18, Langan showed up at the house in Kansas, where he immediately asserted his authority, telling the others that the next hit would occur in about a week in Madison, Wisconsin.

On the surface, the ARA seemed to back to business as usual. But something had changed. Until now, the ARA's goal had been holy revolution, doing the Will of God and waging war on Jews, blacks, banks and the government. All that had faded. Now they were motivated by greed. They needed money.

Now it was all about the money, at least for Langan and Guthrie. The others, though, still believed in the holy revolution. Their motivation was different.

* * * * *

Stedeford and McCarthy jelly-rolled to Elohim City, where they picked up Brescia, who would participate in the robbery. From there the trio of young bank robbing firebrands drove to Missouri, where they met up with Langan and Guthrie at the local WalMart, in Springfield. Then they drove two vehicles to Lincoln, Illinois, checking into a Motel 6.

Langan, McCarthy and Brescia drove to Madison, Wisconsin. There they purchased a $300 drop car from a Mom and Pop used car dealer. At the same time, Guthrie and Stedeford were out buying up supplies for a fake bomb. The two groups convened at the Motel 6 in Janesville, Wisconsin, where Langan clued everyone in on the plan to hit Bank One.

The ARA, for the moment, was acting like professional bank robbers. Even Guthrie, who abstained from getting blotto.

On August 30, they donned their bank robber outfits: body armor, two-way radios and weapons. Langan, being a creature of habit, again chose construction worker disguises for his crew.

Four of the five – Stedeford, Bresica, Guthrie and McCarthy – climbed into the drop car and headed for the bank. Langan remained behind, staying in the Blitzenvagon. This was very unusual and betrayed the mood of the group. On the surface, everything was professional and cool; but underneath, there was a rude, harsh-textured energy. Things weren't as they seemed. Egos, personalities and secret agendas wormed their way into the ARA.

Supposedly, Langan remained behind to monitor the gang's police radios. The idea was that he could give them a heads up if anything unusual happened, like the cops converging on the bank while the robbery was in progress. But that was window-dressing. Langan's heart wasn't in it anymore. His hear belonged to Cheri and their life of bliss.

Stedeford was driving the drop car. He parked, nose out, at the bank. Guthrie, Brescia and McCarthy exited the car, bandannas over their faces. Guns out, they walked through the bank's doors.

Inside, they followed their usual modus operandi. Shouting, "This is a robbery! Get down! Get down, now!"

McCarthy clambered over the counter and began grabbing the cash from the tellers' drawers, while Guthrie moved to the drawer located at the drive-through teller. Brescia's job was to keep the people scared shitless and under control. No heroes. Brescia held the fake bomb in one hand and his gun in the other hand.

Stedeford's panicked voice crackled over the two-way radio, "The alarm went off! Get out!"

Brescia shouted the signal. "Andales! Andales!"

The three men moved toward the exit. That was the moment Brescia fucked up. He was supposed to set the fake bomb down, then as they exited he was to toss a smoke grenade back into the bank. Instead, he set the bomb down and accidentally dropped the smoke grenade onto the fake bomb, which was in a bucket.

"Fuck," said Brescia. But he didn't have time to rectify the situation. He had to get out!

Outside, Stedeford waiting impatiently as the three jumped in the getaway car. When they were all in, he took off like a shot. Minutes passed as Stedeford weaved through traffic to the drop zone, an apartment complex, where Langan waited in the Blitzenvagon.

As Brescia braked to a halt, one of the rear tires exploded. The explosion sounded like a gun shot. In response, Guthrie whipped out his pistol, looking for cops.

"Let's get the hell out of here!" shouted Langan from the Blitzenvagon. The others jumped into the Blitzenvagon and off they went.

* * * * *

Back at Bank One, bomb squads arrived and began carefully examining the bomb in the bucket. Police found the drop car and called for a forensics team. Examination of the car revealed two more fake bombs and a page of a newspaper. The page contained an article about Timothy McVeigh.

In the Blitzenvagon, bitter recriminations were the order of the day. Everybody was pissed off.

"What the fuck was that?" demanded Guthrie, looking at Brescia. "You really fucked that up. Just drop the grenade on the floor, how hard is that? But no, Mr. Wizard drops it in the bucket. You know, it could have exploded, killing one of us. Stupid shit!"

Before Brescia could defend or explain himself, Stedeford jumped in. He was still irate at Guthrie's shenanigans at the Magna Bank.

"Oh, and you're Mr. Fucking Perfect, right? Drunk as a skunk at the last hit. Then moving the fucking car, leaving us hanging in the wind. And all your constant bitching and whining about this that and the other. Fuck you, asshole! Just shut the fuck up!"

They were now in Illinois, where Langan decided to pull into a truck stop. Langan fueled up while McCarthy counted the take -- $9,200. Less than $2,000 apiece, when split five ways.

They drove to Springfield, Illinois, where Stedeford and Brescia took off in the second vehicle, heading to Elohim City. The others drove to the house in Kansas.

Stedeford showed up at the house in Kansas a few days later. Brescia remained at Elohim City.

Stedeford and Guthrie glared at each other, but both decided the ARA had more pressing matters on their hands than a personal beef. Langan announced it was time to hit an armored car, probably in Indiana or Ohio. The hitch was they'd need about $10,000 for operating expenses. And they didn't have it.

"We've hit banks in most of the Mid-West," said Langan. "But we've never hit anything in Indiana. So that's the target, probably Indianapolis. It's big and there's money for the taking. The plan is to hit a bank for walking around money, along with money to fund the armored car hit."

Everybody had something to say, but in the end they all agreed.

"Next is the date," said Langan. "We'll take a break and schedule it for the beginning of October."

"Just in time for Halloween," said Stedeford. "Trick or treat."

They all laughed.

"I got something," said Stedeford.

"Okay, what?"

"Well, I got some connections in Minnesota, from the Aryan Nations. I want to hit a bank in Minnesota with them."

Langan nodded. "Okay. Do a recon and give us a report in October."

"Next is this place," said Langan, referring to the house. "I believe it's time to move. We've been here too long. Sooner or later somebody's going to notice something. Since we're going to hit an armored car, we can kill two birds with one stone. We move and we get closer to the target area. I think Columbus sounds good. It's right in the middle."

Everyone agreed.

"We'll check out rentals on our way to Philadelphia," said Stedeford. He and McCarthy were headed home.

"Good," said Langan. "We'll check out armored cars and their routes and routines." 'We' referred to Langan and Guthrie.

"One more thing," said Langan. "Brescia isn't fitting in. He's making mistakes..."

"Fucking up royally is more like it," interrupted Guthrie.

Langan shrugged the remark off and continued, "He's making mistakes. And we can't afford mistakes, not at this point. I say he's out."

"Second that," said Guthrie.

Everyone agreed. They couldn't take chances. Brescia was out.

At the same time he was being kicked out of the ARA, Brescia was being kicked out of Elohim City, along with Strassmeir. Grandpa Millar, the honcho of Elohim City, considered them both "disappointments." Translation: they were rash, prone to violence and didn't play well with others.

*****

In Columbus, Stedeford and McCarthy looked at a number of properties. Nothing fit their wish-list. The one that came closest was located at 585 Reinhard Avenue. It was a run-down, dilapidated duplex. Not even a house, it was one-step up from a third-world hovel.

In Indianapolis, Guthrie and Langan confronted the Mistress of Disadvantage: all the banks in Indy were interconnected, utilizing a packet-switching computer network. The problem with this type of system was that the computer constantly scanned for open channels. This meant the ARA could not monitor transmissions because the channels were, in effect, random and kept changing.

Langan decided it was too-risky. The plan was a no-go.

In Minnesota, Stedeford hit a brick wall, too. None of the banks presented quick and easy escape routes. Another no-go.

In other words, the gang was faced with a parade of complications. Available funds were almost non-existent and they couldn't locate an acceptable target bank; their vehicles, which had hundreds of thousands of miles on them, needed to be replaced or totally refurbished; finally, the gang's esprit de corps was drooping. The ARA wasn't used to bad luck and adversity.

In Biblical terms, the handwriting was on the wall. Only they couldn't decipher it.

Their most immediate need was money. A description of their financial condition was "dire straits." Money would solve most of their difficulties. To resolve their money problem, Langan decided they should revisit the past: they would jump in a time machine and go back to their most successful robbery – St. Louis.

Thus, November found the gang in The Lou, St. Louis, Missouri. They spent the entire month scouting out banks. In each case, there was some factor that left them less than enthusiastic. Most of the time, Guthrie was tweaking and/or drunk, which meant he was worthless. Stedeford, still nursing a grudge against Guthrie, was fed up with Guthrie's crazy antics.

The palpable tension between the two finally exploded.

"Fuck you, you fucked up piece of shit," hissed Stedeford. They were in the Motel 6. Stedeford was angry because Guthrie was high again.

Guthrie, who was bat-shit crazy even when not stoked on meth, didn't bother to reply. He charged Stedeford, knocking the younger man back into a wall. Punches were thrown.

Langan, who was in the adjoining room, heard the sound of Stedeford crashing into the wall. Jumping to his feet, he raced next door, where he found the two engaged in a John Wayne-esque brawl. Langan couldn't believe this shit.

"Break it up!" he roared.

The two combatants continued to toss wild punches, gouge and kick. Both were breathing heavily.

"Goddammit! Break it up!" Langan moved in and separated the two. Huffing a puffing, Stedeford wanted to finish it. Guthrie did too, but he was exhausted, so he backed off.

Langan demanded to know what was going on. Like little kids in a playground dispute, each accused the other of starting it. McCarthy entered the room and listened to the spat.

"He's either drunk or high every hour of the day," said Stedeford, pointing at Guthrie. "Fucking amateur behavior is what it is." Turning to Langan, he said, "He's putting everything and everybody at risk."

"Am not," said Guthrie. Not much of a defense, but then he was high as a kite. His synapses were fritzing and shorting out.

"He's a major loser," said McCarthy, adding his two-cents.

"Look," said Langan, "this shit has got to stop. If you two can't work together like pros, then we're in trouble." He looked at both of them, hoping his challenge to professionalism would make them both stop and think.

"Fuck it," said Stedeford. "I can't work with him anymore. That's it. Over and out."

McCarthy nodded. "Me neither. Either he goes or I'm out of here too."

Langan didn't know what to say. Things were falling apart and he didn't know how to salvage the situation.

In the end, Langan gave Stedeford and McCarthy their shares of the money that was left – about $2000 a man. Stedeford and McCarthy split.

* * * * *

The dynamic duo – the cross dresser and the tweaker – remained in St. Louis, scouting out banks. Langan was angry and just wanted to go be with Cheri. On his part, Guthrie was only interested in escaping reality through meth or booze.

Determined to find a suitable bank, the two hung in there. Then one day, Guthrie arrived an hour late to case a bank; and when he did finally arrive, he could barely walk. High again. Back at the Motel 6, Langan confronted Guthrie.

"What the hell is your problem?" asked Langan.

Guthrie mumbled something incoherently.

Langan punched him and then proceeded to beat the hell out of him.

Two days later, Langan and Guthrie talked it out in a more civilized manner. Langan adopted stoic resignation; Guthrie, although he now hated Langan, needed Langan. So he did his best to suppress his hatred.

Finally, the located a bank – the Roosevelt Bank.

On November 22, just prior to Thanksgiving, two men walked into the Roosevelt Bank. Instead of being dressed as construction workers, they adopted a new disguise: policemen.

As usual, Langan clambered over the counter. "No alarms! No hostages!" Guthrie stood over the prostrate victims, acting threatening, waving his gun around. Guthrie kept checking his watch. After sixty seconds, he shouted the signal: "Andale, Sanchez! Andale Sanchez!"

Langan responded, clambering back over the counter, while Guthrie placed the fake bomb on a table. As the two walked toward the exit, Guthrie tossed the smoke grenade back into the lobby.

Jumping in the idling drop car, they took off. Twelve hours later they were back at the duplex in Columbus. The take: $2,500.

* * * * *

Richard Guthrie was a liability. Even Langan didn't want to be around him. He was a loose cannon, ready to go off any second. With $2000 to his name, he decided to go solo. Driving to Cincinnati, he scouted out banks and decided to hit the Society Bank. Guthrie's decision was based solely on the bank's location – a strip mall. Guthrie was living in the past, too. Banks at strip malls were inside his comfort zone.

Ever volatile, Guthrie's self-centered megalomania goaded him to overt recklessness. In effect, he said, "Fuck it," and adopted a fatalistic attitude. He wrote and mailed letters to newspapers and the FBI. The letters to the FBI were sneering criticisms of the FBI's abilities. The ARA was invincible; the FBI, full of clowns and incompetents, didn't have snowball's chance in hell of ever catching the ARA. The ARA was simply too smart.

December 8, 1995, a vagrant pulling a trash can walked through the mall in Cincinnati. It was Richard Guthrie doing his best imitation of "slumming." A bank robber in street-person disguise. At the entrance to the bank, he parked his trash can and walked in. No bandanna, no ski-mask. Just a hoodie.

Gun out, he yelled, "Get down! This is a robbery!"

Scrambling over the counter, he grabbed the cash from the drawers, while trying to keep an eye on the prostrate victims. Once all the drawers were empty, he crawled back over the counter and raced out of the bank into the mall, where he slowed to a rapid walk.

Outside the mall, he jumped in the Blitzenvagon and took off. No drop car this time. This was a straight-forward smash and grab. The take: $4,400.

Emotionally deflated and alone, Guthrie drifted on an ocean of self-pity. He realized that without a gang, he was nothing more than a loser, just as McCarthy had said.

* * * * *

A few days after the solo Cincinnati hit, Langan arrived at the hovel in Columbus, where Guthrie was holed up. Langan informed Guthrie that he (Langan), Stedeford and McCarthy had a hit on.

"And you won't be participating," said Langan.

The words slapped Guthrie in the face. When Stedeford and McCarthy arrived, Guthrie swallowed his pride and asked for forgiveness. Then he asked if he could be part of the hit.

"No!"

Guthrie was definitely out. Humiliated, Guthrie decided to hook up with Shawn Kenney and form his own crew. Before he could pack up his gear and leave the house, Langan and the others returned from their hit. They were in high spirits.

Langan and crew had hit the Mid-America Bank just outside Toledo, Ohio. The take: $7,400. The ARA was back in business and back on top of the world.

Depressed and despondent, Guthrie left, driving back to the house in Kansas. It was Christmas Eve and Guthrie was on I-70. Heavy snow was falling, making driving hazardous. Guthrie decided to play it safe, pulling into a run-down motel outside Indy. He spent Christmas Eve in a disgustingly filthy motel room, knocking back a bottle of tequila. Merry Fucking Christmas!

Finally back at the house in Kansas, Guthrie licked his wounds. Then Langan showed up and they talked. Langan told Guthrie the others would never let him back in, but that if he got his shit together, he (Langan) would work with him, doing some hits on the side.

Then they went to work moving all their stuff out of the Kansas house. Renting two storage lockers, they cleared the house out. When they finished, Guthrie left in the Blitzenvagon, heading for Ohio and the duplex in Columbus. The rental agreement on the duplex was in his name, so he figured it was his.

As soon as he arrived, Guthrie began scouting out banks in Dayton. But he would need help. No more of the solo stuff. It was too risky. He needed Shawn Kenney. So he put out feelers and found Kenney in a squalid motel in Cincinnati.

Guthrie told Kenney he wanted him to do a hit. All he had to do was drive the getaway car. Kenney waffled. He was now in the U.S. Army, where he would soon be a sergeant. Kenney's agenda was, once he made sergeant, to become a big-time arms dealer. Lots of money in military-grade weapons. And the white power movement groups and militias would pay beau coup bucks for that kind of ordnance.

What Guthrie proposed was small-time compared to gun running.

Married, with two kids and a wife, Janice, Kenney wanted to move up and become a big fish in a big pond. When her husband informed her he had met with Guthrie, who wanted him to take part in a hit, Janice Kenney didn't like it. So she dropped a dime on Guthrie, placing a call to the FBI. The FBI was very interested in what Janice had to say. Richard Guthrie sat at the top of their wish-list, along with the rest of the Mid-Western Bank Robbers.

The FBI wanted Shawn Kenney to come in and spill the beans, offering a sweet deal if he did. Shawn Kenney took them up on the offer. He met up with an agent, Ed Woods, who told Kenney to play along with Guthrie. Agree to be the getaway driver, and let Woods know what was going on at all times. Kenney agreed.

Kenney called Guthrie and told him he was in. Ecstatic, Guthrie scheduled a meet at a nearby mall. They would talk things over at Papa Dino's Italian Restaurant.

On his way to the mall, Guthrie got a strange feeling, like he was being watched. So he began watching his rear view mirror, checking for tails. Yep, there it was. Rather than turn into the mall, Guthrie drove by the entrance. At the next major intersection, Guthrie turned left and then turned into a residential area, one of those planned living communities.

The tail was closer now, almost on top of him. Guthrie knew the jig was up. And as if synchronized with his realization, the tail's driver hit the siren and announced loudly, "Stop your car and pull over. Now!"

Fuck that, thought Guthrie. He was ARA. The Aryan Republican Army didn't surrender. Making a quick turn, Guthrie found himself on a dead end street. The pursuing tail car cut him off as he tried to evade. Then the tail car concluded the cat and mouse game by the simple expedient of smashing into the Blitzenvagon.

The impact bounced Guthrie's forehead into the steering wheel, opening a gash that, like most head wounds, bled profusely. Whatever anyone had to say about Guthrie, one thing was certain, he wasn't a quitter. Dazed and confused, he still had the chutzpah necessary to exit the Blitzenvagon and take off on foot. Heading for a nearby woodsy area, he got caught up in a snowdrift that came up to his thighs.

The tail car belonged to Ed Woods, the FBI agent working with Shawn Kenney. Kenney had called him and informed him of the meeting at Dino's Italian Restaurant. So Woods had been cruising the main thoroughfare in front of the mall, watching for the Blitzenvagon, which was hard to miss. The instant he spotted the vehicle, Woods had radioed for backup.

Moments before Guthrie got stuck in the snowdrift a dozen FBI agents had arrived, jumped out of their cars and joined the foot race.

Trapped in the snowdrift, Guthrie was out of options. Seconds later, the FBI was all over him. They cuffed him and then pulled him out of the snowdrift.

* * * * *

The following day, Langan arrived at the duplex in Columbus. He had no idea Guthrie was now in custody. While Langan was sitting in the duplex in Columbus having a cold beer, in Cincinnati, a heavily armed SWAT team of FBI agents showed up at his wife's house. Smashing in the door, the SWAT team burst into the house shouting, "FBI! FBI! Get down! Get down!"

The goon squad then proceeded to ransack the house, searching for evidence that Langan had been there. "They scared the hell out of everybody. They had no regard for anything. They just busted up the whole place and traumatized the children," said Leslie Langan.

The SWAT team found nothing. No traces of Langan, no guns, no explosives and no hidden money. As the SWAT team left, one of the honchos informed Leslie, "By the way, your husband is dead. Richard Guthrie killed him."

* * * * *

After cuffing Guthrie and rescuing him from the snowdrift, the FBI agents escorted him to one of their vehicles. Sitting in the back seat, Guthrie was offered champagne in a paper cup. He graciously accepted. The FBI agents were celebrating his capture. And Guthrie was participating in the celebration, which he found surreal.

Guthrie took a sip and smacked his lips in pleasure. "What year is this champagne?"

One of the agents smiled and said, "That's classified information."

Captors and captive laughed.

Sixty minutes later, Guthrie was seated in a room, about to be interrogated. A cake sat on the table in front of him. The frosted inscription said "Welcome Home Bandit." Instead of interrogation, Guthrie was part of another celebration: a capture party! FBI agents stood around the room drinking beer, waiting their turn to get their picture taken with the famous bank robber.

Guthrie was the star of the show. And he was loving it!

It worked. 'It' was a nifty interrogation technique the FBI used to lull criminal suspects into spilling their guts. If Guthrie thought the FBI respected him – and he did, he bought it hook, line and sinker – then he would be willing to cooperate.

Duped and bamboozled, Guthrie began talking to Ed Woods. In reality, Woods was now interrogating Guthrie. But it didn't seem like an interrogation. It was more like a friendly chat between two colleagues who respected each other.

Even though Guthrie had fallen for the ploy, he wasn't stupid. All his answers were posed in hypothetical terms: if that had happened, then it probably happened like this. The ploy had worked, but Guthrie wasn't giving up any solid information, like where the FBI could find Langan.

Guthrie was then moved to the county jail in Covington, Kentucky, where the party was over. No beer, no champagne and no celebratory frosted cake.

It only took one night in jail for Guthrie come to a decision. He would cooperate. Maybe they'd cut him some slack. Guthrie told Woods about the Springdale bank hit. And then he rolled over on Langan, telling the FBI how and where they could locate him.

Guthrie rolled over on Langan out of pure malicious spite. He did it without first asking for an agreement, one stating he would receive a reduced sentence for his cooperation. Guthrie gave up Langan for two reasons: Langan had kicked him out of the ARA, and because Guthrie was aware of Langan's walk on the wild side, his cross dressing and, in Guthrie's eyes, his sexual perversions.

According to Guthrie, Langan would be at a mall in Indianapolis, where Guthrie and Langan were to meet. Guthrie also gave up the address of the duplex in Columbus, where Langan was presently holed up.

The FBI marshaled its forces and surrounded the duplex on Reinhard Street. Agents in plain-clothes went door to door and asked residents in the area to either leave quietly or remain in their homes. Most left.

Then the FBI moved in. Inside the duplex, Langan, seated in a chair by the window, saw something out of the corner of his eye. Black-clad figures in full-tactical gear, holding assault rifles, moving into position.

Without thinking, Langan reacted instantaneously. Rising, he reached for his pistol on the table in front of him. Gun in hand, he moved rapidly to the back door. Opening it just a crack, he peered out. Nothing. Opening the door, he scuttled out of the duplex into the alley, scanning the area for movement.

"FBI!" bellowed a voice. "Put down your weapon and surrender!"

How about I don't, thought Langan. Raising his semi-automatic, he popped off three rounds in the direction of the voice.

All hell broke loose. Assault rifles coughed, spitting death at Peter Langan. Struck twice in the shoulder, Langan fell to his knees. But his gun was up and he blazed away, returning fire.

A few seconds later, Langan's gun was empty. The jig was up and he knew it. Wounded an out of ammo, he, like Guthrie, was out of options. He dropped the weapon and put up his hands.

After spending four days in the hospital, Langan was now the property of the FBI. They interrogated him. But because of the ARA's policy of using only nicknames or first names, Langan honestly did not know the full names of his co-conspirators.

In another interrogation room, Guthrie, who desperately wanted to roll over on anyone and everyone, was stymied by the same problem. He only knew nicknames and first names. When asked to reveal names, he said, "Kevin, Scott and Tim. All three of them were young skinheads, in their twenties."

From the expression on his face, it was obvious Agent Woods thought Guthrie was lying. "That's it? Kevin, Scott and Tim, huh? That narrows it down to just a few million people."

"Really," said Guthrie, "that's all I know. We only used first names or code names to protect ourselves, in case we got caught." He chuckled, thinking about the dramatic irony of his words. "If the feds – you guys – grabbed one of us, the others didn't have to worry about getting rolled up too."

Woods nodded. He could see the wisdom of the tactic. "There's gotta be something else. What about descriptions? Tall, short, thin, fat. Any identifying characteristics?"

Guthrie laughed. "They looked like every skinhead I ever met. Shaved heads, tattoos; young, dumb and full of come. They all look alike." He paused, thinking. "One of them, Scott, lifted weights. Built like a brick shithouse, ya know?"

"Anything else? Think hard."

Guthrie chewed his lip. He really could use a fix or a drink. Something to take the edge off. "Wait a sec. One of 'em, Kevin it was, had a relative who was a cop in Philadelphia. His uncle, I think."

Woods nodded. "Okay, good."

* * * * *

Woods called Gil Hendrickson, who was an FBI agent in Philadelphia. Woods outlined the situation for Hendrickson, and then asked him to look into the Philadelphia cop connection. Woods didn't expect anything to come of it, but he had to play the one card he had. Either that or fold, and Woods refused to fold.

Not long after the phone call with Woods, Hendrickson drove to the Philadelphia Police Department and paid them a friendly visit. Law enforcement officers gossiped a lot.

Hendrickson got lucky beyond belief. In the course of shop-talk with an officer, the topic of the Mid-Western Bank Robbers came up. Hendrickson told the officer that although the media referred to them as the Mid-Western Bank Robbers, it was a misnomer. The fact of the matter was that the Mid-Western Bank Robbers' real name was the Aryan Republican Army, part of the Neo-Nazi movement. They were anarchist skinheads.

Nodding, the cop told Hendrickson he knew all about Neo-Nazis and skinheads. His sister's boy, who was named Kevin, was one of them. A real nutcase; tattoos of swastikas, the whole nine yards. Didn't want a job and even if he'd gotten a job wouldn't be able to hold it very long. Lazy as hell. Still lived with his grandmother; a real Mama's Boy.

Alarm bells went off in Hendrickson's head. "What's the name of the grandmother?"

"O'Neill. Eleanor O'Neill."

The very next day, an FBI surveillance team was camped out across from the old lady's house. The FBI watched every move Kevin McCarthy made from that moment on.

By this time, Kevin McCarthy's paranoia had rendered him taut with indecision. He'd heard that Guthrie and Langan had been captured, as had Stedeford. They didn't know what to do. They had two choices: run and hide or sit tight and see how it all played out. They decided to sit tight.

Michael Brescia had heard the news too. When he found out, he immediately split, crossing over into Canada, where he was now trying to keep a low-profile. McCarthy and Stedeford called him and advised him to hunker down and ride out the storm.

On May 24, 1996, the FBI arrested Kevin McCarthy. A SWAT team surrounded the old lady's house. Rather than kicking in the door and scaring Eleanor to death, they decided to play it smart. The Philadelphia cop, who was indeed Kevin's uncle, simply walked into the house and looked around. He found Kevin sleeping with a .45 caliber Glock nearby. Confiscating the loaded gun, he walked back out of the house and then returned with FBI agents, who handcuffed Kevin.

Kevin was nobody's fool. He knew the only way he'd ever see the light of day again was to talk. So he started talking, revealing everything he knew about the ARA's bank robberies. During the course of singing like a canary, Kevin rolled over on Michael Brescia.

Brescia was in deep shit. He knew Guthrie and Langan had been arrested, but he didn't know the FBI had McCarthy too. And he certainly never believed that McCarthy would roll over on him.

At the same time McCarthy was giving him up to the feds, Michael Brescia decided to go back to the states. With his girlfriend in tow, he headed to Philadelphia, where Brescia landed a gig as a bookkeeper. At all times, wherever he went, whatever he was doing, Brescia was strapped, carrying a fully-loaded 9mm. Determined not to be arrested, Brescia was prepared to die in a shoot-out if need be.

Meanwhile, Stedeford was living with the Palilonis sisters, Susan and Sara. He worked at the Sound Under recording studio, producing music. On May 24, as McCarthy was being arrested, Stedeford was at the recording studio, unaware he was in the FBI's crosshairs.

While Stedeford was listening to the previous day's recording session, a team of FBI agents entered the Palilonis sisters' house with a search and seizure warrant. Going through the house, they discovered and seized Stedeford's weapons: an assault rifle and a shotgun. The agents also seized his body armor, caps, reading material and fake I.D.s.

As the FBI loaded his personal belongings and weapons into an FBI vehicle, another team of FBI agents surrounded the Sound Under recording studio. A pretty, female FBI agent, disguised as a singer/songwriter walked to the studio's front door and knocked. Stedeford answered the door strapped. He wasn't taking any chances. Thankfully, it wasn't the feds. It was just some wannabe singer asking about renting recording time. Stedeford gave her his usual sales pitch and invited her to have a look around. As he led her into the inner sanctum of the studio, FBI agents, who had been standing on either side of the door, swarmed in. Before Stedeford could even consider pulling his gun, he was cuffed and disarmed.

The arrogant exploits of the Aryan Republican Army and its firm belief in and adherence to the concepts of the Phineas Priesthood ended ignominiously. They didn't go out in a blaze of glory. There was no final Gotterdammerung, like Robert Mathews and The Order.

* * * * *

Guthrie kept singing his traitor's tune, rolling over on Scott Stedeford. When he wasn't snitching, Guthrie sat in his cell writing his memoir, entitled *The Taunting Bandits*. Even the title of his book displayed Guthrie's self-centered egotism.

Guthrie, in an attempt to reduce his own sentence – he eventually pled guilty to nineteen bank robberies – consented to testify the other members of the ARA. But in the end, he couldn't do it. Rather than rat-out his friends, he elected to take his own life. On July 12, 1996, Guthrie hung himself in his jail cell.

Peter Langan was convicted of multiple bank robberies, utilizing weapons and bombs. Kevin McCarthy testified against Langan, ratting him out in court, in front of a jury. At his sentencing hearing, Langan, allowed to speak, rambled on at length about how evil governments were and characterized the U.S. government as a "state-sponsored" terrorist group. In addition, he told the court he wanted a sex-change operation so he could finally be the woman he was meant to be. "I want to 'come out' by coming to terms with who I am."

Essentially, Langan blamed his actions as a Phineas Priest and his bank robberies on his transsexualism. He didn't know who he was, so he wasn't responsible for what he did.

Later, Langan asserted that Kevin McCarthy and Richard Guthrie had participated – "played a role in the bombing" – perpetrated by Timothy McVeigh.

Langan was sentence to life in prison without parole. As the years rolled by, Langan forsook Christian Identity and became a convert to the Wicca religion, a religion populated primarily by female witches. He remains adamant that he needs to have a sex-change operation.

Kevin McCarthy, in return for squealing on his comrades in arms, received a five year sentence. And because rats don't last long in prison, McCarthy served his time under an assumed name at a "safe" prison. A "safe" prison was one where most of the inmates were snitches.

McCarthy's testimony against Scott Stedeford resulted in Stedeford's conviction for nine bank robberies. Stedeford received a sentence of twenty years.

Michael Brescia found fame and glory, just not the kind he wanted. The general populace of the U.S. believed Michael Brescia was "John Doe #2," the man who had been in the cab of the Ryder truck with Timothy McVeigh. He bore a striking resemblance to John Doe #2.

On January 30, 1997, Michael Brescia pled guilty to robbing one bank – the Bank One in Madison, Wisconsin, and conspiracy to rob six more banks. Sentenced to six years, Brescia walked free on March 22, 2001.

Both Guthrie and McCarthy rolled over on Mark Thomas. The FBI arrested him and gave him a gift: if he became an FBI informant, he could stay out of prison. Thomas agreed immediately. He was now a Judas goat. Within a very short time, everyone involved in the white power movement was aware Thomas was nothing more than a filthy, traitorous spy. Because his life was now at risk, Thomas was put into the WITSEC (witness protection) program.

Later, on March 19, 1998, Thomas was convicted of conspiring to rob seven banks, for which he received an eight year sentence. Allowed to speak, stricken by remorse and his betrayal of his orthodox Christian beliefs, Thomas lamented the fact he had sinned egregiously in the name of God. In other words, Mark Thomas had assumed the mantle of God, thought he was God, and attacked God's enemies in the name of holy Justice and Righteousness.

Mark Thomas and the other members of the ARA forgot one thing: they weren't God.

Chapter 12

Charleston

The evening air was still warm as Dylann Roof walked up the steps of Emanuel African Methodist Episcopal Church, in Charleston, S.C. He was 21 years old and slender, with a Friar Tuck haircut. He'd been attending the church for a while. Predominantly black, the parishioners were kind, welcoming people who lived their faith. On one level, Dylann actually liked and respected them. But on another level, he hated them. Dylann was white; they were black. In Dylann's mind, they were "kaffirs." Dylann used the South African pejorative for blacks rather than the American "niggers," which according to Dylann's way of thinking had lost much of its derogatory meaning. Depending on how the dreaded N-word was used and who used it, it could even be understood as a compliment. Blacks used it to describe other blacks all the time; and certain white celebrities were allowed to use it freely.

Dylann arrived that night ready to make a statement and take care of business. He carried a .45 caliber Glock, concealed, of course.

It was Wednesday evening, which meant Bible Study. Dylann particularly enjoyed the Bible Study because the discussions were interesting. Besides, it was the perfect time and place to do what he had come to do.

As he joined the Bible Study group, Dylann greeted the others with nods, occasionally saying, "Hi." Everyone took their seats and after a brief opening prayer, the study commenced. Dylann listened attentively. About an hour later, as the study finished, as usual, the group closed with prayer, asking for enlightenment and the blessing of God.

Everyone had their heads bowed and eyes closed during the prayer – except Dylann. His eyes were open and his head was up. Pulling out the Glock, he stood up and, aiming carefully, began pulling the trigger.

The Glock spat death.

To Dylann, it was like watching a movie. In one sense, it was entertaining, interesting to watch. He liked the way the bodies jumped when hit by .45 caliber bullets. There was lots of blood, of course, but that was to be expected. His feelings about the blood were neutral. In fact, the whole thing was neutral – really – in an entertaining way. Just like in a movie theater, he was participating in what was going on, but not really.

This was something that needed to be done. And he had to do it. No one else would.

He reloaded, jamming in a fresh clip. And kept firing. He shot each body several times, not just once. It took a lot of ammo. He didn't know how many times he'd reloaded. Kind of lost track.

* * * * *

Later, during an interview, Felicia Sanders, who was there and miraculously lived, told NBC News, "He caught us with our eyes closed." The hail of gunfire "sounded like a transformer blew."

Dylann aimed and fired, aimed and fired. It went on until he ran out of ammunition. Ejecting the empty clip, he jammed a new, full clip into place. Once again he began pulling the trigger. Finally, there didn't seem to be anyone left to shoot. So he stopped, and gazed around. As far as he could tell, everyone was either dead or dying. Stepping forward, he stood over one of his victims, still conscious and alive.

Looking down at the prostrate figure, Dylann spat out one word: "Kaffir."

Time to go. Dylann walked rapidly out of the church, down the steps and moved to his car. Climbing in, he started the engine and took off. He tossed the gun on the back seat.

* * * * *

A social outcast who didn't really fit in, at least in his own mind, Dylann grew up in an abusive home. He self-medicated, using marijuana and other prescription mind-numbing pain-killers; pretty much anything he could get his hands on. And he drank a lot simply to feel better and make the emotional hurt go away.

A lousy student, he dropped out of high school his sophomore year. He took odd jobs, but none of the jobs lasted long. He either got fired or quit. Bored and looking for something to fill the big empty hole inside, he spent time online, surfing websites and news sites. Alarmed at how the world appeared to be succumbing to people of color, he delved into white power literature. In the course of his reading, he came across articles about Apartheid and Rhodesia, the South African nation that had insisted on the segregation and whites and blacks. According to the white government in Rhodesia (back when it was still Rhodesia), blacks were inferior and incapable of handling any type of responsibility. Blacks only prospered under white rule. Whites provided them – "kaffirs" – with opportunities they could never provide for themselves.

Dylann liked what he read. In fact, he respected and approved of the Rhodesian government's stance. Apartheid was good and necessary, agreed Dylann. The rising tide of color needed to be stopped in its tracks. Somebody needed to do something. People, white people, needed to hear the truth and become aware of what was going on around them.

So he established a website. Through it, he could give voice to his views. Maybe someone would listen. He named his website The Last Rhodesian, a rip off of *The Last Mohican*. In his mind, Dylann was like the last Mohican – the last of his kind, willing to stand up for what he believed in.

He followed the Trayvon Martin tragedy online. This motivated him to do more reading, especially about "black on white violence." What he read about Trayvon Martin astounded him, so much so that he wrote on The Last Rhodesian: "Right away I was unable to understand what the big deal was. It was obvious that [George] Zimmerman was in the right. But more importantly this prompted me to type the words 'black on white crime' into Google, and I have never been the same since that day."

At this point, he came across a group called the Council of Conservative Citizens (CCC). The group maintained a website similar to The Last Rhodesian. They espoused segregation and the purity and superiority of the white race. Once upon a time, the CCC had called itself the White Citizen's Council, but they decided to change the name to something that sounded less radical and extremist. So they did. The thinking was that if they didn't initially appear to be an assortment of right-wing nutcases, they might appeal to more people, people looking for someplace to land and feel at home. Feeling at home and fitting in was a big part of the CCC's propaganda. Like most white power groups, the CCC had long ago recognized that most of their converts and adherents were strangers in a strange land, people who were pariahs and outcasts for one reason or another.

This is an example of the type of racist drivel that the CCC promulgated: "God is the author of racism. God is the One who divided mankind into different types ... Mixing the races is rebelliousness against God." — Council of Conservative Citizens website, 2001

"We believe the United States is a European country and that Americans are part of the European people. ... We therefore oppose the massive immigration of non-European and non-Western peoples into the United States that threatens to transform our nation into a non-European majority in our lifetime. We believe that illegal immigration must be stopped, if necessary by military force and placing troops on our national borders; that illegal aliens must be returned to their own countries; and that legal immigration must be severely restricted or halted through appropriate changes in our laws and policies. We also oppose all efforts to mix the races of mankind, to promote non-white races over the European-American people through so-called 'affirmative action' and similar measures, to destroy or denigrate the European-American heritage, including the heritage of the Southern people, and to force the integration of the races."

The CCC believed that people of color are "retrograde species of humanity." In other words, the CCC was nothing more than a front for the radical, racist doctrinal tenets of the Church of Christian Identity. They were rabid racists, who believe in white supremacy. Non-whites, non-Aryans were nothing more than animals in the CCC's opinion.

Dylann agreed. The CCC's site became his online home. He kept going back and re-reading the racist hyperbole. The site was a hype-machine, designed to seduce individuals like Dylann. Half-truths, misinformation and disinformation formed the gist of the content. The content appealed to anyone who felt out of control, left out, unloved, unwanted. In other words, it appealed to people with unmet expectations – the prime cause of deep-seated anger.

In short, it was indoctrination, a rude, simple form of brain washing.

* * * * *

On his site – the Last Rhodesian – Dylann expressed himself in no uncertain terms, writing that "Niggers are stupid." And later, just prior to his killing spree, "I chose Charleston because it is the most historic city in my state, and at one time had the highest ratio of blacks to Whites in the country. We have no skinheads, no real KKK, no one doing anything but talking on the internet. Well someone has to have the bravery to take it to the real world, and I guess that has to be me."

In other words, Dylann had picked up and donned the robes of the Phineas Priesthood.

* * * * *

A few months before his Phineas action – the slaughter of God's enemies – Dylann was hanging out at a mall in Columbia, acting really weird. He walked into stores in the mall and asked strange questions, like when they opened and closed and how many employees they had. Ridiculous stuff.

Dylann was high on Suboxone, which explained his bizarre behavior. But he felt really good and thought he was being tricky. In his drug-induced altered perception, he didn't realize his behavior was hecka-odd. Anyway, he was creeping out the store owners and cashiers, so one of them called the cops. The cops arrived and questioned him. His answers were random and pretty outlandish. According to Dylann, he was shopping for a birthday present for a friend. When asked the same question later, he was shopping for a Mother's Day present for his mom. Dylann's fritzing synapses precluded his memory; he couldn't remember what lie he'd told moments before.

So the cops asked him to empty his pockets and discovered he had Suboxone strips on his person – and no prescription.

Suboxone contains buprenorphine and naloxone; it's used to treat those addicted to heroin and oxycodone. Suboxone produces what is called an opioid agonist high. It also functions as an anti-depressant in people suffering from chronic depression. Put another way, Suboxone makes you feel really good about yourself and the world around you.

They cuffed him and transported him to jail.

Dylann made bail. So he was released. Upon release, he was informed he was not to go to the mall. He was persona non grata. Out and waiting on his court hearing, Dylann, naturally, went back to the mall. Someone noticed him and the cops were called once again. Dylann was arrested for trespassing.

April rolled around and it was Dylann's birthday. His family gave him cash for his birthday because they knew he needed it. Besides, they didn't know him well enough to know what to get him. He was a stranger to his own family.

Dylann took the cash with pleasure in his heart. He knew just what to do with it. He had plans.

Visiting a local Charleston gun shop, he tried out a number of different semi-automatic pistols. His goal was one that felt right in his hand, one with balance and plenty of hitting power. After handling half a dozen guns, he decided on a Glock model 41, which carried 13 rounds and felt at home in his hand. Added to that was the halo of attraction: Glock sounded cool and macho. Everybody who had ever been to a movie had heard of a Glock. He purchased the gun, along with some extra clips and lots of ammo.

Of course, because of his drug felony charge, Dylann should not have been able to purchase the Glock. Luckily for Dylann, the background check system failed to red-flag his name. So the gun shop happily took his money and sent him on his merry way.

The botched background check proved very unlucky for the parishioners, who would soon die in their church at the hands of a rabid white supremacist.

* * * * *

Now in possession of a weapon, Dylann spent most of his time drinking, taking drugs and hanging out in strip clubs. He favored pain killers, drugs that took away his mental and emotional pain. He wanted to feel good. When he spent time with his friends, no matter what they were doing, Dylann would inevitably find a way to inject his racist beliefs into the conversation. He told friends that "something has to be done," and that he intended to "start a civil war," i.e. a race war. His agenda was the same as every other Phineas Priest, from The Order to Eric Rudolph – to incite RAHOWA.

Most of his friends didn't take him seriously. They all thought he was weird anyway, so they discounted his words of violence. Dylann was just shooting his mouth off again. Same old thing.

He even told his friends he had a plan to infiltrate the campus of the College of Charleston and kill people of color. This was a little crazy even for a weird-o like Dylann, so a couple of his friends got hold of his gun, which everyone knew he had because he was all Chatty Cathy about it and what he wanted to do with it – kill people. They hid the gun at another friend's house. Unfortunately, the other friend didn't want anything to do with hiding a gun at his house. So the gun was returned to Dylann.

Instead of trying to hide the gun, Dylann's friends should have picked up the phone and called the police, telling them about the gun and Dylann's reckless plans. But they didn't. The probably thought they were being loyal friends. But they weren't. They were being stupid. Placing the call would have prevented what was about to occur and might have gotten Dylann the help and medication he needed.

Later, one of the two friends that took the gun and tried to hide it said, "I don't think the church was his primary target because he told us he was going for the school. But I think he couldn't get into the school because of the security. So I think he just settled for the church."

"Just settled" was a scary phrase. Presumably, Dylann, if possible, wanted a much higher body count than nine.

* * * * *

Meanwhile, Dylann was constantly adding material to his website. Somewhere in there, he posted his manifesto, a 2,444 word diatribe against the rising tide of color in the world, especially the U.S., and what needed to be done about it. Dylann hated blacks, Jews, Hispanics and Asians. He included passages about all four racial groups on the Last Rhodesian.

According to Dylann, they all needed to die. Sure and final death of the inferior races – people of color – was the only way to cleanse the world and keep the white race pure and safe.

* * * * *

By 9:11 p.m. on June 17, the police were on their way to the sight of the mass murder – the Emanuel AME Church. When they arrived, the police were appalled by the senseless slaughter. Dead bodies were everywhere. Blood pooled on the floor.

During the shooting, someone inside the church, one of the victims made a call to the police. It was 9:07 p.m. when police dispatchers took a call. The voice on the other end of the line said, "Young white male. Male is reloading."

At 9:09 more calls came in.

By 9:11 the shooting spree was over and Dylann Roof was on the run.

Within hours, the police had a positive identification on the shooter – Dylann Roof. The FBI entered the case.

Meanwhile, Dylann Roof was in his car, a black Hyundai Elantra, headed for North Carolina. BOLOs (be on the lookout) and APBs (all points bulletins) were issued and the manhunt was underway. News coverage of the massacre was massive. Dylann's photo was blasted over the airwaves, along with a description of his car, including his license plate number, which was hard to miss because it had a Confederate flag on it.

Dylann was a poor planner, unlike Robert Mathews, Eric Rudolph and the Aryan Republican Army. He had little money and no escape plan other than just drive and keep on driving. In other words, he had not thought past the actual shooting. He had nowhere to go, nowhere to hide.

* * * * *

245 miles away, in Shelby, North Carolina, Debbie Gillis spotted Dylann's car. She had seen footage from video cameras at the church on television. The footage received constant airplay from the media. Debbie was driving along Route 74 when she saw the car from television. Pressing down on her gas pedal, she moved closer. "I got closer and saw that haircut. I was nervous. I had the worst feeling. Is that him or not him?"

It was him.

Debbie picked up her cell phone and called her boss, explaining what was going on and that she was tailing the car of the church shooter. Her boss immediately called the local police and informed them about what was going on. He gave them Debbie's location and direction of travel.

On her part, Debbie kept following Dylann, wanting to be sure he didn't slip away. She followed him for 35 miles. Meanwhile, the police were converging on her location.

Rack lights flashing, the police jumped in behind Dylann, who pulled over. The police informed him it was a routine traffic stop. They told him he was not under arrest, but was being detained.

One of them asked, "Do you know why we stopped you?"

Dylann nodded.

Then Dylann said, "There's a gun on the back seat." The police looked and there it was – a .45 Glock.

Dylann's very undramatic surrender took place for a number of reasons: he had no money and nowhere to go; in addition, now that the adrenaline high was gone, he felt deflated. And he didn't have any drugs to jack him back up. Moreover, his Phineas action had not resulted in a race war. Throngs of armed citizens had not flowed out to the streets to kill, kill, kill. He had failed. All he had done was slaughter nine innocent people. Depressed and emotionally quashed, Dylann just wanted to rest.

The police arrested him and transported him. The FBI arrived and questioned him. At first, Dylann maintained he was just driving to Nashville, when he had been stopped and arrested in Shelby. Further questioning revealed that Dylann had been thinking about his killing spree for at least six months.

* * * * *

That's when things got complicated.

South Carolina wanted Dylann back so they could charge him with murder. But he had been arrested in North Carolina. North Carolina assigned Dylann an attorney, who explained extradition to him. After discussing the situation with his attorney, Dylann agreed to waive his extradition rights. He could have stalled and fought extradition, but it was inevitable, so why bother?

Dylann was transported by airplane back to Charleston, where he was placed in the Sheriff Al Cannon Detention Center. It was still June 18, the day of his capture. Things were moving rapidly.

In jail, Dylann was once again questioned by investigators. Not only were the investigators trying to get him to confess to the murders, they were very interested in his motivations for such an orgy of cold-blooded killing.

In the end, Dylann told the two investigators he killed the nine people at the church.

When asked, "Why?"

Dylann replied, "To start a race war."

In the same interview, Dylann told the investigators he hesitated about attending the Bible Study. The people in the Bible Study group were so nice to him. He didn't know if he could go through with it.

Presumably, the question confronted by his conscience was yes, or no. Do it or don't do it. Of course, he decided to do it. But the question was what tipped the scales in the positive direction? No one knew for sure, not even Dylann. However, a simple religious explanation may provide an answer to the hypothetical question.

Most conservative, fundamentalist Christians are believers of the tale propounded by the "Devil" in the Garden of Eden, when he told Adam and Eve that if they ate of the Tree of the Knowledge of Good and Evil "they would be as gods." Somewhere deep inside his head, Dylann Roof believed that. Oh, if asked if he thought he was a god, he would have said no. But the energy was there; the idea was there. What do gods do? They decide who is right and who is wrong; what is right and what is wrong. They judge. And they punish.

Dylann Roof decided what was right and what was wrong. The rising tide of color was wrong. Blacks were judged guilty. Their punishment, according to Dylann Roof, was death. So he executed them. In his own mind, Dylann Roof was doing what any god would do. And that meant he was doing what God would do. With just a slight twist, Dylann defended his actions by asserting he was carrying out the Will of God. He was killing God's enemies.

The previous hypothesis is simply that – a hypothesis. There is no solid proof. But if conspiracists want to speculate about a grand, overarching conspiracy, this one deserves time and attention.

* * * * *

On the following day, June 19, Dylann attended his bail hearing, kind of. The hearing was held but Dylann was not personally in attendance. Instead, he was linked to the court by means of a video conference. The court could see and hear him; Dylann could hear but not see the court.

Judge James Gosnell presided. Dylann was formally charged with nine counts of murder, and possession of a firearm while perpetrating a crime of violence. Judge Gosnell asked Dylann a few perfunctory questions about his age, name, employment, etc.

Then survivors of the church shooting, along with the families of those murdered were allowed to speak. Most of the victims stated that they had already forgiven him for what he did and were praying for his redemption.

Judge Gosnell told the court and Dylann that he was setting bail at $1 million for the weapon charge. For the murder charges, bail was precluded.

With the authority of his office surrounding him, Judge Gosnell spoke about the victims, citing two sets of victims – those who died and those who lived.

"There are victims on this young man's side of the family. Nobody would have ever thrown them into the whirlwind of events that they are being thrown into," said Judge Gosnell.

His words, acknowledging victims on both sides, infuriated many people. He was accused of being a white bigot, a good ole boy, and exceeding his authority. In other words, people didn't like it because he was doing his job. Demonstrating sympathy and even empathy for any and all victims, physical or emotional, did not make him a white bigot. Indeed, it simply demonstrated his ability to think clearly and perceive all sides of the tragedy.

A few weeks later, on July 7, Dylann was charged with three counts of attempted murder.

One week later, events descended to the ridiculous. A letter, supposedly written to Andrew Dodge appeared online. The letter was being auctioned off. The asking price was $1000.

Dodge ran a site called True Crime Auction House, which catered to "gear queers," people who like to read about and possess items from actual serial killers. Kind of like the true-crime version of *Hoarders* on steroids or the collectors in the movie *Hannibal*. Of course, these people were called collectors rather than hoarders or nutcases. The letter and the auctioning off of the letter, of course, hit the national news.

When interviewed, Dodge stated that he was not sympathetic to the white power movement; he was simply interested in "serial killers." He liked to know what made them "tick." To that end, he reached out to Dylann via the mail and received a reply. In his reply, Dylann wrote that he was "doing fine," but went on to request books to read. Frankly, to all intents and purposes, it appeared to be a normal letter.

The big question was: was it real? Did Dylann really pen the letter? No one knew for sure. Dodge, of course, claimed it was authentic.

The result of the media furor surrounding the alleged letter was that the court issued a gag order. No one could talk about the case in any manner, including the letter. Later, the gag order was amended. 911 transcripts and certain other documents pertaining to the case could be released and discussed.

* * * * *

Meanwhile, the court provided Dylann with a top notch litigator, David Bruck, which was usual in such cases. On July 31, Dylann pled not guilty. According to his attorney, Dylann wanted to plead guilty, but Bruck indicated he couldn't in good conscience allow his client to do so, until the prosecution's intentions were clear. In other words, was the prosecution going to seek the death penalty?

"Mr. Roof has told us that he wishes to plead guilty," stated Bruck. "Until we know whether the government will be seeking the death penalty, we are not able to advise Mr. Roof."

Therefore, the Judge, U.S. Magistrate Bristow Marchant, accepted Dylann's not guilty plea.

Dylann Roof was there. When addressed directly by the Judge, he answered with 'yes' or 'no.' Otherwise, his attorney did the talking. This, too, was normal modus operandi.

By this time, the charges against Dylann had grown in number. He now faced 33 counts: hate crimes, weapon possession and obstructing the practice of religion, along with nine murder charges, attempted murder charges, and civil rights violations.

Essentially, Dylann and his legal team were looking for a plea deal. Dylann would plead guilty, if the prosecutors and the state agreed to drop the death penalty. No deal would be forthcoming, as on September 3, the state prosecutor, Scarlett Wilson, stated that she was going after a death penalty.

* * * * *

Dylann Roof's trial is scheduled to begin in July 2016. Maybe. Further motions for continuance may push the date back. At this point in time, for all intents and purposes, Dylann will more than likely be found guilty and sentenced to death, unless, of course, he is considered mentally unstable and thus unable to stand trial.

Psychiatrists are presently evaluating Dylann's mental stability.

How did the community of white supremacists react to Dylann's killing spree? Two days after Dylann was arrested, on June 20, the Council of Conservative Citizens temporarily removed its website. They did this because of all the negative media publicity, which cited Dylann's association with the group.

The CCC's honcho, Earl Holt, issued a statement saying the CCC was not "responsible" for the murders committed by Dylann Roof. The statement went on to acknowledge that Dylann couldn't be faulted for his "legitimate grievances" with people of color, especially blacks.

By the way, the CCC's website is now back in business.

Northwest Front's front man, Harold Covington, denounced Dylann's extremist violent behavior, but referred to the murders as "a preview of coming attractions." Northwest Front was another white supremacist site that spewed racial hatred and indirectly promoted violence against blacks and people of color; it also espoused the Phineas Priesthood and its righteous agenda.

The editor of The Daily Stormer, another racist, white power site stated that he "repudiated Roof's crime and publicly disavowed violence, while endorsing many of Roof's views."

In each instance cited above, the initial public statement slammed Dylann for what he had done, but then added qualifiers tantamount to approval. The white power groups were playing the PR game. On the one hand they condemned racist violence, but on the other hand they were sympathetic. Simply put, behind the scenes, they were applauding Dylann for his Phineas actions. They thought it was good, right and proper. Who cared if a bunch of sub-humans were exterminated? They were vermin anyway.

In other words, they were spectators, urging others to Phineas actions. In a sense, they were just as vile and evil as Dylann Roof, Robert Mathews, the Aryan Republican Army and Eric Rudolph. Like high school cheerleaders, they rooted for their Phineas heroes, while remaining a safe distance from the action.

Chapter 13

Yahweh's Elite

R ichard Kelly Hoskins' Phineas Priesthood was nothing more than a "literary invention." Hoskins took an obscure passage from the Bible – Numbers 25 – and interpreted it to meet his needs. He twisted and distorted the passage to fulfill his personal agenda – the creation of a silent order of priests who would identify, track and kill the enemies of God. And of course, Hoskins was there to point the way, to give direction, to tell the Phineas Priests who they should seek out and exterminate – Jews, blacks, Asians, anyone of the so-called "Mud People," those inferior to whites.

Hoskins aggrandized himself to the position of Pope of the Phineas Priesthood.

And the white supremacist movement accepted Hoskins' literary nonsense, his twaddle, as Holy Scripture, the Word of God. They accepted it because it gave them permission to rape, pillage and plunder. It was just what the doctor ordered, a prescription to arrogantly wipe out anyone who wasn't white, or established laws and policies they didn't like or agree with.

According to George M. Fredrickson, "The identification of the Jews with the devil and witchcraft in the popular mind of the thirteenth and fourteenth centuries was perhaps the first sign of a racist view of the world. Official sanction for such attitudes came in sixteenth century Spain when Jews who had converted to Christianity and their descendants became the victims of a pattern of discrimination and exclusion."

Thus, Richard Kelly Hoskins just took an old, old idea, wrapped it with a pretty literary bow and presented it as a gift to the white power movement. In reality, racism arrived with the appearance of mankind on the planet earth. Both ancient history and the Bible are rife with racism.

But the concept of the Phineas Priesthood – Yahweh's Elite – came forth from the mind and pen of Hoskins. He gave it corporeality. He provided the concept with modern clothing, clothing a select few were willing to don. And ever since then, Yahweh's Elite – the Phineas Priesthood – have taken up the divine raiment – and heard God's call to arms.

Like the holy warriors of Islam, Yahweh's Elite believe they will be rewarded by God for doing His work here on earth.

*****

Hoskins' literary invention was based on Numbers 25 and Psalm 106. Psalm 106 reads: "Then stood up Phineas, and executed judgment: and so the plague was stayed. And that was counted unto him for righteousness unto all generations for evermore."

According to Hoskins, these two passages established a perpetual priesthood. And this priesthood is populated by a few men who act on their own initiative to carry out God's judgment on those who break God's law. This notion of "initiative" implies direct and personal contact with the Holy Spirit, who provides the Phineas Priest with exclusive information and insight unavailable to the rest of mankind.

What Hoskins and other wannabe theological interpreters always fail to mention is Numbers 25 does not make any reference to miscegenation. In fact, the Moabites and Midianites mentioned in the passage were both the descendants of Lot and Abraham, respectively. There was no racial mixing taking place in Numbers 25. What God was pissed off about was that His people had begun worshipping another god, a pagan god by the name of Baal Peor.

Of course, this is mechanically dismissed by Phineas Priests, who are misguided and misinformed religious zealots obsessed with the so-called "abominable sins of mankind." Phineas Priests like Buford Furrow, Jr., who shot up a Jewish day care center in Los Angeles. Furrow justified his act saying, "It's time for America to wake and kill the Jews."

Ben Smith, who targeted people of color in Indiana and Illinois, killed two people and wounded another ten. Then he turned his gun on himself. Then there was William King, the Texas racist, who wanted to spark a race war. So he kidnapped a black man, hooked the man up to the back of his truck and dragged him to death. Prior to the gruesome murder, King told his victim, "We're going to start *The Turner Diaries* early."

Most, if not all, of these religious nutcases are aroused by either Hoskins book, or by William Pierce's *The Turner Diaries*, or both. *The Turner Diaries* is a fiction novel describing a fantasy world. In effect, it's apocalyptic fiction, end of the world stuff, like *Alas, Babylon*.

Phineas Priests view themselves as initiators of the race war that leads to Armageddon, the final battle against The Devil or Satan. According to their interpretation of the last book of the Bible – Revelation – which describes Armageddon and the events presaging the great battle, the government of the United States aligns itself with Satan in the last days. This gloom-and-doom religious perspective was described by Kerry Noble thusly: They (the nutcases) "envision a dark and gloomy end time scenario, where some Antichrist makes war against Christians."

The perfect example of this peculiar and wacky perspective was The House of Yahweh, a group of fundamentalist extremists in Texas. The group asserted that the Israeli Peace Accord of 1993 marked the beginning of the Tribulation, which was a seven-year period of suffering and strife prior to Armageddon or, depending on one's theological stance, prior to the Rapture. In other words, The House of Yahweh was certain that the true Messiah (a white, Aryan Messiah) would descend from heaven to the earth in the year 2000. The House of Yahweh, in accord with this belief, referred to the U.S. government as "the beast."

Political policies serve to exacerbate the beliefs of the white supremacists. White supremacists are very superstitious and perceive signs and portents everywhere. Gun control, which white supremacists view as nothing less than civilian disarmament, plays a major role in *The Turner Diaries*. In that sense, the book is comprehended as prophetic. The last days are looming. More restrictions on gun sales means the last days, along with Armageddon, are nigh.

* * * * *

White supremacist groups, like the Aryan Nations and all the rest, are religious cults, wherein the leader of the cult is recognized as messianic. God speaks to him and he in turn speaks to the cult members, who seek to serve God by serving the cult leader. The cult leader preaches the Word of God, makes prophetical announcements and sets forth objectives that are – supposedly – God-inspired.

Within these religious cults lies another cult, a cult within a cult. This cult is the Phineas Priesthood. Phineas Priests are the recipients of special dispensations from God. God elects only a few to this specialized priesthood. They are the "gibbor chayyil" – the Might Men of God – who carry out God's Will on earth. They right the wrongs committed by so-called evil men, wrongs such as miscegenation, abortion, gun control, immigration, homosexuality and taxation. God gives his Phineas Priests permission to utilize violence to right these wrongs. Essentially, Phineas Priests are similar to 007. They are licensed to kill God's enemies.

It's all balderdash! A factitious display of a peculiar brand of hate that finds its denouement in violent bloodshed.

In the end, the rationale of the Phineas Priesthood is an industrial-strength version of the typical white supremacist mentality: formless, chaotic and devious. This half-bucolic botchery reflects the caprice of intrinsic deviancy.

White supremacist cult groups, such as the Aryan Nations, The Order, the Aryan Republican Army, Elohim City, et al, are betwixt and between: they have one foot in the Old Testament of the Bible and the other foot in a pseudo-macho philosophy gleaned from old-fashioned Western movies, John Wayne stuff. The gap in between the two feet is where amalgamation occurs. Old Testament passages are appropriated and propounded as the Way of God, the path to righteousness, which is subsequently transmuted into violent criminality. The transmutation process, as in the story of Rumpelstiltskin, who turned straw into gold, is irrational and almost magical.

The magical process takes place in a cultural matrix, where money and celebrity become society's modern gods and goddesses. Bravura effects and eccentric mannerisms are worshipped above humanity, kindness and love. Essentially the tastes and preferences of the rich and famous, derived from mass media, television and the internet, are aggrandized and glorified. In reality, these tastes and preferences are false, shrill, shallow and insincere. The white power movement reacts to the new cultural icons, which are perceived as perverted abominations. Yet simultaneously, those caught up in white supremacism cannot escape the influence of their culture. For example, the ARA became enamored with their own celebrity, their fame, their money, their misperceived invincibility. In their eyes, they achieved the status of rock stars; they were celebrities. In effect, they were part and parcel of a subculture modeled after the prevailing universal culture.

The desire to be famous celebrities was the focal point of their lives. Being a violent renegade was the new cool. But it was an illusion.

Still, the white power movement is not dead. Even though the old guard has passed into history, new skinhead groups, Anti-Semitic groups and racists have sprouted up like weeds in an untended garden. The marginalized, radical, fringe groups are out there, growing and plotting ways to release their inner rage against the perceived abominations of mankind. They, too, will use God as their patsy, their excuse for righteous violence. Similar to Islam, which sees the eradication of infidels as justifying any means to attain their goal, the Phineas Priesthood searches for any pretext to kill God's enemies.

Index

The True Story of the Bilderberg Group

by Daniel Estulin   *North American Union edition*

More than a center of influence, the Bilderberg Group is a shadow world government, hatching plans of domination at annual meetings ... and under a cone of media silence.

THE TRUE STORY OF THE BILDERBERG GROUP goes inside the secret meetings and sheds light on why a group of politicians, businessmen, bankers and other mighty individuals formed the world's most powerful society. As Benjamin Disraeli, one of England's greatest Prime Ministers, noted, "The world is governed by very different personages from what is imagined by those who are not behind the scenes."

Included are unpublished and never-before-seen photographs and other documentation of meetings, as this riveting account exposes the past, present and future plans of the Bilderberg elite.

Softcover: **$24.95** (ISBN: 9780979988622) • 432 pages • Size: 6 x 9

America's Nazi Secret
An Uncensored History of the US Justice Department's Obstruction of Congressional Investigations into Americans Who Funded Hitler, Postwar Immigration of Eastern European War Criminals to the US, and the Evolution of the Arab Nazi Movement into Modern Middle Eastern Terrorists

by John Loftus

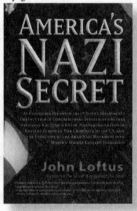

Fully revised and expanded, this stirring account reveals how the U.S. government permitted the illegal entry of Nazis into North America in the years following World War II. This extraordinary investigation exposes the secret section of the State Department that began, starting in 1948 and unbeknownst to Congress and the public until recently, to hire members of the puppet wartime government of Byelorussia—a region of the Soviet Union occupied by Nazi Germany. Now available with a chapter previously banned from release by authorities and a foreword and afterword with recently declassified materials.

John Loftus is a former U.S. government prosecutor, a former Army intelligence officer, and the author of numerous books, including *The Belarus Secret, The Secret War Against the Jews, Unholy Trinity: How the Vatican's Nazi Networks Betrayed Western Intelligence to the Soviets,* and *Unholy Trinity: The Vatican, the Nazis, and the Swiss Banks.* He has appeared regularly as a media commentator on ABC National Radio and Fox News. He lives in St. Petersburg, Florida.

Softcover • $24.95 • ISBN 978-1-936296-04-0 • 288 Pages

Dr. Mary's Monkey
How the Unsolved Murder of a Doctor, a Secret Laboratory in New Orleans and Cancer-Causing Monkey Viruses are Linked to Lee Harvey Oswald, the JFK Assassination and Emerging Global Epidemics
by Edward T. Haslam, Foreword by Jim Marrs

Evidence of top-secret medical experiments and cover-ups of clinical blunders
The 1964 murder of a nationally known cancer researcher sets the stage for this gripping exposé of medical professionals enmeshed in covert government operations over the course of three decades. Following a trail of police records, FBI files, cancer statistics, and medical journals, this revealing book presents evidence of a web of medical secret-keeping that began with the handling of evidence in the JFK assassination and continued apace, sweeping doctors into cover-ups of cancer outbreaks, contaminated polio vaccine, the genesis of the AIDS virus, and biological weapon research using infected monkeys.

Hard Cover 24.95 Softcover: **$19.95** • 399 pages • Size: 5 1/2 x 8 1/2

New World Order
A Strategy of Imperialism
by Sean Stone

While preparing his Senior Thesis in American History at Princeton University, Sean Stone came across the name of William Yandell Elliott, Professor Emeritus of history and government at Harvard through the first half of the 20th century. Stone found that Elliott had created a virtual "kindergarten" of Anglo-American imperialists among his students, who included Henry Kissinger, Zbigniew Brzezinski, Samuel P. Huntington, and McGeorge Bundy. Upon further investigation, Stone came to understand Elliott's own integral role, as an advisor to six presidents, in connecting the modern national-security establishment with the British Round Table Movement's design to re-incorporate America into the British "Empire." Whether that goal has been achieved will be left to the reader to decide. But through this sweeping overview of world affairs, it cannot be denied that W.Y. Elliott's life and intellectual history demonstrate the strong interlocking relationship between academia, government, big business and ... our future.

Sean Stone has grown up in the film-world, having acted since childhood in his father Oliver Stone's films, including The Doors, JFK, Natural Born Killers, and Wall Street: Money Never Sleeps, before becoming a director in his own right with Greystone Park. The movie was based on Stone's experiences of exploring haunted mental asylums.

Stone studied at Oxford and Princeton University, graduating with a BA in American History from Princeton in 2006.

Softcover: $19.95 (ISBN: 9781634240901) • 240 pages • Size: 6 x 9

Esoteric Hollywood
Sex, Cults and Symbols in Film
by Jay Dyer

Like no other book before it, this work delves into the deep, dark and mysterious undertones hidden in Tinsel Town's biggest films. Esoteric Hollywood is a game-changer in an arena of tabloid-populated titles. After years of scholarly research, Jay Dyer has compiled his most read essays, combining philosophy, comparative religion, symbolism and geopolitics and their connections to film. Readers will watch movies with new eyes, able to decipher on their own, as the secret meanings of cinema are unveiled.

Jay Dyer is a writer and researcher from the Southern US with a B.A. in philosophy, his graduate work focused on the interplay of literary theory, espionage and philosophy.

Softcover: $19.95 (ISBN: 9781634240772) • 382 pages • Size: 6 x 9

The Franklin Scandal
A Story of Powerbrokers, Child Abuse & Betrayal
by Nick Bryant

A chilling exposé of corporate corruption and government cover-ups, this account of a nationwide child-trafficking and pedophilia ring tells a sordid tale of corruption in high places. The scandal originally surfaced during an investigation into Omaha, Nebraska's failed Franklin Federal Credit Union and took the author beyond the Midwest and ultimately to Washington, DC. Implicating businessmen, senators, major media corporations, the CIA, and even the venerable Boys Town organization, this extensively researched report includes firsthand interviews with key witnesses and explores a controversy that has received scant media attention.

The Franklin Scandal is the story of a underground ring that pandered children to a cabal of the rich and powerful. The ring's pimps were a pair of Republican powerbrokers who used Boys Town as a pedophiliac reservoir, and had access to the highest levels of our government and connections to the CIA.

Nick Bryant is a journalist whose work largely focuses on the plight of disadvantaged children in the United States. His mainstream and investigative journalism has been featured in Gear, Playboy, The Reader, and on Salon.com. He is the coauthor of America's Children: Triumph of Tragedy. He lives in New York City.

Hardcover: $24.95 (ISBN: 0977795357) • 480 pages • Size: 6 x 9

A Terrible Mistake
The Murder of Frank Olson and the CIA's Secret Cold War Experiments
by H.P. Albarelli Jr.

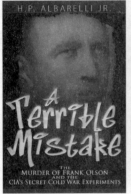

In his nearly 10 years of research into the death of Dr. Frank Olson, writer and investigative journalist H.P. Albarelli Jr. gained unique and unprecedented access to many former CIA, FBI, and Federal Narcotics Bureau officials, including several who actually oversaw the CIA's mind- control programs from the 1950s to the early 1970s. A Terrible Mistake takes readers into a frequently bizarre and always frightening world, colored and dominated by Cold War concerns and fears. For the past 30 years the death of biochemist Frank Olson has ranked high on the nation's list of unsolved and perplexing mysteries. *A Terrible Mistake* solves the mystery and reveals in shocking detail the identities of Olson's murderers. The book also takes readers into the strange world of government mind-control programs and close collaboration with the Mafia.

H. P. Albarelli Jr. is an investigative journalist whose work has appeared in numerous publications and newspapers across the nation and is the author of the novel The Heap. He lives in Tampa, Florida.

Hardcover $34.95 • Softcover $29.95 • 852 pages

Me & Lee
How I Came to Know, Love and Lose
Lee Harvey Oswald
by Judyth Vary Baker

Foreword by
Edward T. Haslam

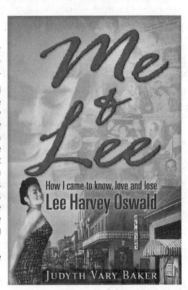

JUDYTH VARY WAS ONCE A PROMISING science student who dreamed of finding a cure for cancer; this exposé is her account of how she strayed from a path of mainstream scholarship at the University of Florida to a life of espionage in New Orleans with Lee Harvey Oswald. In her narrative she offers extensive documentation on how she came to be a cancer expert at such a young age, the personalities who urged her to relocate to New Orleans, and what lead to her involvement in the development of a biological weapon that Oswald was to smuggle into Cuba to eliminate Fidel Castro. Details on what she knew of Kennedy's impending assassination, her conversations with Oswald as late as two days before the killing, and her belief that Oswald was a deep-cover intelligence agent who was framed for an assassination he was actually trying to prevent, are also revealed.

JUDYTH VARY BAKER is a teacher, and artist. Edward T. Haslam is the author of *Dr. Mary's Monkey*.

Hardcover • $24.95 • Softcover $21.95 • 580 Pages

Betrayal
A JFK Honor Guard Speaks
By Hugh Clark with William Matson Law

The amazing story that William Law has documented with his historical interviews helps us to understanding our true history. This compelling information shreds the official narrative.In 2015, Law and fellow researcher Phil Singer got together the medical corpsman, who had been present at Bethesda Naval Hospital for President Kennedy's autopsy with some of the official honor guard, who had delivered the president's coffin. What happened next was extraordinary. The medical corpsmen told the honor guards that they had actually received the president's body almost a half-hour before the honor guard got there. The honor guard couldn't believe this. They had met the president's plane at Andrews, taken possession of his casket and shadowed it all the way to Bethesda. The two sides almost broke into fisticuffs, accusing the other of untruths. Once it was sifted out, and both sides came to the understanding that each was telling their own truths of their experience that fateful day, the feelings of betrayal experienced by the honor guards was deep and profound. This is dynamic first person testimony.

Softcover • $19.95 • 144 pages • 6 x 9

PERFECTIBILISTS
The 18th Century Bavarian Illuminati
by Terry Melanson

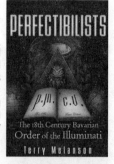

The shadowy Illuminati grace many pages of fiction as the sinister all-powerful group pulling the strings behind the scenes, but very little has been printed in English about the actual Enlightenment-era secret society, its activities, its members, and its legacy … until now.

Presenting an authoritative perspective, this definitive study chronicles the rise and fall of the fabled Illuminati, revealing their methods of infiltrating governments and education systems, and their blueprint for a successful cabal, which echoes directly forward through groups like the Order of Skull & Bones to our own era.

Softcover: $19.95 • 9780977795381 • 530 pages • Size: 6 x 9

Sinister Forces
A Grimoire of American Political Witchcraft
Book One: The Nine
by Peter Levenda, Foreword by Jim Hougan
A shocking alternative to the conventional views of American history.

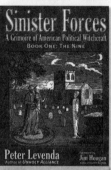

The roots of coincidence and conspiracy in American politics, crime, and culture are examined in this book, exposing new connections between religion, political conspiracy, and occultism. Readers are taken from ancient American civilization and the mysterious mound builder culture to the Salem witch trials, the birth of Mormonism during a ritual of ceremonial magic by Joseph Smith, Jr., and Operations Paperclip and Bluebird. Not a work of speculative history, this exposé is founded on primary source material and historical documents. Fascinating details are revealed, including the bizarre world of "wandering bishops" who appear throughout the Kennedy assassinations; a CIA mind control program run amok in the United States and Canada; a famous American spiritual leader who had ties to Lee Harvey Oswald in the weeks and months leading up to the assassination of President Kennedy; and the "Manson secret."

Softcover: **$24.95** • 396 pages • Size: 6 x 9

Book Two: A Warm Gun

The roots of coincidence and conspiracy in American politics, crime, and culture are investigated in this analysis that exposes new connections between religion, political conspiracy, terrorism, and occultism. Readers are provided with strange parallels between supernatural forces such as shaminism, ritual magic, and cult practices, and contemporary interrogation techniques such as those used by the CIA under the general rubric of MK-ULTRA. Not a work of speculative history, this exposé is founded on primary source material and historical documents. Fascinating details on Nixon and the "Dark Tower," the Assassin cult and more recent Islamic terrorism, and the bizarre themes that run through American history from its discovery by Columbus to the political assassinations of the 1960s are revealed.

Softcover **$24.95** • 392 pages • Size: 6 x 9

Book Three: The Manson Secret

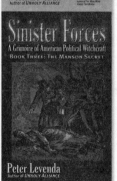

The Stanislavski Method as mind control and initiation. Filmmaker Kenneth Anger and Aleister Crowley, Marianne Faithfull, Anita Pallenberg, and the Rolling Stones. Filmmaker Donald Cammell (Performance) and his father, CJ Cammell (the first biographer of Aleister Crowley), and his suicide. Jane Fonda and Bluebird. The assassination of Marilyn Monroe. Fidel Castro's Hollywood career. Jim Morrison and witchcraft. David Lynch and spiritual transformation.The technology of sociopaths. How to create an assassin. The CIA, MK-ULTRA and programmed killers.

Softcover $24.95 (ISBN 9780984185832) • 422 pages • Size: 6 x 9